Cybercafes

Cybercafes

A Worldwide Guide for Travelers

THIRD EDITION

cyberkath@traveltales.com

TEN SPEED PRESS
Berkeley, California

A Kirsty Melville Book

Ten Speed Press
PO Box 7123
Berkeley, California 94707
www.tenspeed.com

Distributed in Australia by Simon and Schuster Australia, in Canada by Ten Speed
Press Canada, in New Zealand by Southern Publishing Group, in South Africa by
Real Books, in Southeast Asia by Berkeley Books, and in the United Kingdom and
Europe by Airlift Books.

Cover Design by Kathy Warinner
Interior Design by Catherine Jacobes
Illustrations by Kathy Warinner
Typeface used in this book is Officina Sans

Library of Congress Cataloging-in-Publication Data
cyberkath@traveltales.com
        Cybercafes: a worldwide guide for travelers / cyberkath@traveltales.com.
    —3rd ed.
            p. cm.
    ISBN 1-58008-070-7
    1. Cybercafes Directories.   I. Title.
    HE7581.5.C93   1999
    910'.2'02—dc21   99-14287   CIP

First printing, 1999
Printed in Canada
1 2 3 4 5 6 7 8 9 10 — 03 02 01 00 99

Special thanks to:

Bert Bulder

Craig and Carolyn

Susan Gray

David Jose

Hideki Kato

Marc Lagies

Steven Pierce

Shirlee Sacks

Peter Stanton

PLEASE NOTE: All the information in this book is as accurate as we could get it when we went to press. Every effort has been made by the publisher and author to verify information. Please inform the author at cyberkath@traveltales.com if you find any incorrect items in this book. Thank you and enjoy.

Contents

Introduction

Hi from cyberkath—

How does an anti-computer, non-computer-literate, non-typist get to be the author of a book that encourages people to use computers? Especially considering this book is particularly for people traveling, when actually, my belief is that travelers should be meeting new people, opening their eyes to the environment, forgetting about work, and remembering how to be real, living, spontaneous creatures again. Well, the answer is, I really don't have a clue. It was one of those things that happened when I was traveling around and nothing I had done up to that point could have prepared me for it.

Three other factors are relevant: money, dependence, and joy. I'm not rich enough to make endless long-distance phone calls. Sometimes I need to make endless long-distance phone calls. And I get sheer joy when I see messages to me from people I love, and who love me. :)

So, attempting to pass through California, I got snared there and discovered e-mail. I tasted the pleasure of the creative ramblings of this new form of exchange and it seemed to me that it was unnecessary to go without. Well, one thing led to another, and finally to this little book, which is designed to help other travelers, wherever they are, find their way to their stash of messages.

How to Use This Book

This guide attempts to cover the world. The entries are arranged into five vaguely geographic regions—I say "vaguely" because you just try to get people to agree about which countries should fit into which divisions. Here are the regions as I have grouped them:

AFRICA & THE MIDDLE EAST
ASIA & THE PACIFIC
CENTRAL & SOUTH AMERICA (INCLUDES THE CARIBBEAN)
EUROPE
NORTH AMERICA (INCLUDES HAWAII AND MEXICO)

The listings within each region are alphabetical by country. In most cases, the name of the state, province, canton, county, or whatever follows the city name, in parentheses. Within each city the cybercafes are listed in alphabetical order. The quickest way to find a specific cafe is to go to the index at the back and look up the city you are going to visit.

The Index by Cafe Name (page 332) is alphabetized by cafe name. The Index by City Name (page 339) is alphabetized by city or town name first, then the country name. You can also look up each U.S. and Canadian state to find all the cafes within its boundaries (page 344).

The entry for each cybercafe will show you the following:

- The name of the cybercafe/establishment.

- The address, phone number, and fax number. You will notice that the country code is preceded by a +. If there are numbers in parentheses, you only use these if you are in the country but out of the local telephone area.

- E-mail address and World Wide Web address, if any.

- Where it is and how to get there. In this section I have tried to provide landmarks, plus up-to-date transportation information. The info. here varies enormously. Cybercafe owners are usually car owners too, and at times find it difficult to realize that often travel means actually catching those things called buses and trains. Short of going to all the cybercafes myself, I have done my best to drag as much information out of them as possible. Maybe let the owner know what you think of his or her directions, if you want a potentially lively conversation. Or e-mail me with better directions and I'll put them in the next edition.

- Hours. If hours for a particular day are not listed, then it is closed that day. Also be aware that some cafes may suddenly get seasonal on you, especially in seaside or skiing resorts.

- How much it costs per half hour and per hour to be online, generally in the local currency. If the local currency is not used, it may mean they prefer to accept U.S. dollars only. This section also indicates what credit cards are accepted. Major credit cards are listed by the following abbreviations: Visa=V, Mastercard=MC, American Express =AmEx, Diners Club=DC, Discover=D.

- If student discounts are available. If you are interested in discounts of any kind (senior, school, or unemployed) do ask, but make sure that you have some proof of your status with you. Most cafes ask for International Student Identification Cards (ISIC) from university students.

- Places to visit nearby. I asked cybercafe staff to let me know of interesting places in the vicinity. Some did not offer any suggestions so nothing appears here, but this does not necessarily mean that there's nothing to see in that location. Some cybercafe owners made extensive suggestions, about which they will probably be able to give you more information when you get there.

The Facilities Available Symbols

With each listing you will see symbols indicating some basics that cybercafes have to offer.

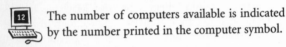 The number of computers available is indicated by the number printed in the computer symbol.

Black-and-white or color printer available (if you need good-quality prints you should phone to check if they have a laser printer). Printing allows you to cut down the amount of time you spend on-line because you can print out your mail and read it later.

Scanner available. This may not seem essential, but your loved ones might be amused if you scan in holiday snaps and e-mail them home.

Everything in this book is as accurate as we could get it at press time. I am fully aware that there are literally hundreds more cybercafes in the world, but the instability of the business and the lack of actual proof of continued existence at this time has meant that I'm only putting into this guide cybercafes that have replied to my e-mails. They may have an active virtual presence (a website that works), but there's nothing more frustrating than trekking all the way to a cafe, only to find that it went out of business months or even years before. So quality not necessarily quantity is my philosophy here.

Cybercafe Basics

If you are a cybercafe first-timer, you may be put off by the initial contact. In a way, there's a whole other culture involved here. To help you familiarize yourself with this new world, here's my mini-guide to cybercafe types:

The Pure Cybercafe. This is the original-style nerd hangout, completely devoid of any resemblance to cafe ambiance. The order of the day is lines of computer terminals staring blankly at lines of computer nerds. Your reaction to this cybercafe may range from horrified to stunned to strongly attracted, depending on your personal bent. Actually, I have developed a fondness for this kind of cafe; it may seem bleak, but the futuristic spirit is often there, with a pseudo hi-tech/sci-fi flavor.

The Nonchalant Cybercafe. Here the cybercafe message is understated. Real live people are having in-the-flesh chats around tables without screens, while at the back, to the side, or 'round the corner lurk the keyboards and their users. There is much of the cafe spirit as we know it here. Although the blue glow is still present, computer literacy doesn't seem to be absolutely de rigueur.

The Cafe with Computer. This type is your regular coffee shop or cafe with a computer thrown in, much as a telephone would be. Here you may not even notice the presence of our one-eyed friend; it possibly could be out of commission. Alternatively though, the owner may be all enthused about this new attraction, having recently been converted from the joys of java (coffee, not the language) to the ecstasy of e-mail.

Other types of cyber-stations or cyber-points also exist, and new cyber-environments are being dreamed up every day. There are already quick-fix kiosks (computer terminals in boxes like slot machines) at airports around the globe and on-line terminals in copy shops. Many libraries, especially in North America, Europe, and Australia, have free Internet access, although this is generally intended for research purposes. There are hotels boasting bedside services and soon, no doubt, we will have in-flight surfing (Will the flight attendants come 'round offering mice in little hermetically sealed plastic bags?).

From Entrance to E-mail

So once you have selected and located your cybercafe, how do you make the transition from the door to sitting at your computer and accessing your mail or surfing the Web? What do you say to the person behind the counter? How do they know how long you've been on? Here are some tips to help you get started.

- Don't be afraid to ask questions. Every cybercafe is different and the systems they use can vary enormously. Sound as awkward as you like; there's still no real set way to do things.

- If the staff are experts, all the better. Just bear in mind that they have chosen to work in this setting and that part of their job is helping customers. If we are beginners, so what?

- Each cafe has its own system for timing your time on-line. Some have software and others have a sheet of paper on which you sign in and out. Let them explain all that to you.

E-mail and the Internet on the Road

First of all, I must remind all English speakers that the instructions and prompts on the browsers and keyboards in other non-English speaking countries will almost certainly be in foreign languages. I would suggest you learn the common phrases before you go, or just hope that someone there speaks your language. In my experience, staff often do know how to translate Internet terms for any lazy language learners, but you shouldn't take this for granted. It can be disconcerting to be faced with a keyboard and monitor you can't understand, so you might want to be prepared.

Reconfiguring for a Standard POP Account (Post Office Protocol—a regular non-web-based e-mail account)

These days this option is not usually necessary because other easier options are available, which you will read about in the next sections. The only advantage that I know of in reconfiguring is that you can download your mail if you need to. If you don't have a computer or an e-mail account, go straight to the section called Web-Based E-mail (page 10) for how to get a free e-mail account.

The rest of you probably access your e-mail at home or work by downloading your mail and storing it in your computer. Now, when you are traveling and using a different machine, you have to tell the browser (Netscape or Microsoft Explorer) to pick up your stash from your server. Obviously, if your e-mail account is at work, you need to make sure that it's not only available when you are at work. In other words, that it is not an Intranet system (internal system accessible only from your computer at work) or that your work e-mail

7

is not protected by a firewall that you cannot get through from outside.

Depending on how technically savvy you are and on what resources you have at your disposal, you may find entering the relevant information a problem. If you do, read on to the next sections or ask for help from a cafe staff member.

If you are like me, you like to be shown what to do, not just have it explained. If you can't reconfigure the setting on your own, I suggest you get the staff member to show you how. In any case, you will need to know these things to get your mail:

- Your domain name. This is the name of the computer that holds your e-mail for you. Usually your e-mail address is something like name@whatever.com. It's the part after the "@" that you need to tell the staff member. So first, you have to put in the server name, for example "whatever.com". This is also referred to as the "server name" or the "domain name" of your server.

- Then you need to know your user name; mine is cyberkath, because that's what comes before the "@" in my address— yours is what comes before the "@" in your e-mail address.

- Last, you need to remember your password. You may have forgotten this because your e-mail program may remember it for you, so just make sure you have it with you.

First, you will need to have a staff member help you go into the configuration settings in the e-mail client software. To try it yourself, you would use the browser (Netscape or Microsoft Explorer) and go into the e-mail programs there. For Netscape, for example, you would go to the "Options" menu.

There you will find a file called "Server," and you put in the name of your Internet provider's mail server next to where it asks for the POP server. You then fill in your user name, and when you click on the e-mail icon it will ask you for your password. Then, bingo!, it should actually go and grab your mail! You will probably want to alter the "Identity" settings so that your e-mail will have your own address at the top. Some cafes may not particularly want you to do this, but most won't care. You should change the identity settings back before you leave so that the next person on that terminal won't send e-mail from your address. Also, remember to remove all information that relates to you to make sure that no one else can get at your mail.

NOTE: If you are an AOL user, you should check the AOL website and find out about AOL NetMail, which allows you to access your AOL mail from anywhere (in theory). All you need is your user name and your password and you'll be able to read your AOL mail on the road. If you want to use AOL NetMail, you should look up the required specifications before you leave on your trip so that you aren't stuck somewhere that isn't equipped for this feature.

Getting Your E-mail without Reconfiguring

As long as your e-mail account is not protected by your company, you should be able to obtain your mail without going through the more complicated process of reconfiguring. Some cybercafes do not allow users to reconfigure the e-mail software in the browsers. This happened to me in one cafe in Germany; they said I could only get my mail if I had a web-based account. This is because they don't want you messing with settings that will then have to be changed with each user.

An easier way to access your regular e-mail account is to use one of the following nifty websites which allow you to access your account from wherever you are:

www.mailstart.com
www.thatweb.com
www.readmail.com

If you go to these websites you will see instructions on how to get your mail from any account (except for AOL users). All you'll need is your e-mail address and your password. You can send mail from there too, so it really makes life easy. The only slight misgiving I have about these very useful services is that you do have to give over your password in the process. As with most of these different options, I would suggest testing these websites with your e-mail address before leaving on your trip to make sure they will interface well. You'll also need to make sure you manage your e-mail well. Read on for more tips on this.

Web-Based E-mail: Getting a Free Roving E-mail Account

For those of you who are going away for a long time and who don't have an e-mail account or don't own a computer, there is good news. Another option exists: web-based e-mail. Just go to one of the web page addresses listed below and you can open yourself an account for free.

www.excite.com
www.hotmail.com
www.rocketmail.com
www.yahoo.com

I'm just giving you these four, although there are many nowadays. They make their money by advertising and I'm not really sure what they do with the information you give them, but you should read the terms of your account carefully if you are worried. Hotmail.com asks for a lot of info.; others like yahoo.com don't ask for much.

When you get to their web page, just click where it says "E-mail" to open an account, and it will take you to a registration form. They will ask you to choose a user name and a password. Then there are a bunch of other questions. The whole thing takes about ten minutes if you're lucky. You can do this from any computer, anywhere.

When you've followed all their instructions, you have a new e-mail address. All you need to do now to pick up your mail is go back to the web page and click on "E-mail" again, but this time not as a new user. You will be asked for your user name and password. Enter these and then it will show you your mail. The mail stays on the web page; it does not get downloaded into your computer, this makes it possible for you to access it from anywhere that has Internet access. Just remember to close the browser or log out when you leave the terminal so that the next person can't read your mail.

With web-based e-mail there's no nasty reconfiguring and some providers can even forward mail from your regular account to your roving one while you are away. The only thing you need to know is where to go to get on-line—hence this list of cybercafes.

Managing Your E-mail

Once you have figured out how to access your e-mail, you have to decide how to manage it: either you can leave your mail on the server and download a copy, or download the originals. These settings are in the e-mail software too. You usually have to click a button in the "Server" settings that says "Leave on the Server" or "Remove from the Server." If you want to get it again later, click "Leave on the Server"; if not, and you don't mind only seeing it once, click "Remove from the Server." Either way, do remember to delete your e-mail from the computer you are using so that other people can't read it. You can always print out your mail in the cybercafe if you want to keep a copy.

Want to Start a Cybercafe?

If you are interested in opening your own cybercafe, get in touch with the International Association of Cybercafes (IAC), which is a self-help group for cybercafe owners. It's "small but perfectly formed (and gradually growing)," to quote one of its leading members. For details, go to http://www.theiac.org. There is also a cybercafe newsgroup (alt.cybercafes), a listserv, and a live discussion group available. The Cybercafe Ring, hosted in Cardiff, Wales, connects cybercafe homepages and cybercafe-related sites; check out http://www.cardiffcyber-cafe.co.uk/cafe-ring.

How You Can Make This Guide Better

Well, that just about covers it—until you let me know that's not the case. Remember to send all feedback, angry or appreciative, to cyberkath@traveltales.com, so the next edition of this book can be bigger and better thanks to you. In particular, let us know about cybercafes in South America and Asia. I'm well aware that there are lots more to add to our list and those of you actually on the road now are best placed to help.

All I need is the name of the cafe, the city, the country, the URL, and—most importantly—the email address of a staff member or the cafe's general e-mail address.

So that's all. Have a trip and a half, and may your java be hot and your e-mails cool. Bonne cyberoute!

—cyberkath

HANDY ADDRESSES AND WEB RESOURCES FOR THE TRAVELER

Other Ways to Find Cybercafes

If you can't find the place you need in this book, you might be able to locate it on one of the following lists. However, if you select a place from these lists, do try to check by phone that the establishment is still open.

Worldwide

Two extensive lists covering the globe are currently maintained by Kireau in the U.S. and Ernst in Norway. The web addresses are as follows:

Kireau-http://www.cybercaptive.com

Ernst-http://www.netcafeguide.com/index.htm

They both have searchable databases.

Another possible worldwide resource is the Yahoo Cybercafe page, which just lists the names of cybercafes submitted and links to the cybercafes' homepages. You can search it too. The address is http://www.dir.yahoo.com/Business_and_Economics/Companies/Internet_Services/Internet_Cafes/Complete_Listing

Asia and the Pacific

Australia: Vicnet will tell you about libraries on-line in Victoria. Just go to http://www.vicnet.net.au/vicnet/libraries/library.htm.

Http://www.gnomon.com.au/publications/netaccess is another good site for information in Australia. I have heard that there are also many Internet kiosks in Australia.

Japan: The biggest list I know of is the Japanese Yahoo page of cybercafes at http://yahoo.co.jp/Society_and_Culture/Cyberculture/Internet_Cafes. It is in Japanese but when you go to the URL's, the address is often in roman script and the phone number is usually there. In addition, as has happened in North America, copy shops are increasingly offering on-line access. Try Ernst (see above) too.

Thailand: Martin & Goi have a list at http://www.thailine.com/edh/cafes.htm. They cover East Asia.

Europe

Bert Bulder in The Netherlands has the most comprehensive searchable list of European cybercafes, with links to their URL's or e-mail addresses for places with no homepage. It's at http://www.xs4all.nl/~bertb/cybercaf.html. Try Virgin Megastores in Europe too.

Austria, Germany, and Switzerland: Cyber Ryder in Frankfurt keeps a decent list at http://www.cyberyder.de.

Belgium: Pot-Au-Lait cybercafe maintains the Belgian resource at http://cybercafe.potaulait.be.

France: Yahoo's small list is at http://www.yahoo.fr/Sujets_de
_societe/Cyberculture/Cybercafes, but your best bet is to go
to Bert's list (see above). Alternatively, Cyberis is a company
that has "cyberstations" in various locations around the
country—cinemas, pubs, pizzerias, Novotels, and Burger
Kings (especially in Paris). You buy a "cybercarte" from the
place that hosts the cyberstation. For locations, go to
http://www.cyberis.fr/info-cyberis/carte.htm.

Italy: Italian lists are hard to find. The ones I was using are
now dead and as far as I know no one has taken on the bur-
den of keeping things updated Anyway, try Bert (see above)
or you may have some luck with kiosks, see http://www.
netkiosk.it/utenti.html.

Spain: Joan at TangaWorld, a cybercafe near Barcelona
(Casteldefels), has a list at http://www.tangaworld.com/_
cyberca.htm. And at http://www.andal.es/guiaCiberCafes/
indexComAut.html there's yet another great list of Spanish
cybercafes, this time from Seville.

Switzerland: There's a supermarket chain called Migros that
has cafes or connections in many of its stores, so it's well
worth asking if the local one is connected.

UK & Ireland: *Internet Magazine* has quite a good list at
http://www.internet-magazine.com/resources/welcome.html.
TNT magazine (a free "what's on" travelers magazine) also
has an up-to-date list in every edition and at their website,
see http://www.tntmag.co.uk.

Mexico, Central America, & South America

Ron Mader compiled a useful list with contributions from travelers in these regions. That's at http://www2.planeta.com/mader/ecotravel/coffeeag/cybercafe.html. A recent traveler to South America told me that she experienced the biggest problems getting on-line in Brazil. However, generally she was able to find venues, some weird and wonderful, in even quite remote places.

USA and Canada

I highly recommend using one of the worldwide searchable databases for cybercafes if you need extra help in this region. However, if there's no cybercafe nearby, you will probably be able to find a photocopy shop (for example, the Kinko's chain; see http://www.kinkos.com for locations) that is wired, or your hotel may very well have access. The fact that local phone calls tend to be free means that it's sometimes even worth asking a native that happens to be on-line if you can just send a quick message.

Kiosks, Copy Shops, Libraries, and Tourist Offices

Here are some handy resources for locating other ways of getting on-line.

> http://www.kinkos.com
> http://www.atcominfo.com
> http://www.touchnet.com
> http://www.quickaid.com (shows airport
>   locations with maps)

Most developed countries are now getting copy shops on-line, and above all libraries are becoming more and more connected. You can often find computers on-line in cultural outposts in more remote areas; for example, the British Council has cybercafes in many of its libraries worldwide. Even the post office in Jakarta is on-line. Lastly, one of the best resources for Internet access is the local tourist information office, and increasingly they are on-line so you can e-mail them for up-to-date details. See below for Tourist Office Resources.

Business Travelers

A number of airports worldwide now have on-line access, so it's always worth asking ground staff when you arrive if there is an Internet point available.

Generally, most hotels in the U.S. and Canada, at least ones for which you pay over $100 a night, will have either a business center, with a computer on-line and photocopy facilities, or fax/modem jacks for laptops in the rooms.

Those who have laptops no doubt know that if you go to a cybercafe whose connection to the Internet is through a router (an ISDN or T1 line), you will probably need an Ethernet card/port and cable in order to be able to hook up your laptop. Not every cybercafe accommodates laptops and you will have to make sure you know what connections you need.

On the Road at http://www.roadnews.com may be of interest to business travelers too. They have a bookstore and will send you a free leaflet containing tips for taking your laptop with you on international trips, but be aware that they will only send stuff to your business address. Other resources for wired business travelers exist on the Net and it's well worth exploring these before you go.

Choosing Your Destination

City.Net Travel by Excite
http://www.city.net
Links to thousands of cities worldwide, including weather, cultural, and historical information.

MapQuest!
http://www.mapquest.com
Well known site providing extensive map support for the would-be traveler.

Lonely Planet
http://www.lonelyplanet.com
Great information, tips, pictures, and books. Nice picture previews of your destination and hot tips from travelers (from visas to viruses).

Tickets, Flights, Cars, and Hotels

Travelocity air car hotel on-line reservations
http://www.travelocity.com
Definitely not the only on-line travel booking service, but it has been around for a while and in Internet terms is well established.

Tourist Information

Tourism Office Worldwide Directory
http://www.towd.com
A searchable site that links to tourism offices in cities all over the globe, giving addresses, phone, fax, and e-mail information.

Currency

Oanda Currency Converter
http://www.oanda.com
One of many sites that lets you choose your home currency
and endlessly compare it with other countries'.

The Lingo

Travlang
http://www.travlang.com
Great resource for basic survival expressions (which you can
even hear spoken) in a huge variety of languages.

Public Transportation

Railroad, Subway, and Tram Maps
http://www.gamayun.physics.sunysb.edu/RR/maps.html
Remarkable resource for journey planning within a country
or city, if you won't have a car. Gives underground maps and
links to local regional transport sites.

Hostels

The Internet Guide to Hostelling™
http://www.hostels.com/hostel.menu.html
A worldwide guide with useful contact information, including e-mail addresses and prices in some cases.

Camping

CampNet America Campground, RV, and Camping
Directory
http://www.kiz.com/campnet/html/campnet.htm

Unlike the name suggests, this is actually a worldwide site with links to reviews of campgrounds and a myriad useful links for the outdoorsy dweller.

Don't Go There!

State Department-Services-Travel Warnings and Consular
  Information Sheets
http://travel.state.gov/travel_warnings.html
The U.S.'s official site covering country descriptions, entry requirements, and areas of instability, plus information on medical facilities, crime, drug penalties, and so on.

Travel Magazines

Travelmag—The Independent Travel Magazine
http://www.travelmag.co.uk/travelmag
A monthly travel magazine with pieces on the latest, the remotest, the cheapest, and the best, plus links to other travel reading materials.

Journeywoman

http://www.journeywoman.com/journeywoman
Gal-oriented travel site with chunky info. on female-friendly travel spots.

International Media

E & P Directory of On-line Media
http://www.mediainfo.com/emedia
Want to see the latest headline in your country of choice? Or even see TV and radio listings? This expanded site links to local media throughout the world.

Africa & the Middle East

The Idea Gallery—Cafe Internet & Discovery Unlimited—1057 Road 3831 • tel: +973 714828 • fax: +973 771-847 • balles@ideagal.com • www.ideagal.com

Location and Access
Located near the Gulf Hotel, Palace Inn Hotel, and the Carlton Hotel.
Bus: 6 from Manama city center, ask for Palace Inn Hotel.
Nearest cross street is Sheikh Isa Avenue.

Hours
Mon-Thu & Sat-Sun 10am–midnight

Fri   4pm–midnight

Prices
BD1.250 per half hour
BD2.000 per hour
V, MC, AmEx
Student discount available

Nearby Places to Visit
The House of the Quran, the Bahrain National Museum, the Arabic Souk, mosques, Adhari Park

ACCESS Cybercafe
Main Shopping Mall, Shop No. 68, Semouha • tel: +20 (0)3 4255766 • No fax • access@dataxprs.com.eg • www.cyberaccess.com.eg

Location and Access
Located near the Hatim Mosque.
Bus: 206, ask for Vector Amanowel.
Train: Ask for Sidi Gaber.
Nearest cross street is Vector Amanowel Square.

Hours
Mon-Sun 9am–midnight

Prices
£E10 per half hour
£E15 per hour
No credit cards
Student discount available

Nearby Places to Visit
Alexandria Zoo, Semouha Club

Netsonic—Internet Club and Computer Services
72 Ammar Ibn Yasser Street, Heliopolis • tel: +20 (0)2 6420134 •
fax: +20 (0)2 6420133 • netsonic2000@usa.net •
http://come.to/netsonic

Location and Access
Location behind the Military
  Academy.
Tram/Trolley: El-Nozha
  metro, ask for Hassan
  Kamal.

Hours
Mon-Sun   10am-4pm &
          7pm-midnight

Prices
£E7 per half hour
£E10 per hour
No credit cards

Nearby Places to Visit
Sinbad City Amusement Park

Rainbow Internetcafe
Military Club, Nile St. • tel: +20 (0)95 372320/377800 •
fax: +20 (0)95 370499 • rainbow@link.com.eg • No website

Location and Access
Located near Military Club.
Nearest cross street is El-
  Sayed Yosef Square.

Hours
Mon-Thu &
  Sat-Sun 9am–11pm
Fri   9am–noon &
         2pm–11pm

Prices
£E20 per half hour
£E40 per hour
No credit cards

Nearby Places to Visit
Luxor Museum, Momification
  Museum, Karnak Temple

ISRAEL, JERUSALEM

Strudel Internet Cafe and Wine Bar—11 Monbaz
Street • tel: +972 (0)2 623-2101 • fax: +972 (0)2 622-1445 •
strudel@inter.net.il • http://home.palnet.com/strudel

Location and Access
Located near Zion Square.
Bus: All buses to the center
of town, ask for Zion
Square.
Nearest cross street is
Hahavazelet Street.

Hours
Mon-Fri &
  Sun   10am-2am
Sat   3pm-2am

Prices
NIS12 per half hour
NIS24 per hour
V, MC, AmEx, DC

Nearby Places to Visit
Underground Museum,
  Russian Orthodox Church,
  Prophets Street

ISRAEL, TEL AVIV

EBC Executive Business Center
99 Hayarkon Street • tel: +972 (0)3 522 6999 •
fax: +972 (0)3 522 5795 • ebc_tlv@netmedia.net.il • No website

Location and Access
Located near the Tel Aviv
beach.
Bus: 4 from Central Bus
Station, ask for Mendele
Street.
Nearest cross street is Ben
Yehuda Street.

Hours
Mon-Thu &
  Sun   8am-8pm
Fri   8am-2pm

Prices
NIS25.5 per half hour
NIS51 per hour
V, MC, AmEx, D

InBar Internet—2 Shlomo Hamelech •
tel: +972 (0)3 5282228 • fax: +972 (0)3 5282225 •
barak@isralink.co.il • www.isralink.co.il/inbar999

Location and Access
Located near Diezengoff
  Center.
Bus: 5, 13, 18, 23, 25, ask
  for Diezengoff Center.
Nearest cross street is King
  George.

Hours
Mon-Fri &
  Sun   9am-1am
Sat   4pm-1am

Prices
NIS30 per half hour
NIS40 per hour
V, MC, AmEx

Books@Café
1st Circle, Omar Bin Khatab Street • tel: +962 6 4650457 •
fax: +962 6 4650458 • contact@books-cafe.com • www.books-cafe.com

Location and Access
Located at the end of
  Rainbow Street, next to a
  fries shop called Batata.
Nearest cross street is
  Rainbow Street, Jabal
  Amman.

Hours
Mon-Sun 9am-midnight

Prices
JD2.500 weekends (Wed,
  Thu, Fri), weekdays 50%
  off per half hour
JD4 weekends (Wed, Thu,
  Fri), weekdays 50% off per
  hour
V, MC, AmEx

Nearby Places to Visit
Roman Citadel and
  Amphitheatre

KENYA, MOMBASA (COAST PROVINCE)

Hard Rock Cyber Cafe—Electricity House, Nkurumah Road •
tel: +254 011 229722 • fax: + 254 011 227172 •
cybercafe@form-net.com • www.kenyaweb.com/cybercafe

Location and Access
Located near TSS Towers.
Bus: All buses, ask for Coast
   General Post Office.
Nearest cross street is
   Kenyatta Avenue.

Hours
Mon-Sat   10am-7pm

Prices
Kshs300 per half hour
Kshs500 per hour
No credit cards

Nearby Places to Visit
Fort Jesus, Mombasa Old
   Town, the shipping docks

KENYA, NAIROBI

The Global Access Centre, Ltd.—Harambee Avenue,
Kenyatta International Conference Centre • tel: +254 (0)2 248539/42 •
fax: +254 (0)2 248539/42 • robert@gacl.com • www.gacl.com

Location and Access
Located in the Kenyatta
   International Conference
   Centre.

Hours
Mon-Fri   8am-7pm
Sat   8am-2pm

Prices
Kshs400 per half hour
Kshs500 per hour
No credit cards
Student discount available

Nearby Places to Visit
National Park, Carnivore
   Restaurant, Rift Valley
   Escarpement

Hard Rock Cyber Cafe—Mezzanine 2, Loita Street •
tel: +254 (0)2 220802 • fax: +254 (0)2 240870 •
cybercafe@form-net.com • www.kenyaweb.com/cyber-cafe

Location and Access
Located near Florida
  Niteclub and Grand
  Regency Hotel.
Nearest cross street is Loita
  Street.

Hours
Mon-Sat   10am-7pm

Prices
Kshs300 per half hour
Kshs500 per hour
No credit cards
Student discount available

Nearby Places to Visit
Nairobi National Park,
  markets

Hotel Intercontinental Cyber Cafe
City Hall Way • tel: +254 (0)2 26100 • fax: +254 (0)2 240870 •
cybercafe@form-net.com • www.kenyaweb.com/cyber-cafe

Location and Access
Located near Kenyatta
  Mausoleum.
Nearest cross street is City
  Hall Way Near.

Hours
Mon-Sat   8am-7pm

Prices
Kshs500 per half hour
Kshs1000 per hour
V
Student discount available

Nearby Places to Visit
Nairobi National Park,
  markets

L'Odeon Cyber Cafe

Loita Street • tel: +254 (0)2 245630 • fax: +254 (0)2 240870 •
cybercafe@form-net.com • www.kenyaweb.com/cybercafe

Location and Access
Located next to Florida
  Casino.
Nearest cross street is
  Uhuru Highway/University
  Way/Waiyaki Way/State
  House Road Roundabout.

Hours
Mon-Sun 11am-7pm

Prices
Kshs300 per half hour
Kshs500 per hour
V
Student discount available

Nearby Places to Visit
Nairobi National Park,
  markets

MIPS Netcafe

1st Floor, Kampus Towers, University Way • tel: +254 (0)2 335639 •
fax: +254 (0)2 335639 • netcafe@netcafe.co.ke • www.netcafe.co.ke

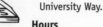

Location and Access
Located opposite Central
  Police Station.
Bus: All buses to the Central
  Bus Terminal, ask for
  Central Bus Station.
Nearest cross street is
  University Way.

Hours
Mon-Fri   8am-7pm
Sat-Sun   9am-2pm

Prices
Kshs200 per half hour
Kshs300 per hour
No credit cards
Student discount available

Nearby Places to Visit
Nairobi National Park,
  Nairobi Museum, Bomas of
  Kenya

Café Olé

Salhiya Complex • tel: +965 2436344 • No fax •
webmaster@ole.com.kw • www.cafe-ole.com

Location and Access
Located near Salhiya
  Complex.
Bus: 505, ask for Salhiya
  Complex.
Nearest cross street is Fahad
  Al-Salem Street.

Hours
Mon-Thu &
  Sat-Sun 10am-1am
Fri   noon-1am

Prices
US$3 per half hour
US$6 per hour
V, MC

Nearby Places to Visit
Kuwait Towers

Café Olé

Salem Al-Mubarak Street • tel: +965 5715595 • fax: +965 5715593 •
webmaster@ole.com.kw • www.cafe-ole.com

Location and Access
Located near Sultan Center,
  Al-Fanar, Laila Galleria.
Bus: 505, ask for Sultan
  Center.
Nearest cross street is Gulf
  Road.

Hours
Mon-Thu &
  Sat-Sun 10am-1am
Fri   noon-1am

Prices
US$3 per half hour
US$6 per hour
V, MC

Nearby Places to Visit
Kuwait Towers

LEBANON, BEIRUT (HAMRA)

Web C@fe

Makhoul Street • tel: +961 (0)1 348881 • No fax •
cafe@mail.webc.com.lb • www.webc.com.lb

Location and Access
Located near American
   University of Beirut.
Bus: Ask for BLISS bus stop.
Nearest cross street is Jean
   D'Arc.

Hours
Mon-Sun noon-midnight

Prices
LP6000 per half hour
LP8000 per hour and five
   minutes (LP7000 per hour
   for more than two hours)
V, MC

MOROCCO, MARRAKESH (MARRAKESH)

04 Multimedia

14, Bd. Yacoub El Mansour, Gueliz • tel: +212 (0)4 439117 •
fax: +212 (0)4 438411 • info@cybernet.net.ma • www.cybernet.net.ma

Location and Access
Located near the famous
   Majorelle Garden.
Nearest cross street is
   Mohamed V Avenue.

Hours
Mon-Sat 8:30am-9pm
Sun   10am-1pm &
         3pm-7pm

Prices
DH10 per half hour
DH20 per hour
No credit cards
Student discount available

Nearby Places to Visit
Koutobia Minaret, Jamaa El
   Fna Square

interPLANET—6 Rue Ibn El-Yasmine, Avenue de la Victoire •
tel: +212 (0)7 68 22 44 • fax: +212 (0)7 68 22 55 •
planet@maghrebnet.net.ma • www.cafeplanet.com

Location and Access
Located near Fath soccer
   stadium and BAB Rouah
   Art Gallery.
Bus: 11, ask for Fath soccer
   stadium.
Nearest cross street is
   Avenue de la Victoire.

Prices
MDH10 per half hour
MDH15 per hour
No credit cards

Hours
Mon-Sat   9am-9pm
Sun   9:30am-3:30pm

sett@net
15, Bd Zerktouni • tel: +212 (0)3 40 01 70 • fax: +212 (0)3 40 01 71 •
settanet@settanet.net.ma • www.settanet.net.ma

Location and Access
Located near the Chamber
   of Commerce and the train
   stop.
Bus: Ask for Bd Zerktouni.
Train: Ask for Settat.
Nearest cross street is Bd
   Hassan II.

Prices
MDH15 per half hour
MDH20 per hour
No credit cards
Student discount available

Nearby Places to Visit
Kasbah, cafes

Hours
Mon-Sat   9am-11pm
Sun   9am-10pm

MOROCCO, TANGIERS

Cyber Espace Pasteur
rue Pasteur • tel: +212 9 33 11 67 • fax: +212 9 33 24 49 •
majidh@mailcity.com • No website

Location and Access
Located near BCM Banque.

Hours
Mon-Sun   8am-2am

Prices
US$1.50 per half hour
US$2.50 per hour
No credit cards
Student discount available

Nearby Places to Visit
The whole city

MOROCCO, TETOUAN

Cyber Mania—68, Avenue Mohamed V •
tel: +212 (0)9 961141/704987 • fax: +212 (0)9 965883 •
info@cybermania.net.ma • www.cybermania.net.ma

Location and Access
Please phone for directions.

Hours
Mon-Sun   9am-1pm &
            3pm-10pm

Prices
MDH15 per half hour
MDH15 per hour
No credit cards

Nearby Places to Visit
Archaeological Museum,
    Ethnographic Museum

Cyberworld—PO Box 196, P.C. 116 Mina Al Fahal •
tel: +968 566740 •fax: +968 566741 • powar@rocketmail.com •
parent page: www.imtac.com

Location and Access
Located near Pizza Hut
  Qurum.
Bus: Ask for Qurum
  Roundabout.
Nearest cross street is
  Qurum.

Hours
Mon-Wed &
  Sat-Sun 9am-9pm
Thu   9am-1pm &
          4pm-9pm

Fri   4:30pm-9pm

Prices
Cents$2.60 per half hour
Cents$5.20 per hour
V
Student discount available
  for members

Nearby Places to Visit
National Garden, Gulf Hotel
  Beach, Muscat Intercon
  Beach

Carma Cyber Club—6th Floor, Lo'loat Al-Manarah Building,
Manarah Square • tel: +972 (0)2 29848547 • fax: +972 (0)2 2447703 •
ccc@al-carma.com • www.al-carma.com

Location and Access
Located near Manarah
  Square.
Bus: Nablus-Ramallah,
  Jerusalem-Ramallah lines,
  ask for Manarah Square.
Nearest cross street is
  Manarah Square.

Hours
Mon-Sun 8am-midnight

Prices
One hour minimum for non-
  members
NIS12.00 per hour from 5pm
  to 9pm
NIS10.00 per hour from 8am
  to 5pm & from 9pm to
  midnight
No credit cards

Nearby Places to Visit
City Centre

PALESTINE, RAMALLAH (WEST BANK)

K5M Internet Cafe
Main Street • tel: +972 (0)2 2956813 • fax: +972 (0)2 2954835 •
k5m@palnet.com • www.palnet.com/k5m

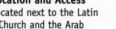

Location and Access
Located next to the Latin
   Church and the Arab
   Episcopalian Centre and
   Church.

Prices
NIS15 per half hour
NIS25 per hour
V
Student discount available
   sometimes

Hours
Mon-Sat   11am-11pm

SENEGAL, DAKAR

Metissacana
30 rue de Thiong • tel: +221 822 20 43 • fax: +221 822 20 23 •
webmaster@metissacana.sn • www.metissacana.sn

Location and Access
Bus: 7, 9, 18, ask for stop
   Ponty-LGM.
Nearest cross street is
   Avenue Georges
   Pompidou.

Prices
FF10 per half hour
FF15 per hour
V

Nearby Places to Visit
Marché Sandaga market

Hours
Mon-Sun midnight-
            midnight

Futurix

Centre Commercial Plein Sud • tel: +221 957 30 99 •
fax: +221 628 20 95 • futurix@metissacana.sn • No website

Location and Access
Nearest big city is Mbour.
Phone for directions.

Hours
Mon-Sun 9am-11pm

Prices
fcfa2500 per half hour
fcfa3000 per hour
No credit cards

SOUTH AFRICA, CAPE TOWN (WESTERN CAPE)

The Blue Lizard Internet Cafe

45 de Villiers Street, Zonnebloem • tel: +27 (0)21 461 9535 •
fax: +27 (0)21 465 3099 • info@lizard.co.za • www.lizard.co.za

Location and Access
Located near Parliament,
  Cape Technicon, Table
  Mountain.
Train: All lines, ask for Cape
  Town Station.
Nearest cross street is
  Roeland Street.

Prices
R12 per half hour
R24 per hour
V, MC, AmEx, DC
Student discount available

Hours
Mon-Fri   10am-2 or 5am
Sat-Sun   6am-2 or 5am

SOUTH AFRICA, CAPE TOWN (WESTERN CAPE)

iJunction Internet Cafe
12A Marine Circle, Table View • tel: +27 (0)21 557 9402 •
fax: +27 (0)21 557 9402 • james@ijunction.co.za • www.ijunction.co.za

Location and Access
Located near the beach-
front.
Nearest cross street is
Blouberg Road.

Hours
Mon-Sat 10am-9pm

Prices
R15 per half hour
No credit cards

Nearby Places to Visit
West Coast

SOUTH AFRICA, DURBAN (KWAZULU-NATAL)

Java @ JAVA Cyber Cafe
13 Marriott Road • tel: +27 (0)31 309 1575 • fax: +27 (0)31 309 3653 •
junaid@javajava.co.za • www.javajava.co.za

Location and Access
Located near Greyville Race
Course.
Bus: Botanic Gardens Mynah
Bus, ask for Caltex Garage
on Cowey Road.
Nearest cross street is
Cowey.

Hours
Mon-Sun 9am-midnight

Prices
R10 per half hour
R20 per hour
V, MC, AmEx, DC
Student discount available

Nearby Places to Visit
Botanic Gardens

Gateway Internet Services

Shop 5, New Colonnade, Vincent • tel: +27 (0)431 726 8030 •
fax: +27 (0)431 726 8082 • sroux@gis.co.za • www.gunny.gis.co.za

Location and Access
Located next to BP garage
  and opposite Vincent Park
  Shopping Centre.
Bus: Ask for Vincent Park
  Shopping Centre.
Nearest cross street is
  Devereux Avenue.

Hours
Mon-Sat   8am-8pm

Prices
R10 per half hour
R20 per hour
V, MC
Student discount negotiable

Nearby Places to Visit
Vincent Park Shopping
  Centre, mall, cinema

Westdene Internet Cafe

21 Thornton Road, Westdene • tel: +27 (0)11 477 4511 •
fax: +27 (0)11 477 4511 • steve@westcafe.co.za • www.westcafe.co.za

Location and Access
Located near Rand Afrikaans
  University.
Bus: Ask for Westdene.
Nearest cross street is 5th
  Avenue.

Hours
Mon   7pm-midnight
Tue-Sat   noon-midnight
Sun   1pm-midnight

Prices
R12 per half hour
R24 per hour
V, MC, AmEx, DC

SOUTH AFRICA, JOHANNESBURG (GAUTENG)

The MilkyWay Internet Cafe—204 Times Square
(2nd floor), 38 Raleigh Street, Yeoville • tel: +27 (0)11 487 1340 •
fax: +27 (0)11 648 1616 • info@milkyway.co.za • www.milkyway.co.za

Location and Access
Located near Times Square.
Bus: 19, ask for Eloff Street.
Nearest cross street is
Fortesque.

Hours
Mon-Thu 8:30am-8pm
Fri   8:30am-midnight
Sat   9am-7pm

Prices
R5 or R10 (depending on
computer) per half hour
R10 or R20 (depending on
computer) per hour
V, MC
Student discount available

Nearby Places to Visit
Rockey Street neighborhood

SOUTH AFRICA, PORT ELIZABETH (EASTERN CAPE)

Cyberjoe's Internet Cafe
4 Buckingham Road • tel: +27 (0)41 3741911 •
fax: +27 (0)41 3738928 • pluto@cyberjoe.co.za • www.cyberjoe.co.za

Location and Access
Phone for directions.

Hours
Mon-Sun 8am-7pm

Prices
R12 per half hour
R18 per hour
V, MC, AmEx

Nearby Places to Visit
Beaches, clubs, etc.

SOUTH AFRICA, PORT ELIZABETH (EASTERN CAPE)

Cyberscape
D39 Shop, The Bridge, Greenacres • tel: +27 (0)41 341399 •
fax: +27 (0)41 331544 • nikki@cyberscape.co.za • No website

Location and Access
Located in a well-known
  shopping center—The
  Bridge.
Nearest cross street is Cape
  Road.

Prices
R15 per half hour
R24 per hour
V, MC, DC

Hours
Mon-Thu 9am-5:30pm
Fri   9am-6pm
Sat   9am-2pm

SOUTH AFRICA, PRETORIA (GAUTENG)

The Net Café—Hatfield Square, corner of Prospect/Hilda Streets •
tel: +27 (0)12 362 6459 • fax: +27 (0)12 362 6459 •
jshutte@netcafe.co.za • www.netcafe.co.za

Location and Access
Located opposite the
  women's residences of the
  University of Pretoria.
Bus: Brooklyn 8, ask for
  Burnett and Hilda Streets.
Nearest cross street is
  Bennett Street.

Prices
R9 per half hour
R18 per hour
V, MC, AmEx

Nearby Places to Visit
Union Buildings, Hatfield
  Plaza, Hatfield Square,
  Magnolia Dale Park

Hours
Mon-Fri 9am till late
Sat-Sun 10am till late

SOUTH AFRICA, STELLENBOSCH (WESTERN CAPE)

CyberSonic
36 Market Street • tel: +27 (0)21 887 4022 • No fax •
info@winelands.co.za • No website

Location and Access
Bus: All the buses to
  Stellenbosch, ask for
  Information Centre.
Train: Stellenbosch Line,
  Stellenbosch Station.
Nearest cross street is N1.

Hours
Mon-Sun 7am-11pm

Prices
R10 per half hour
R20 per hour
V, MC, DC

Nearby Places to Visit
The Cape Winelands

SOUTH AFRICA, VANDERBIJLPARK (GAUTENG)

CyberServ Internet—Corner of FW Beyers and DF Malan
Streets • tel: +27 (0)16 981 4525 • fax: +27 (0)16 981 4535 •
pieterv@cyberserv.co.za • www.cyberserv.co.za

Location and Access
Nearest large city is
  Johannesburg.

Hours
Mon-Sat 8am-8pm

Prices
R12 per half hour
R16 per hour
V, MC
Student discount available

Nearby Places to Visit
Hotels, casino on the bank
  of the Vaal River

TANZANIA, ARUSHA

Cybernet—India Street • tel: +255 57 3149 •
fax: +255 57 3525 • guest@cybernet.co.tz or guest1@cybernet.co.tz •
http://home.twiga.com/about-ar.html

Location and Access
Nearest large city is Dar-es-salaam.
Located near Clock Tower.
Nearest cross street is Sokoine Road.

Hours
Mon-Fri   9am-5pm
Sat   9am-1pm

Prices
/-1800 per half hour
/-3600 per hour
No credit cards

Nearby Places to Visit
Ngorogoro National Park,
Manyara National Park,
Serengeti National Park

TANZANIA, DAR-ES-SALAAM

Cyberspot Ltd.
Jamhuri Street • tel: +255 51 121425/121427 • No fax •
info@cyberspot.co.tz • www.cyberspot.co.tz

Location and Access
Located near Chick King Restaurant.
Nearest cross streets are Morogoro Road or Zanaki Street.

Hours
Mon-Sat   9am-midnight
Sun   9:30am-midnight

Prices
/-1500 per half hour
/-2000 per hour
No credit cards

UNITED ARAB EMIRATES, ABU DHABI

Cyber Cafe Inc.
Zayed the 2nd Street • tel: +971 (0)2 319000 • fax: +971 (0)2 312323 •
maher@cyber-cafe.com • ww.cyber-cafe.com/abudhabi

Location and Access
Located at the Sahara
   Residence Complex.
Best transport is taxi.
Nearest cross street is Al
   Najda Street.

Hours
Mon-Sun 8:30am-midnight

Prices
dirhams10.00 per half hour
dirhams20.00 per hour
V, MC, AmEx

Nearby Places to Visit
Downtown Abu Dhabi

ZIMBABWE, HARARE

Cyber Cafe—1st Floor, Nhaka Parade •
tel: +263 (0)4 781684/781686/775632 • fax: +263 (0)4 781687 •
sales@alphatech.co.zw • www.alphatech.co.zw/alphatechweb

Location and Access
Located near the Harare
   Central Post Office.
Nearest cross streets are
   Angwa Street and George
   Silundika Avenue.

Hours
Mon-Fri   8am-8pm
Sat   8am-4pm

Prices
Z$45 per half hour
Z$90 per hour
No credit cards
Student discount available

Nearby Places to Visit
1st Street Shopping Mall

Asia & the Pacific

AUSTRALIA, ALBURY (NEW SOUTH WALES)

Albury Local Internet Pty Ltd.

Shop 2, 326 Griffith Road, Lavington • tel: +61 (0)2 6040 2692 •
fax: +61 (0)2 6025 7144 • enquiries@albury.net.au • www.albury.net.au

Location and Access
Located opposite Coles
  carpark and the Lavington
  Library and next to the
  ANZ bank.
Bus: Ask for Lavington
  Square.
Nearest intersection is
  Urana Road/Griffith Road.

Prices
A$5 per half hour
A$10 per hour
V, MC, AmEx, DC

Hours
Mon-Fri   9am-5:30pm
Sat   9:30am-1pm

AUSTRALIA, BONDI BEACH (NEW SOUTH WALES)

phone.net.cafe

73-75 Hall Street • tel: +61 (0)2 9365 6100 •
fax: +61 (0)2 9365 6570 • No e-mail address • No website

Location and Access
Located near Bondi Beach.
Bus: Ask for Bondi Beach.

Nearby Places to Visit
Bondi Beach (backpackers
  heaven)

Hours
Mon-Sun 9am-9pm

Prices
A$6 per half hour
A$10 per hour
No credit cards

The Hub Internet Cafe—125 Margaret Street •
tel: +61 (0)7 3229 1119 • fax: +61 (0)7 3229 3566 •
info@thehub.com.au • www.thehub.com.au/cafe

Location and Access
Located near Brisbane
  Botanical Gardens.
Bus: Route 333, ask for
  near Albert and Margaret
  Streets.
Nearest cross street is
  Albert Street.

Hours
Mon-Fri   8am-8pm
Sat-Sun   9am-9pm

Prices
A$6 weekday and A$4.50
  weekend per half hour
A$12 per hour weekday and
  A$9 weekend per hour
V, MC
Student discount available

Purrer's Cyber Space Cafe—751 Stanley St., Woolloongabba •
tel: +61 (0)7 3392 1377 • fax: +61 (0)7 3392 1377 •
cyber@cyber-s-cafe.com.au • www.cyber-s-cafe.com.au/cyber

Location and Access
Located near Gabba Cricket
  Ground.
Bus: Ask for bus stop 9.
Train: Ask for Park Road.
Nearest cross street is
  Stanley Street.

Hours
Mon-Fri   7am-11pm
Sat-Sun   9am-11pm

Prices
A$5 per half hour
A$10 per hour
V, MC, AmEx, DC
Student discount available

AUSTRALIA, CANBERRA (CAPITOL TERRITORY)

cyberchino—33 Kennedy Street, Kingston •
tel: +61 (0)2 6295 7844 • fax: +61 (0)2 6295 7844 •
admin@cyberchino.com.au • www.cyberchino.com.au

Location and Access
Bus: Action buses, ask for
  Kennedy Street or
  Kingston Shops.

Hours
Mon-Fri   10am-midnight
Sat-Sun   9am-midnight

Prices
A$6 per half hour
A$10 per hour
V, MC, AmEx

AUSTRALIA, CLAREMONT (WESTERN AUSTRALIA)

Smileys Internet Cafe—Shop 18, 337 Stirling Highway •
tel: +61 (0)8 9385 5520 • fax: +61 (0)8 9385 5520 •
smileys@smileys.net • www.smileys.net

Location and Access
Located near Body Club
  gym.
Bus: Ask for Stirling
  Highway.

Train: Perth-Fremantle line,
  ask for Claremont.

Hours
Mon-Fri   9am-7pm
Sat   10am-5pm

Prices
A$7 per half hour
A$12 per hour
V, MC

Nearby Places to Visit
Perth and Fremantle

AUSTRALIA, COFFS HARBOUR (NEW SOUTH WALES)

Happy PlaNet—3/13 Park Avenue •
tel: +61 (02) 66 517520 • fax: +61 (02) 66 517522 •
hpcafe@happyplanet.com.au • www.happyplanet.com.au

Location and Access
Located near City Centre
  Mall.

Nearby Places to Visit
Rainforest, beach

Hours
Mon-Fri   9am-5pm
Sat   9am-midnight

Prices
A$6 per half hour
A$10 per hour
V, MC

AUSTRALIA, GREENSBOROUGH (VICTORIA)

Hard Drive Internet Cafe
98 Grimshaw Street • tel: +61 (0)3 9432 7866 •
fax: +61 (0)3 9432 7866 • harddrive@hdic.net.au • www.hdic.net.au

Location and Access
Nearest large city is
  Melbourne.
Located near Kentucky Fried
  Chicken.
Bus: Ask for Greensborough.
Train: Ask for
  Greensborough.
Nearest cross street is Henry
  Street.

Hours
Mon-Sat   noon-11pm
Sun   noon-6pm

Prices
A$5 per half hour
A$10 per hour
No credit cards
Student discount available

AUSTRALIA, KATHERINE (NORTHERN TERRITORY)

Homestead Cafe—Lot 102, Third Street •
tel: +61 (0)8 8972 3390 • fax: +61 (0)8 8972 3391 •
tammie@inspirit.com.au • www.inspirit.com.au/homestead/default.htm

Location and Access
Three blocks from the only
   traffic light in town.
   Nearest cross street is Giles
   Street.

Hours
Mon-Sun   6:30am-9pm

Prices
A$5 per half hour
A$10 per hour
No credit cards

Nearby Places to Visit
Railway Museum, School of
   the Air, Historical
   Museum, Katherine Gorge

AUSTRALIA, MELBOURNE (VICTORIA)

Binary Bar—243 Brunswick Street, Fitzroy •
tel: +61 (0)3 9419 7374 • fax: +61 (0)3 9419 7348/7347 •
info@binary.net.au • www.binary.net.au

Location and Access
Located near Vasettes
   Flowers.
Tram: 11 tram (Brunswick
   Street) or 96 tram
   (Nicholson Street), ask for
   Virgona's.
Located at the corner of
   Brunswick Street and
   Grieves Street.

Hours
Mon-Sun   3pm-1am

Prices
A$6 per half hour
A$12 per hour
V, MC

Nearby Places to Visit
Brunswick Street shopping
   and High Street

Cybernet Cafe—789 Glenferrie Road, Hawthorn •
tel: +61 (0)3 9818 1288 • fax: +61 (0)3 9818 1252 •
cybercaf@hilink.com.au • www.cyber.aus.net/home.htm

Location and Access
Located near Glenferrie rail-
way station.
Tram: 69, ask for stop 76.
Train: Alemain, Lilydale, or
Belgrave trains, ask for
Glenferrie Station.
Located between Burwood
Road and Barkers Road.

Hours
Mon-Thu &
   Sun   11am-10pm
Fri-Sat   11am-11pm

Prices
A$6 per half hour
A$12 per hour
V, MC, AmEx

Internet Cafe St. Kilda
9 Grey Street • tel: +61 (0)3 9534 2666 • fax: +61 (0)3 9534 2666 •
anthonydillon@hotmail.com • www.web.access.net.au/kennel

Location and Access
Located near the George
Hotel.
Tram: 16, 96, ask for Fitzroy
Street.
Nearest cross street is
Fitzroy Street.

Hours
Mon-Sun   9:30am-11pm

Prices
A$3 per half hour
A$6 per hour
No credit cards
Student discount available

Nearby Places to Visit
Fitzroy Street, St. Kilda

Melbourne Central Internet Cafe—Shop 133, Level 2,
Melbourne Central, 300 Lonsdale Street • tel: +61 (0)3 9663 8410 •
No fax • info@melbint.com.au • www.melbint.com.au

Location and Access
Located near Melbourne
  Central Shopping Centre.
Underground: City Loop, ask
  for Melbourne Central.
Tram: Swanston Street
  routes 1, 3, 5, 6, 8, 16,
  22, 25, 64, 67, 72, ask for
  Melbourne Central.
Nearest cross street is inter-
  section of Latrobe and
  Swanston Streets.

Hours
Mon-Fri   10am-6pm
Sat   11am-5:30pm
Sun   11am-5pm

Prices
A$5 per half hour
A$10 per hour
No credit cards

Nearby Places to Visit
Queen Victoria Market

Myer RMIT Computer Learning Centre—Level 4, 295
Lonsdale Street • tel: +61 (0)3 9661 1700 • fax: +61 (0)3 9661 1701 •
myerrmit@rmit.edu.au • www.training.rmit.edu.au/myer

Location and Access
Located near 1000-1800.
Bus: Ask for Lonsdale Street.
Tram: Ask for Lonsdale Street.
Underground: Ask for
  Melbourne Central.
Nearest cross street is the
  corner of Swantson and
  Lonsdale Streets.

Hours
Mon-Wed &
  Sat   10am-6pm

Thu-Fri   10am-7pm

Prices
A$5 per half hour
A$10 per hour
V, MC, AmEx, DC
Student discount available
  for members

Nearby Places to Visit
Victorian Arts Centre, Crown
  Casino, Southbank

Mukinbudin Telecentre
8 White Street • tel: +61 (0)8 9047 1129 • fax: +61 (0)8 9047 1088 •
muktelec@merredin.agn.com.au • No website

Location and Access
Located opposite The
  School.
Bus: Westrail bus, ask for
  Mukinbudin, opposite the
  pub.
Nearest cross street is
  Shadbolt Street.

Prices
A$6 per half hour
A$12 per hour
No credit cards

Nearby Places to Visit
Eagle Rock, Turtle Rock,
  Eluchbutting Rock,
  Berenbooding Rock

Hours
Mon-Fri   9am-5pm

Newcastle West Internet Cafe—538 Hunter Street •
tel: +61 (0)2 4929 7601 • fax: +61 (0)2 4929 6054 •
nwcafe@aaa.com.au • www.aaa.com.au/online/newcastle

Location and Access
Train: Newcastle, ask for
  Civic.

Hours
Mon-Fri   9am-7pm
Sat   9am-3pm
Sun   9am-5pm

Prices
A$5 per half hour
A$10 per hour
No credit cards

AUSTRALIA, NOOSA HEADS (QUEENSLAND)

NoosaNetCafe—Palms Arcade Shopping Centre, 2 Lanyana Way •
tel: +61 (0)7 5474 5770 • fax: +61 (0)7 5474 5771 •
info@noosa.com.au • www.noosa.com.au

Location and Access
Located near Coles-
Supermarket.
Bus: Sunbus from Caloundra
& Maroochydore, ask for
Noosa Fair.
Nearest cross street is
Sunshine Beach Road.

Hours
Mon-Sun   9am-6pm

Prices
A$6 per half hour
A$12 per hour
V, MC, AmEx

Nearby Places to Visit
Resort Town, national parks,
beaches

AUSTRALIA, PERTH (WESTERN AUSTRALIA)

Traveller's Club
499 Wellington Street • tel: +61 (0)8 9226 0660 •
fax: +61 (0)8 9226 0661•pstravel@git.com.au • www.travellersclub.com

Location and Access
Located near Perth Central
Train Station.
Bus: Central Area Transit,
ask for Forrest Place.
Train: All lines, ask for
Central Station.
Nearest cross street is
William Street.

Hours
Mon   9am-7pm
Tue-Fri   9am-6pm

Sat   10am-4pm
Sun   noon-4pm

Prices
A$3 per half hour
A$4 per hour
V, MC

Nearby Places to Visit
Art Gallery, Western
Australian Museum, Perth
Mint

AUSTRALIA, SOUTHPORT (QUEENSLAND)

Sugar Shack Internet Cafe
9 Nerang Street • tel: +61 (0)7 5532 4495 • No fax •
sugar@fan.net.au • www.sugarshack.com.au

Location and Access
Located near Australia Fair
Shopping Centre.
Bus: Surfside buses, ask for
Australia Fair, main bus
terminus.
Nearest cross street is
Scarborough Street or
Marine Parade.

Hours
Mon-Fri   9am-8pm
Sat   9am-5pm

Prices
A$5 per half hour
A$10 per hour
No credit cards

Nearby Places to Visit
The Gold Coast is
Queensland's major tourist
destination with many
attractions, such as
Dreamworld, Seaworld,
Movieworld, Currumbin
Bird and Animal Sanctuary.

AUSTRALIA, SYDNEY (NEW SOUTH WALES)

Digi.Kaf
174 St Johns Road, Glebe • tel: +61 (0)2 9660 3509 •
fax: +61 (0)2 9660 6405 • info@digikaf.com.au • www.digikaf.com.au

Location and Access
Located between the Nags
Head and British Lion
pubs.
Bus: 470 from Central
Station, ask for Glebe
Town Hall.
Nearest cross street is Ross
Street.

Hours
Mon-Thu   8am-6pm

Fri   8am-4pm &
           7pm-11pm
Sat-Sun   9am-6pm

Prices
A$5 per half hour
A$10 per hour
V, MC, AmEx
Student discount available

Nearby Places to Visit
Ten minutes from the center
of Sydney

overdose—135-137 Macquarie Street •
tel: +61 (0)2 9251 1968 • fax: +61 (0)2 92411996 •
overdosecafe@hotmail.com.au • No website

Location and Access
Located near Sydney Opera
House.
Underground: Ask for
   Circular Quay or Martin
   Place.
Nearest cross street is
   Bridge Street.

Hours
Mon-Sat   8am-3:30pm

Prices
Free

Nearby Places to Visit
Botanic Gardens, Rocks,
   Opera House

Shearers Cybercafe—99 Norton Street, Leichhardt •
tel: +61 (0)2 9572 7766 • fax: +61 (0)2 9572 7755 •
ausgard@cia.com.au • www.shearersbookshop.com.au/cyber

Location and Access
Located near Leichhardt
   Council, Paramatta Road,
   and Comedy Store.
Train: Ask for Stanmore.
Nearest cross street is
   Marion Street.

Hours
Mon-Fri &
   Sun   10am-10pm
Sat   10am-11pm

Prices
A$4 per half hour
A$8 per hour
V, MC, AmEx, DC

The SurfNet Cafe—Manly
5A Market Lane, Manly • tel: +61 (0)2 9976 0808 •
fax: +61 (0)2 9976 0505 •info@surfnet.net.au • www.surfnet.net.au

Location and Access
Located near Manly Library.
Transportation: 144 bus,
  Manly Ferry, Manly JetCat,
  ask for Manly Wharf.
Nearest cross street is
  Sydney Road.

Hours
Mon-Thu   9am-9pm
Fri-Sun   9am-7pm

Prices
A$3 per half hour
A$7 per hour
V, MC, AmEx, DC
Student discount available

Nearby Places to Visit
Manly Beach, Manly Corso,
  Marineland, Manly Wharf

Java Bay—Shop 4, 33 Wharf Street •
tel: +61 (0)7 5599 3232 • fax: +61 (0)7 5599 3477 •
info@javabay.com.au • www.javabay.com.au

Location and Access
Located opposite the
  Maritime Sculpture.
Bus: Surfside Bus Line &
  Interstate carriers, ask for
  Tweed Heads.

Hours
Mon-Fri   8am-6pm
Sat-Sun   10am-6pm

Prices
A$6 per half hour
A$10 per hour
V, MC
Student discount available

CHINA, URUMQI (XINJIANG)

Mark's Internet Center—19, Guangming Road •
tel: +0086-991-2317686 • fax: +0086-991-2619694 •
markinfo@xj.cninfo.net • www.markguide.com

Location and Access
Located near the Hongshan
Hotel.
Bus: 1, 7, 17, 101, 902, ask
for Xidaqiao stop.
Nearest cross street is
Xinhua Road.

Hours
Mon-Sun   midnight-
          midnight

Prices
RMB5 per half hour
RMB10 per hour
No credit cards

Nearby Places to Visit
Hongshan (Red Hill) Park

COOK ISLANDS, AVARUA (RAROTONGA)

Pacific Computers Ltd
Browns Arcade, Beach Road • tel: +682 20727 • fax: +682 20737 •
email@pacific.co.ck • www.pacific.co.ck

Location and Access
Located near Trader Jack's
Waterfront Bar and Grill.
Bus: Round the Island Bus,
ask for Browns Arcade.
Nearest cross street is
Beach Road.

Hours
Mon-Fri   8am-4pm
Sat   8am-noon

Prices
NZ$15 per half hour
NZ$30 per hour
No credit cards

COOK ISLANDS, AVARUA (RAROTONGA)

TCI Cyberbooth
Telecom Centre, Parekura • tel: +682 29 680 • fax: +682 21 123 •
info@oyster.net.ck • www.oyster.net.ck

Location and Access
Bus: Cooks buses, ask for
  Cooks Corner.

Nearby Places to Visit
Perfume Factory

Hours
Mon-Sun   midnight-
              midnight

Prices
NZ$10.50 per half hour
NZ$21 per hour
V, MC, AmEx, DC

FIJI ISLANDS, SUVA

The Republic of Cappuccino—Corner of Loftus Street and
Victoria Parade • tel: +679 300-333 • fax: +679 361-035 •
jp@internetfiji.com • No website

Location and Access
Located near Shell Hibiscus
  Service Station, Victoria
  Parade.
Bus: Any city-bound bus,
  ask for Dolphins
  Foodcourt.

Prices
F$6.60 per half hour
F$13.20 per hour
No credit cards

Nearby Places to Visit
Fiji Museum, Traps NiteClub

Hours
Mon-Thu &
  Sat   7am-11pm
Fri   7am-midnight
Sun   10am-7pm

Cyber Mall—138 Saphlya, Samarth Nagar, Varad Ganesh
Mandir Road • tel: +91 (0)240 350007 • fax: +91 (0)240 331191 •
vatan@bom3.vsnl.net.in • www.cybermallindia.com/cm/tariff

Location and Access
Located near Central Bus
stand road, Varad Ganesh
Mandir Road, and Hotel
IRA.
Auto rickshaw: Ask for
Samarth Nagar.
Nearest cross street is Varad
Ganesh Mandir Road.

Hours
Mon-Sun   8am-10pm

Prices
Rs80 per half hour
Rs150 per hour
V, MC
Student discount available
  for registered members

Nearby Places to Visit
Bibika Makbara, Panchakki,
Paithan, Nipat Niranjan,
Ellora, Ajanta, Mhaismal,
Shani Shignapur,
Pitalkhora

Maegabytes Cyber Cafe—9 Shriram Colony Samarth Nagar •
tel: +91 (0)240 331036/335304/330422 • fax: +91 (0)240 331036 •
jverghese@yahoo.com • No website

Location and Access
Located behind Hotel
Aurangabad Ashok.
Bus: All buses to
Aurangabad, ask for
Samarth Nagar.

Hours
Mon-Sun   8am-midnight

Prices
Rs40 per half hour
Rs75 per hour
V, MC, AmEx, DC
Student discount available

Nearby Places to Visit
The world-famous Ajantha &
Ellora caves

INDIA, BANGALORE (KARNATAKA)

Le Web—15/E. 2nd Floor, facing Church Street, Shrungar Shopping Centre, M.G. Road • tel: +91 (0)80 5091115/5587471 • No fax • leweb@blr.vsnl.net.in • No website

Location and Access
Located near Coffee House and FoodWorld.
Bus: Ask for Brigade Road.
Nearest cross streets are Brigade Road and Church Street.

Hours
Mon-Sat   8am-8pm
Sun   9am-5pm

Prices
Rs30 per half hour
Rs50 per hour
No credit cards

Nearby Places to Visit
Cubbon Park and Vidhana Soudha

INDIA, CALCUTTA (WEST BENGAL)

future.com—31, Raja Manindra Road • tel: +91 (0)33 5566072/5570932 • fax: +91 (0)33 5562689 • ganesh@giascl01.vsnl.net.in • www.india-future.com

Location and Access
Located near Belgachia Metro Station and opposite Ashu Babu Bazaar.
Bus: 3B, 3C/1, 3D, 3D/1, 47A, 47B, 219, 227, ask for Tala Park or Ashu Babu Bazaar.
Underground: Metro, ask for Belgachia.
Nearest cross street is near Tala Park.

Hours
Mon-Sun   10am-10pm

Prices
Rs60 per half hour
Rs120 per hour
No credit cards

Nearby Places to Visit
Calcutta itself

INDIA, CHENNAI (TAMIL NADU)

Netcafe@india—6 Kanaksri Nagar, Cathedral Road •
tel: +91 (0)44 8263779/8225427 • fax: +91 (0)44 8223286 •
netcafe@cyberidentity.com • www.cyberidentity.com

Location and Access
Located near Music Academy
and Hotel Chola Sheraton.
Bus: 23A, 27D, 29C, 29M,
ask for Music Academy.

Hours
Mon-Sun   7am-11pm

Prices
Rs50 at non-peak (7am-11
am, 1pm-4pm, 9pm-11
pm), Rs60 at peak

(11am-1pm, 4pm-9pm)
per half hour
Rs100 non-peak, Rs120
peak per hour
V, MC, AmEx, DC
Student discount available
for members

Nearby Places to Visit
Kalpa Druma, a shop for
buying Indian handicrafts,
etc.

INDIA, COCHIN (KERALA)

BTH Cyber Café—Gandhi Square, Durbar Hall Road •
tel: +91 (0)484 353501/361415 • fax: +91 (0)484 370502 •
bthekm@md2.vsnl.net.in • www.bharathotel.com

Location and Access
Located near the Shiva
Temple and the Indian
Airlines Office.
Bus: All buses through
Menaka Junction, ask for
Durbar Hall or TDM Hall.
Train: Allepey Express,
Rajadhani Express, Madras
Mail, ask for Ernakulam
Junction (EKM Junction).

Nearest cross street is M.G.
Road.

Hours
Mon-Sun   midnight-
midnight

Prices
Rs50 per half hour
Rs75 per hour
V, MC, AmEx, DC, D

Nearby Places to Visit
Kochi Backwaters

Cyberland—The Internet Cafe
38/384, near South Railway Flyover • tel: +91 (0)484 315217/313371 •
No fax • cyberland@keralahome.com • www.keralahome.com/cyberland

Location and Access
Located near Manorama
  Junction.
Bus: All buses going to
  Vytilla, Thripunithura from
  Cochin City, ask for
  Manorama Junction.
Train: All trains going to
  Cochin, ask for Ernakulam
  South Junction.

Hours
Mon-Sat   10am-10:30pm
Sun   2pm-10:30pm

Prices
Rs40 per half hour
Rs60 per hour
No credit cards

Nearby Places to Visit
Fort Cochin, Bolghatty
  Palace, Marine Drive,
  Jewish Church,
  Mattancherry Fort

Raiyaan Communication Service—Raiyaan Complex, M.G.
Rd., Padma Junction • tel: +91 (0)484 351387/354808/370671/
361029 • fax: +91 (0)484 380052 • raiyaan@giasmd01.vsnl.net.in •
www.richsoft.com/raiyaan

Location and Access
Located near City Hospital,
  Padma Junction.
Bus: All Padma route buses,
  ask for Padma Junction.

Prices
Rs30 per half hour
Rs60 per hour
No credit cards

Hours
Mon-Sat   8am-10pm
Sun   9am-1pm

INDIA, MUMBAI (MAHRASHTRA)

Online Cybercafe—82, Veer Nariman Road •
tel: +91 (0)22 2844716/23 • fax: +91 (0)22 2088350 •
onlinecybercafe@usa.net • www.online-cybercafe.com

Location and Access
Located between Churchgate
  Railway Station and Hotel
  Ambassador.
Bus: 81, 83, 84, 85, 89,
  101, 103, 106, 108, 121,
  122, 123, 132, 134, 137,
  138, ask for Churchgate.
Train: Western Railway, ask
  for Churchgate.

Hours
Mon-Sun   8am-1am

Prices
Rs80 per half hour
Rs160 per hour
No credit cards
Student discount available

Nearby Places to Visit
Gateway of India, CST (VT
  railway station)

INDIA, NEW DELHI (UTTAR PRADESH)

Cafe Wired World—2nd Floor Leisure Bowl, 34/35 Bawa
Potteries Complex, Aruna Asaf Ali Marg, Kishnagarh, Vasant Kunj •
tel: +91 (0)11 6122942/945 • No fax • webmaster@cafeww.com •
www.cafeww.com

Location and Access
Phone for directions.

Hours
Mon-Sun   11:30am-
          midnight

Prices
Call for prices
No credit cards

INDONESIA, DENPASAR (BALI)

Bali@Cyber Cafe & Restaurant—Jalan Pura Bagus Taruna
tel: +62 (0)361 761326 • fax: +65 2341024
(virtual fax in Singapore) • bl-cafe1@idola.net.id •
http://sunflower.singnet.com.sg/~hchua/cafe.htm

Location and Access
Located near Hotel
  Jayakarta-Bali.
Nearest cross street is
  Double Six Street.

Prices
Rp15.000 per half hour
Rp30.000 per hour
V, MC
Student discount available

Hours
Mon-Sun   8:30am-11pm

Nearby Places to Visit
Beach, main shopping street

INDONESIA, KUTA (BALI)

Legian Cyber—21st, Sahadewa Street •
tel: +62 (0)361 761804 • fax: +62 (0)361 752455 •
cyleg1@idola.net.id • www.idola.net.id/~cyleg1

Location and Access
Nearest cross street is Raya
  Legian Street.

Nearby Places to Visit
Kuta Beach

Hours
Mon-Fri   8am-10pm
Sat-Sun   8am-5pm

Prices
Rp15.000 per half hour
Rp30.000 per hour
No credit cards

INDONESIA, SENGGIGI LOMBOK (NUSA TENGGARA BARAT)

Bulan Cybercafe & Business Centre—Jalan Raya
Senggigi KM 1 • tel: +62 (0)370 693663 • fax: +62 (0)370 693832 •
Bulan@mataram.wasantara.net.id • www.angelfire.com/sd/pardi

Location and Access
Located near Dream Divers
   Diving Club.
Bus: Bemo from Ampenen
   by asking for Senggigi.
Nearest cross street is
   Senggigi Main Street.

Hours
Mon-Sat   8:30am-11pm
Sun   8:30am-9pm

Prices
Rp13.000 per half hour
Rp30.000 per hour
No credit cards
Student discount available

Nearby Places to Visit
Senggigi Beach and the Gili
   Islands

INDONESIA, UBUD (BALI)

Pondok Pekak Library
Monkey Forest Road • tel: +62 (0)361 976194 • No fax •
pondok@denpasar.wasantara.net.id • No website

Location and Access
Located on the east side of
   the soccer field; follow
   the path around the field.

Hours
Mon-Sat   9am-9pm
Sun   noon-5pm

Prices
Rp10.000 per half hour
Rp20.000 per hour
No credit cards

Nearby Places to Visit
Monkey Forest Sanctuary

JAPAN, KYOTO (NAKAGYO-KU)

Cafe Aspirin—3F A-Break Blvd 302 Higashidaimonji-cho
Shijo agaru teramachi-dori • tel: +81 (0)75 251 2351 •
fax: +81 (0)75 251 2336 • info@aspirin.co.jp • www.aspirin.co.jp

Location and Access
Located near Fujii-Daimaru
  Department.
Bus: Ask for Shijo-
  kawaramachi.
Underground: Ask for Shijo-
  karasuma.
Train: Kawaramachi to
  Hankyu line, ask for
  Kawaramachi.
Nearest cross street is Shijo-
  teramachi Crossing.

Hours
Mon-Sun   11am-9pm

Prices
¥300 per half hour
¥500 per hour
No credit cards

Nearby Places to Visit
Yasaka Shrine

JAPAN, OIZUMI-MACHI, ORA-GUN (GUNMA-KEN)

Internet Cafe GLOBAL
2-16-20 Fuji • tel: +81 (0)276 62 0885 • fax: +81 (0)276 40 3361 •
global@crscc.com • No website

Location and Access
Nearest cross street is
  National Route 354.

Hours
Tue-Sun   2pm-10pm

Prices
¥300 per half hour
¥600 per hour
No credit cards

Bean's Bit Cafe

6-2-29 Uehommachi Tennoji-ku • tel: +81 (0)6 6766 3566 •
fax: +81 (0)6 6766 3567 • bbc@interfarm.co.jp • www.interfarm.co.jp

Location and Access
Located near Kintetsu
   Department Store.
Bus: 1, 2, ask for
   Uehommachi 6-chome.
Underground: Tanimachi
   line, ask for Tanimachi 9-
   chome.
Train: Kintetsu line, ask for
   Uehommachi.
Nearest cross street is
   Sennichimae Street.

Hours
Mon-Sun   8:30am-9pm
(closed 1st & 3rd Sundays)

Prices
¥400 per half hour
¥500 per hour for members
No credit cards

Nearby Places to Visit
Osaka Castle, International
   House

Internet Cafe Web House Umeda

1-17 Kakuda-cho 3F Kita-ku • tel: +81 (0)6 6367 9555 •
fax: +81 (0)6 6361 7555 • office@netpower.co.jp • www.webhouse.co.jp

Location and Access
Located near Umeda Center
   Building and Hep Five
   Umeda.
Underground: Midohsuji
   (Red) line, Hankyu rail-
   ways, ask for Umeda.
Nearest cross street is Shin-
   Midohsuji.

Hours
Mon-Sun   11am-9pm

Prices
¥600 per half hour
¥1,200 per hour
V, MC, AmEx, DC

JAPAN, TOKUSHIMA

Cafe B—1-7 Suketo-bashi •
tel: +81 (0)886 53 4856 • fax: +81 (0)886 53 4856 •
tyoun@nmt.ne.jp • www.nmt.ne.jp/~tyoun/upload/b.html

Location and Access
Located near Suketo-bashi
  Park Hotel, Tokushima
  Park, Tokushima
  University.

Hours
Mon	noon-5:30pm
Tue-Sat	8am-11pm
Sun	noon-11pm

Prices
¥60 per half hour
¥160 per hour
No credit cards

Nearby Places to Visit
Castle hill

JAPAN, TOKYO

Cyberia Tokyo—Nishi-azabu 1-14-17 (Minato-ku Tokyo) •
tel: +81 (0)3 3423 0318 • fax: +81 (0)3 3423 3774 •
cyberia@cyberia.co.jp • www.cyberia.co.jp/tokyo

Location and Access
Located near Aoyama
  Cemetery.
Underground: Chiyoda Line,
  ask for Nogizaka Station.
Nearest cross street is
  Roppongi Avenue.

Hours
Mon-Sun   11am-11pm

Prices
¥500 per half hour (or free
  with one drink)
¥1,000 per hour (or free
  with two drinks)
No credit cards

Nearby Places to Visit
Roppongi

BaekRyong PC Bang—615-28 Hyoja 3 Dong, 200-093 •
tel: +82-361-255-9770, +82-11-731-8133 (for English) • No fax •
baekryong@hotmail.com • www.shinbiro.com/~brpc

Location and Access
Nearest big city is Seoul.
Located near HyoJa Tang
Sauna.
Bus: 20, 9 (or bus for
KangDaeHooMoon), ask for
HyoJa Mokyok Tang
(KwaHakKwanIpKu).
Located between Palho
Kwang Jang and
KangDaeHooMoon.

Hours
Mon-Sun   midnight-
midnight

Prices
W1,000 per half hour
W2,000 per hour
No credit cards
Student discount available

Nearby Places to Visit
Kangwon University, Eui-am
Lake, So-yang Lake

Net Cafe
300-2 Chongjin-dong Chongno-gu • tel: +82 (0)2-733-7973 •
fax: +82 (0)2-738-5794 • info@net.co.kr • www.net.co.kr

Location and Access
Located on the second floor
of the Knaghan Building
near Kyobo Book Center.
Subway: Purple line, ask for
Kwangwhamun, exit num-
ber 3.
Nearest cross street is
Kwangwhamun.

Hours
Mon-Fri   9:30am-midnight
Sat   10am-midnight
Sun   noon-10pm

Prices
W1,500 per half hour
W3,000 per hour
V, MC

Nearby Places to Visit
Kyongbok Palace

Starlet

591, Shinsadong, Kangnamgu • tel: +82 (0)2-546-5677 • No fax •
yoocw@link.co.kr • www.link.co.kr/starlet

Location and Access
Underground: Line 3, ask for
  Apgujeong Station.
Nearest cross streets are
  Tosan-no and Nonhyun-no.

Hours
Mon-Sat   11am-midnight

Prices
Free as long as no one is
  waiting
No credit cards

Nearby Places to Visit
Apgujeongdong—Cultural
  Center of River South

LAOS, LUANG PRABANG (LUANG PRABANG PREFECTURE)

PlaNet Cybercentre—Phothisalat Road •
tel: +856-71-252291 • fax: +856-21-216387 •
info@planet.laonet.net • www.planetcafe.net

Location and Access
Located near the royal
  palace.
Phothisalat Road is the
  main street down the center of the peninsula.

Hours
Mon-Sun   9am-8pm

Prices
kip36,000 or B240 per half
  hour
kip60,000 or B400 per hour
No credit cards

Nearby Places to Visit
Everything is beautiful in
  the Luang Prabang; World
  Heritage Village is in
  walking distance of the
  cafe.

LAOS, VIENTIANE (VIENTIANE PREFECTURE)

PlaNet Cafe
205 Setthatirath Road • tel: +856-21-218974 • fax: +856-21-216387 •
info@planet.laonet.net • www.planet.laonet.net

Location and Access
Located between Nam Phu
    Fountain and Wat Mixay.

Hours
Mon-Fri   9am-8pm
Sat   9am-2pm

Prices
kip27,000 or B240 per half
    hour
kip45,000 or B400 per hour
No credit cards

Nearby Places to Visit
Wat Mixay, Lao-Chinese
    Cultural Center,
    Revolutionary Museum,
    Nam Phu Fountain, Carol
    Cassidy Lao Textiles

MALAYSIA, DAMANSARA UTAMA (SELANGOR)

The Java Shoppe—No. 23 Jalan SS21/60,
Petaling Jaya, Selangor • tel: +60 (0)3 734-5362/712-2576/737-1943 •
fax: +60 (0)3 734-9150 • java@shoppe.com.my • www.shoppe.com.my

Location and Access
Located near Damansara
    Utama uptown foodcourt.
Bus: Intrakota 4, 10, 11,
    ask for DU Uptown.
Train: Putra, LRT, ask for
    Damansara Utama/Taman
    Megah.
Nearest cross street is
    Federal Highway.

Hours
Mon-Thu &
    Sun   noon-3am
Fri-Sat   10am-3am

Prices
M$2 per half hour
M$3 per hour
No credit cards

Nearby Places to Visit
One Utama Shopping Mall

The Java Shoppe, KLCC

Lot 346, Level 3, Suria • tel: +60 (0)3 734-5362/737-1943 •
fax: +60 (0)3 734-9150 • java@shoppe.com.my • www.shoppe.com.my

Location and Access
Located in the KLCC Suria
  Shopping Mall (Petronas
  Twin Towers).
Bus: Intrakota 259, 270, ask
  for KLCC, Twin Towers.
Nearest cross street is Jalan
  Ampang, Jalan P. Ramlee.

Hours
Mon-Thu &
  Sun   11am-10pm
Fri-Sat   11am-midnight

Prices
M$5 per half hour
M$10 per hour
No credit cards
Student discount available

Nearby Places to Visit
KLCC, Petronas Twin Towers,
  Suria shopping mall, KLCC
  Park

MALAYSIA, MALACCA (MALACCA STATE)

Stream Cafe—203F1 Jalan Kenanga 3/29A, Jalan Gajah Berang •
tel: +60 (0)6 284-7889 • fax: +60 (0)6 284-5539 •
stream@icon.com.my • www.stream.com.my

Location and Access
Located near Great Wall
  Supermarket.
Bus: Ask for main city bus
  terminus.
Nearest cross street is Jalan
  Gajah Berang.

Hours
Mon-Thu   11am-10pm
Fri-Sat   11am-midnight
Sun   11am-6pm

Prices
M$3 per half hour
M$6 per hour
DC

Nearby Places to Visit
Jonker Street (or Jalan
  Hang Jebat) and Heeren
  Street or (Jalan Tan Cheng
  Lock). Both known as the
  streets of antiques.

MALAYSIA, SHAH ALAM

The Java Shoppe, Shah Alam—No. 11A, Jalan Pinang E,
Section 18/E • Tel : +60 (0)3 541-1882 • No fax •
java@shoppe.com.my • www.shoppe.com.my

Location and Access
Bus: Cityliner 222, ask for
   Giant Grocery store.
Nearest cross street is
   Section 18/A.

Hours
Mon-Thu &
   Sun   10am-10pm
Fri-Sat   10am-midnight

Prices
M$2 per half hour
M$4 per hour
No credit cards
Student discount available

Nearby Places to Visit
Shah Alam Stadium, Masjid
   Sultan Azlan Shah (largest
   mosque in the world)

MALAYSIA, SUBANG JAYA (SELANGOR)

The Java Shoppe
No. 8, Jln SS15/8B • tel: +60 (0)3 734-5362/712-2576/737-1943 •
fax: +60 (0)3 734-9150 • java@shoppe.com.my • www.shoppe.com.my

Location and Access
Located near Subang Parade
   Shopping Mall.
Bus: Metro 3.
Train: Kommuter (Sabang
   Jaya), ask for SS15,
   Taylor's College.
Nearest cross street is
   Federal Highway.

Hours
Mon-Thu &
   Sun   noon-3am
Fri-Sat   10am-3am

Prices
M$2 per half hour
M$4 per hour
No credit cards

Nearby Places to Visit
Subang Parade Shopping
   Mall

NEPAL, KATHMANDU (BAGMATI ZONE)

EasyLink Cyber Cafes—Thamel PO Box 5273 •
tel: +977 1 420985/416239 • fax: +977 1 412178 •
easylink@visitnepal.com • www.visitnepal.com/easylink

Location and Access
Located behind Hotel
  Vaisali.
Bus: 10, 23.
Nearest cross street is
  Bhagawatisthan.

Hours
Mon-Fri &
  Sun   8am-11pm

Prices
Rs60 per half hour
Rs120 per hour
V, MC, AmEx
Student discount available

Nearby Places to Visit
Kathmandu, temples, and
  much more

NEPAL, POKHARA

Quick Link
6-Lakes side • tel: +977 61 24600/26723 • fax: +977 61 26839 •
qlink@mos.com.np, qlink@cnet.wlink.com.np • www.visitnepal/easylink

Location and Access
Located near Hotel the
  Mountain Top.
Bus: Toward the lake side,
  ask for Barahi chowk.
Nearest cross street is
  Hallane Chowk.

Hours
Mon-Tue &
  Thu-Sun 8am-9pm
Wed   8am-6pm

Prices
Rs150 per half hour
Rs300 per hour
No credit cards
Student discount available

Nearby Places to Visit
Phewa Lake, Devi's
  Waterfall, Mahendra Gupha
  Cave

LiveWire—239 Queen Street, Level 1, Mid City Cinema Complex •
tel: +64 (0)9 356 0999 • fax: +64 (0)9 356 0999 •
livewire@livewire.co.nz • www.livewire.co.nz

Location and Access
Located near McDonald's.
Bus: Toward center of town,
    ask for Queen Street near
    McDonald's.
Nearest cross street is
    Wellesley Street.

Hours
Mon-Wed 9am-11pm
Thu-Fri 9am-midnight
Sat 10am-midnight
Sun 10am-10pm

Prices
NZ$6 per half hour
NZ$12 per hour
V, MC

Nearby Places to Visit
Museum, waterfront, Sky
    Casino and Tower, shop-
    ping

Net Central Cybercafe

Lorne Street • tel: +64 (0)9 373 5186 • fax: +64 (0)9 373 5216 •
info@netcentral.co.nz • www.netcentral.co.nz

Location and Access
Bus: Ask for Victoria Street.
Nearest cross street is
    Victoria Street.

Hours
Mon-Sun 9:30am-10pm

Prices
NZ$7.20 per half hour
NZ$14.40 per hour
V, MC

InternetP@L—158 Manchester Street •
tel: +64 (0)3 366 2222/363 1133 • fax: +64 (0)3 377 2570 •
atul@netpal.co.nz • www.netpal.co.nz

Location and Access
Bus: Toward town center,
  ask for the square.
Nearest cross street is
  Hereford Street.

Hours
Mon-Sun   7am-11pm

Prices
NZ$6 per half hour
NZ$12 per hour
No credit cards

Nearby Places to Visit
Asia Pacific Travel

Coromandel Cyberplace—390 Pagitt Street •
tel: +64 (0)7 866 7377 • fax: +64 (0)7 866 7377 •
coromandelcyberplace@yahoo.com • http://members.tripod.com/
coromandelcyberplace/coromandelcyberplace.html

Location and Access
Located near Coromandel
  Information Centre.
Train: Drive Creek Railway
  and Potteries, ask for
  Driving Creek.
Nearest cross street is Rings
  Road.

Hours
Mon-Fri   10am-when last
                  customer
                  leaves

Sat-Sun   by appointment
                  only

Prices
NZ$6 per half hour
NZ$12 per hour
V, MC, AmEx, DC

Nearby Places to Visit
Coromandel Forest Reserves,
  Hauraki Gulf, Driving
  Creek Small Gauge
  Railway, native Maori sites

Vudu Cafe Queenstown

23 Beach Street • tel: +64 (0)3 442 5357 • fax: +64 (0)3 441 8899 •
cafe@vudu.co.nz • www.vudu.co.nz

Location and Access
Phone for directions.

Hours
Mon-Sun   8am-10pm

Prices
NZ$6 per half hour
NZ$10 per hour
V, MC
Student discount available

Cybersurf Internet Café—Shop 11, Piccadilly Arcade, Grey

Street • tel: +64 (0)7 579 0140 • fax: +64 (0)7 571 2580 •
cybersf@cybersurf.co.nz • www.cybersurf.co.nz

Location and Access
Located near New Zealand
Post.
Bus: From Auckland, ask for
   Tauranga Information
   Center. Then ask inside for
   directions to the cafe.
Nearest cross street is
   Devonport Road.

Hours
Mon-Fri   9am-6pm

Sat   10am-4pm
Sun   11am-4pm

Prices
NZ$7 per half hour
NZ$12 per hour
No credit cards

Nearby Places to Visit
Rotorua, Maori Pa meeting
   house, mud pools, hot
   springs, geyser pools

Waipu Cyber Centre—15-17 The Centre •
tel: +64 (0)9 432 0225/432 0045 • fax: +64 (0)9 432 0225 •
anpicket@igrin.co.nz • www.geocities.com/thetropics/paradise/6223
or www.igrin.co.nz/~anpicket

Location and Access
Located opposite the Lotto
  Shop.
Bus: Auckland/Whangarei
  route, ask for the Cyber
  Centre.

Hours
Mon-Thu	9:30am-6:30pm
Fri-Sat	9:30am-7pm
Sun	open by appointment

Prices
NZ$5 per half hour
NZ$10 per hour
V, MC, AmEx

Nearby Places to Visit
Waipu House of Memories,
  beaches, horse trekking,
  walks, camping grounds,
  NZ Oil Refinery Visitors
  Centre

Net Arena
115 Cuba Street • tel: +64 (0)4 384 1185 • fax: +64 (0)4 384 1187 •
cybercafe@netarena.co.nz • www.netarena.co.nz

Location and Access
Located near Burger King.
Nearest cross street is
  Manners Street.

Hours
Mon-Fri	9:30am-10pm
Sat-Sun	10am-10pm

Prices
NZ$2 per six minutes
NZ$10 per hour
V, MC, AmEx

Nearby Places to Visit
Te Papa (New Zealand's
  national museum)

CyberHeads Cafe

2nd Floor, LD Centre, Lacson-7th Streets • tel: +63 (0)34 433 1604 • No fax • cybheads@mozcom.com • www.lasaltech.com

Location and Access

Located near Provincial Capitol Lagoon.

Bus and Jeepney: Bata or Mandalagan route; taxis are also available.

Nearest cross street is Lascon Street.

Hours

Mon-Sun   3pm-midnight

Prices

P37.50 per half hour
P75 per hour
V, MC, DC
Student discount available

Nearby Places to Visit

Capitol Lagoon and Negros Museum, Mt. Kanlaon National Park, Lakawon Island, Mambucal Mountain Resort, Balay Negrense

CyberHeads Cafe—2nd Floor, MC Metroplex, BS Aquino Drive • tel: +63 (0)34 433 1604 • No fax • cybheads@lasaltech.com • www.lasaltech.com

Location and Access

Located near Provincial Capitol Lagoon.

Jeepney: Bata or Mandalagan route; taxis are also available.

Hours

Mon-Sat   9am-7pm

Prices

P25 per half hour
P50 per hour
V, MC, DC
Student discount available

Nearby Places to Visit

Mt. Kanlaon National Park, Lakawon Island, Mambucal Mountain Resort, Balay Negrense

Cyberpoint Cafe

R.N. Abejuela-Pabayo Streets • tel: +63 (0)88 857 2320 • No fax •
thebin@cyberpoint-cafe.com • www.cyberpoint-cafe.com

Location and Access
Located opposite Magsaysay
  Monument.
Bus and Jeepney: Pier,
  Lapasan, and Bugo Liners
  route, ask for opposite the
  Magsaysay Monument.

Hours
Mon-Sat   9:30am-midnight

Prices
P25 per half hour
P50 per hour
V, MC

Nearby Places to Visit
Xavier University Museum,
  Golden Friendship Park

Coffee California at Powerbooks—SM Megamall, Ground

Floor, Building A • tel: +63 (0)2 635 2898 • fax: +63 (0)2 725 6583 •
beanme@coffeecalifornia.com • www.coffeecalifornia.com

Location and Access
Located near the Megamall.
Bus: Ask for Megamall.
Nearest cross street is EDSA.

Hours
Mon-Sun   10am-9pm

Prices
P50 per half hour
P90 per hour
No credit cards
Student discount available

CyberNet Cafe—036-120/121 Terminal 2 Changi International Airport • tel: +65 5461968 • fax: +65 5461969 • admin@cybertrek.com.sg • www.cybertrek.com.sg

Location and Access
Located in the airport
Viewing Mall.
Bus: Ask for the airport.

Hours
Mon-Sun   8am-10pm

Prices
S$4.50 per half hour
S$8 per hour
V, MC
Student discount available

CyberNet Cafe—036-120/121 Terminal 2 Changi International Airport • tel: +65 5461968 • fax: +65 5461969 • admin@cybertrek.com.sg • www.cybertrek.com.sg

Location and Access
Located in the airport
Transit Lounge.
Bus: Ask for the airport.

Prices
S$4.50 per half hour
S$8 per hour
V, MC
Student discount available

Hours
Mon-Sun   7am-11:30pm

Icon Bytes Bug

39 Stamford Road, #02-12 Stamford House • tel: +65 3339027/8 •
fax: +65 3339029 • petrina@pacific.net.sg • No website

Location and Access
Phone for directions.

Hours
Phone for hours.

Prices
S$2 per fifteen minutes
No credit cards

Nearby Places to Visit
CHIJMES, City Hall, Arts
  Centre, YMCA

Internet Centre

32 Wallich Street, #01-63 Wallich Building • tel: +65 3244361 •
fax: +65 3244362 • admin@cybertrek.com.sg • www.cybertrek.com.sg

Location and Access
Located near Tanjong Pagar
  MRT Station.
Underground: MRT (Mass
  Rapid Transit), ask for
  Tanjong Pagar Station.

Prices
S$4.50 per half hour
S$8.50 per hour
No credit cards
Student discount available

Hours
Mon-Fri   9am-7pm
Sat   9am-5pm

THAILAND, BANGKOK

Cyberia Internet Cafe—654-8 Sukhumvit Rd., Corner Soi 24 •
tel: +66 (0)2 2593356 • fax: +66 (0)2 2593358 •
kulthep@cyberia.co.th • www.cyberia.co.th

Location and Access
Located near the Emporium
Shopping Complex.
Bus: Ask for the Emporium
Shopping Complex.

Hours
Mon-Sun   9:30am-midnight

Prices
B125 per half hour
B250 per hour
V, MC, AmEx, DC
Student discount available

THAILAND, BANGKOK

Explorer Internet Café
Surawong Road • tel: +66 (0)2 6340944 • No fax •
w_watchara@hotmail.com • www.cvp.co.th/gigared

Location and Access
Located near Patpong.
Bus: 16, ask for Patpong.

Hours
Mon-Fri	2pm-1am
Sat	2pm-10pm
Sun	5pm-1am

Prices
B120 per half hour
B240 per hour
No credit cards

Nearby Places to Visit
Patpong

THAILAND, BANGKOK

Pumpkin Netc@fe—410/3-4 Suriwong Road, Bangrak •
tel: +66 (0)2 2335000 ext 409 • fax: +66 (0)2 2371482 •
narin@cbu.net • www.members.xoom.com/pumpkincafe

Location and Access
Located near Suriwongse
  Tower Inn.
Bus: 16, 35, 75, 136, ask
  for Mahesak Road.

Prices
B90 per half hour
B150 per hour
V, MC, AmEx

Hours
Mon-Sun   9:30am-midnight

THAILAND, CHIANGMAI

Future Pacific Internet Center—89/2 Galare Food
Center, Night Bazaar, Changklan Road Muang • tel: +66 (0)53 818787•
fax: +66 (0)53 818787 • f-pac@cmnet.co.th • No website

Location and Access
Located near Galare Food
  Center, Night Bazaar.
Bus: Ask for Galare Food
  Center, Night Bazaar.

Prices
B90 per half hour
B180 per hour
AmEx
Student discount available

Hours
Mon-Sun   11am-11pm

THAILAND, KOH PHANGAN (SURATTHANI)

Phangan Batik Internet Service—79/10-12 Thongsala
Town • tel: +66 (0)77 238401 • fax: +66 (0)77 238401 •
internet@kohphangan.com • www.kohphangan.com/batik/internet

Location and Access
Pickup, Motorcycle, and
    Taxis: Ask for Thongsala
    Town.
Nearest cross street is Krung
    Thai Bank Street.

Hours
Mon-Sun   10am-10pm

Prices
B120 per half hour
B200 per hour

No credit cards
Student discount available

Nearby Places to Visit
Koh Phangan is an island in
    the Gulf of Thailand. It's
    about 40 minutes by boat
    from Koh Samui. Very
    famous Full Moon Party
    (300,000 visitors each
    year).

THAILAND, PASANG-MAECHAN (CHIANGRAI)

Hilltribe-Internet-Cyber-Kitchen—360 Moo. 3-Soi 1 •
tel: +66 (0)1 8827279 • fax: +49 (0)89 66617/40866 •
cyberkitchen@gmx.net • www.welcome.to/chiangmai+chiangrai

Location and Access
Located behind the Esso
    Station in Pasang-
    Maechan–Chiangri
    Province.
Bus: From Chiangrai or
    Maesai, ask for Pasang
    Esso Pump Station.
Nearest cross street is
    Maesalong junction.

Hours
Mon-Sun   midnight-
                midnight

Prices
B80 per half hour
B140 per hour
No credit cards

Nearby Places to Visit
The Golden Triangle

CONNECT Internet Coffee Bar & Restaurant with Guesthouse & Laundry—125/8-9 Rath-U-Thit Road •
tel: + 66 (0)76 294195 • fax: + 66 (0)76 294195 •
connect@beachpatong.com • www.beachpatong.com/connect

Location and Access
Located in Paradise Complex near James Dean Bar.
Bus: Phuket Town-Patong Beach line, ask for Paradise Complex.

Hours
Mon-Sun   10am-midnight

Prices
B120 per half hour
B200 per hour
V, MC

Nearby Places to Visit
The beach

VIETNAM, HANOI (HOAN KIEM)

Queen Cafe Travel—Internet
65 Hang Bac Street • tel: +84 4 8260860 • fax: +84 4 8260300 •
queenaz@fpt.vn • www.queencafe.com.vn

Location and Access
Phone for directions.

Hours
Mon-Sun   6am-11pm

Prices
US$1.50 per half hour
US$3 per hour
V, MC, AmEx

333 Restaurant/Cybercafe
201 De Tham Street, District 1 • tel: +84 8 8360205 •
fax: +84 8 8360205 • hue@hcmc.netnam.vn • No website

Location and Access
Located near the main Pham
  Ngu Lao travelers area.

Nearby Places to Visit
Ben Thanh Market

Hours
Mon-Sun   very early to very
              late

Prices
VND12.000 per half hour
VND24.000 per hour
V, MC, AmEx

Central &
South America
with the
Caribbean

ARGENTINA, BUENOS AIRES (BUENOS AIRES)

CyberCafe
1886 Maure • tel: +54 (0)14 7713030 • fax: +54 (0)14 7742419 •
info@cybercafe.com.ar or info@cyber.com.ar • www.cybercafe.com.ar

Location and Access
Located near La Abadia
  Shopping Mall and Central
  Military Hospital.
Bus: 15, 29, 55, 59, 60, 64,
  118.
Subway: Linea D.
Train: Ferrocarril Mitre line,
  Lisandro de La Torre sta-
  tion.
Nearest cross street is
  Avenida Luis Maria
  Campos.

Hours
Mon-Fri   9am-midnight
Sat   6pm-midnight

Prices
Arg$5 per half hour
Arg$7.50 per hour
V, MC, AmEx
Student discount available

Nearby Places to Visit
La Abadia Shopping Mall, La
  Imprenta Shopping Center,
  Belgrano University

ARGENTINA, CORDOBA (CORDOBA)

Peperina Cyber Café
Maipu 264 • tel: +54 (0)351 4283407 • No fax • contacto@peperina.
com or peperina@peperina.com • www.peperina.com

Location and Access
Bus: Ask for downtown.
Nearest cross street is
  Avenida Olmos.

Hours
Mon-Sat   8am-midnight
Sun   6pm-midnight

Prices
Arg$5.20 per half hour
Arg$8.70 per hour
No credit cards
Student discount available

Nearby Places to Visit
Cathedral of Cordoba

Krackers Cafe Informatico

2069 Mitre • tel: +54 (0)223 4946121 • No fax • hack@argenet.com.ar • www.krackers.com.ar

Location and Access

Located near Peatonal San Martin.

Bus: All buses to Luro and Mitre, ask for Monument to San Martin.

Nearest cross street is Avenue Colon.

Hours

Mon-Fri	9am-3am
Sat	9am-5am
Sun	3pm-3am

Prices

Arg$4 per half hour
Arg$6 per hour
No credit cards
Student discount available

Nearby Places to Visit

Monument to San Martin, the Cathedral

Cyb@r Café

264 Espejo • tel: +54 (0)61 233224/292880 • No fax • abrunet@lanet.com.ar • www.mendozaweb.com

Location and Access

Located near Plaza Independencia.

Bus: 80, 60, 90, 100, 120, ask for Parada Plaza Independencia.

Nearest cross street is Patricias Mendocinas (Plaza Independencia).

Hours

Mon-Fri	8am-11pm
Sat	8:30am-2pm

Prices

Arg$3.50 per half hour
Arg$6 per hour
No credit cards
Student discount available with ISIC

Nearby Places to Visit

Peatonal Sarmiento, Plaza España

ARUBA, ORANJESTAD

Cafe Internet

#204, Royal Plaza Mall, LG Smith Boulevard • tel: +297 824500 •
fax: +297 828534 • bizopp@cybercafe.aw • www.cybercafe.aw

Location and Access
Located opposite the Cruise
  Terminal gate in down-
  town Oranjestad, inside
  the Royal Plaza Mall.
Bus: Ask for Downtown
  Oranjestad.

Prices
US$5.75 per half hour
US$11.50 per hour
V, MC, AmEx

Hours
Mon-Sat   10am-9:30pm
Sun   noon-8pm

BELIZE, SAN IGNACIO (CAYO)

EVAS cafe

22 Burns Avenida • tel: +501 922267 • No fax • evas@btl.net •
http://member.spree.com/evasonline

Location and Access
Bus: Ask for Batty San
  Ignacio.
Nearest cross street is Burns
  Avenida.

Hours
Mon-Sun   7am-11pm

Prices
US$4 per half hour
US$8 per hour
No credit cards

90

BOLIVIA, LA PAZ (MURILLO)

Cibercafe MoNET
Calle 11 Obrajes • tel: +591 (0)2 785541 • fax: +591 (0)2 785541 •
rodasbun@mail.cafe-monet.com • www.cafe-monet.com

Location and Access
Located near Plaza de
  Obrajes between Avenidas
  Ormachea and Villamil.
Bus: Trufi A, ask for Plaza
  de Obrajes.
Nearest cross street is
  Avenida Hernando Siles.

Hours
Mon-Fri	9am-9pm
Sat	9am-noon

Prices
BS7.5 per half hour
BS15 per hour
No credit cards

Nearby Places to Visit
Valle de la Luna

BOLIVIA, LA PAZ (MURILLO)

TorinoNet Internet Solutions
457 Calle Socabaya • tel: +591 (0)2 364333 • No fax •
cyber-cafe@torino-net.com • www.torino-net.com/cybercafe.htm

Location and Access
Located near Hotel Torino,
  Plaza Murillo (Goverment
  Palace).
Bus: CH, H, M, 254, ask for
  Plaza Murillo.
Nearest cross street is Calle
  Potosi, Plaza Murillo.

Hours
Mon-Sat	9:30am-10pm
Sun	9:30am-3pm

Prices
US$2 per half hour
US$4 per hour
No credit cards

Nearby Places to Visit
Plaza Murillo (Goverment
  Palace), Museo de la
  Catedral, Museo Nacional
  del Arte

BRAZIL, BELO HORIZONTE (MINAS GERAIS)

Pegasus Cafe

57 Rua Sergipe • tel: +55 (0)31 213 1088 • fax: +55 (0)31 273 7527 •
cafe@pegasus.com.br • www.pegasus.com.br

Location and Access
Phone for directions.
Ask here for more cafes in
 Brazil connected to
 Pegasus.

Hours
Mon-Sun   8am-10pm

Prices
Br$3.50 per half hour
Br$3.50 per hour
No credit cards

BRAZIL, JUIZ DE FORA (MINAS GERAIS)

ArtNet Sistemas Internet Ltda.

2281/513, Rio Branco • tel: +55 (0)32 215 5202 •
fax: +55 (0)32 215 0438 • artnet@artnet.com.br • www.artcafe.com.br

Location and Access
Located near Halfeld Park.
Bus: Any bus which goes
 along Rio Branco Avenue,
 ask for Halfeld Park.
Nearest cross street is
 Halfeld Street.

Prices
Br$3.50 per half hour
Br$7 per hour
V, MC, AmEx, DC

Hours
Mon-Fri   8am-6pm
Sat   8am-noon

Arroba Cafe Ltda—Avenida das Americas 4666 luc B215/216
Barra Shopping • tel: +55 (0)21 431 9727 • fax: +55 (0)21 431 9840 •
webmaster@arrobacafe.com.br • www.arrobacafe.com.br

Location and Access
Located near Rock in Rio
Cafe.
Bus: 175, 179, 233, 234,
524, 701, 702, 703, 742,
748, 753, 754, 755, 852,
853, 854, 855, 882, ask
for Barra Shopping.
Nearest cross street is
Avenida das Americas.

Hours
Mon-Wed   noon-midnight
Sat   noon-3am
Sun   noon-11pm

Prices
Br$6 per half hour
Br$12 per hour
V, MC, DC

Nearby Places to Visit
Barra Shopping–the biggest
mall in Latin America.

Internet House—195, Nossa Senhora de Copacabana Avenue,
Shop 106-Copacabana • tel: +55 (0)21 542 3348 •
fax: +55 (0)21 542 3348 • internethouse@openlink.com.br • No website

Location and Access
Located near Copacabana
Palace Hotel and the
Meridien Hotel.
Bus: Ask for Copacabana.
Underground: Ask for
Copacabana.

Hours
Mon-Sat   9:30am-10pm

Prices
Br$5 per half hour
Br$10 per hour
V, MC, AmEx, DC

Nearby Places to Visit
Copacabana Beach, Sugar
Loaf

BRAZIL, SAO PAOLO (SAO PAOLO)

Cafe com Leiternet
Rua Cel. Camisao 226 B • tel: +55 (0)11 867 0739 •
fax: +55 (0)11 816 0289 • artagent@that.com.br • www.midia.com/cafe

Location and Access
Located near the University of Sao Paolo.
Bus: Vila Gomes, ask for the terminus, last stop.

Hours
Mon-Thu &
  Sat   by appointment
            only
Fri   8pm-11:30pm

Prices
Br$3.50 per half hour
Br$7 per hour
No credit cards

Nearby Places to Visit
University of Sao
  Paolo–Butanta

CHILE, PUERTO BARAS (LLANQUIHUE)

2nd Floor E-mail @ Internet
Avenida Gramado • tel: +56 (0)2 311901 • No fax •
pvarasint@yahoo.com • No website

Location and Access
Located near Supermarket Vyhmeister.
Bus: Varmont-Expresso, ask for Avenida Gramado and San Bernardo.
Nearest cross street is San Jose.

Hours
Mon-Sun 9am-midnight

Prices
Ch$2.000 per half hour
Ch$4.000 per hour
No credit cards

Nearby places to visit
Volcano Osorno, Volcano Calbuco, Lake Llanquihue, District of the Lake

CHILE, SANTIAGO (PROVIDENCIA)

Cafe Internet Cybercenter

170 General Holley • tel: +56 (0)2 2314207 • fax: +56 (0)2 2314209 •
info@cybercenter.cl • www.cybercenter.cl

Location and Access
Located near Suecia Street.
Metro: Ask for Los Leones
   station.
Nearest cross street is
   Providencia Ave.

Hours
Mon-Sat   10am-10pm

Prices
Ch$1.800 per half hour
Ch$3.600 per hour
V, MC, AmEx, DC
Student discount available

Nearby Places to Visit
San Cristobal Hill,
   Providencia Ave. shopping

CHILE, SANTIAGO (PROVIDENCIA)

Cafe Virtual—145 Alameda, Plaza Italia •
tel: +56 (0)2 6386846 • fax: +52 (0)2 6873996 •
webmaster@cafe-virtual.cl • www.cafe-virtual.cl

Location and Access
Located near Plaza Italia, in
   front of Hotel Crowne
   Plaza.
Underground: Ask for
   Baquedano.
Train: Ask for Plaza Italia.

Hours
Mon-Thu	10am-11pm
Fri	10am-2am
Sat	5pm-2am
Sun	5pm-11pm

Prices
US$3 per half hour
US$6 per hour
V, MC

CHILE, VALDIVIA

Centro @ Internet
236 Letelier • tel: +56 (0)63 294300 • fax: +56 (0)63 294300 •
centro@libertad7.com • www.libertad7.com

Location and Access
Located near La Plaza.
Bus: All buses, ask for the
town center.
Nearest cross street is
Central Place.

Hours
Mon-Sat   11am-8pm

Prices
Ch$1.100 per half hour
Ch$2.200 per hour
No credit cards
Student discount available

Nearby Places to Visit
The Church

CHILE, VILLARRICA

La Torre Suiza
969 Francisco Bilbao • tel: +56 (0)45 411213 • fax: +56 (0)45 411213 •
info@torresuiza.com • www.torresuiza.com

Location and Access
Bus: From all the major
cities of Central Chile, ask
for the main bus terminal.
Nearest cross street is Pedro
de Valdivia.

Hours
Mon-Sun   11am-11pm

Prices
Ch$1.500 per half hour
Ch$3.000 per hour
No credit cards

Nearby Places to Visit
Volcano and Lake Villarrica,
Pucón

COLOMBIA, CALI (VALLE)

Hotel Residencial JJ—14-47 Avenida 8A Norte •
tel: +57 (09)2 661 2964/661 8979 • fax: +57 (09)2 661 2964/661
8979 • jjjhotel@hotmail.com • No website

Location and Access
Located near Bolivar
  Theater.
Bus: All city lines, ask for El
  Cam and La Ermita.
Nearest cross street is Sixth
  Avenue.

Hours
Mon-Fri   6am-midnight
Sat-Sun   8am-midnight

Prices
Col$2.500 per half hour
Col$5.000 per hour
MC, DC
Student discount for guests

Nearby Places to Visit
Gold Museum, Cali Zoo,
  History Museums,
  Chipichape Shopping
  Center. Tours of "El
  Paraiso" for visitors
  arranged by the Hotel.

COLOMBIA, CARTAGENA (BOLIVAR)

Hotel Chalet Suizo—Calle de la Media Luna 10-36 •
tel: +57 (09)5 6647861 • fax: +57 (09)5 6647861 •
chalet@col3.telecom.com.co • www.salelawrence.com/chome.htm

Location and Access
Located near Parque
  Centenario.

Hours
Mon-Sun   7:30am-9pm

Prices
Col$3.000 per half hour
Col$6.000 per hour
No credit cards

Nearby Places to Visit
Barrio Getsemaní, Castillo
  San Felipe

COLOMBIA, PEREIRA (RISARALDA)

Cafenet

Calle 3 #13-28, local 2 • tel: +57 (09)63 313149 •
fax: +57 (09)63 314844 • info@cafenet.avan.net • www.cafenet.net.co

Location and Access
Located near Comfamiliar, a
supermarket.
Bus: 23, ask for Avenida
   Circunvalar near
   Comfamiliar Supermarket.
Nearest cross street is
   Avenida Circunvalar.

Hours
Mon-Sat   9am-8pm

Prices
US$2 per half hour
US$4 per hour
No credit cards
Student discount available

COSTA RICA, PORT OF GOLFITO (GOLFITO)

Land Sea Services (Servicios Tierra Mar, S.A.)

500 meters south of Central Park on the waterfront •
tel: +506 775 1614 • fax: +506 775 1300 • landsea@sol.racsa.co.cr •
www.costaricasur.com/landsea

Location and Access
Located between the Yellow
   Yacht Marina and the
   cemetery on the main
   road in town.
Bus: Ask for Cemetario.

Hours
Mon-Sat   7am-5pm with
               after-hours
               service bell

Prices
US$.10 per minute for
general computer use
US$.20 per minute while
   on-line
V

Nearby Places to Visit
National parks and Jungle
   Refuge, deep sea fishing,
   rainforest lodges, river
   and sea kayaking, famous
   surf breaks, historic
   Banana Port, duty free
   shopping

ATEC (Talamancan Assoc. of Ecotourism & Conservation)—Across the street from Soda Tamara • tel: +506 750 0398 • fax: +506 750 0191 • atecmail@sol.racsa.co.cr • www.greencoast.com/atec.htm

Location and Access
Located next to Casa de
   Cultura.
Bus: From San Jose and
   Limon to Manzanillo and
   Sixaola, ask for Puerto
   Viejo.
On the main street, this is a
   very small town.

Hours
Mon-Tue &
   Thu-Fri   7am-9pm

Wed	7am-noon & 2pm-9pm
Sat	8am-noon & 1pm-9pm
Sun	8am-noon & 4pm-8pm

Prices
US$3 per half hour
US$6 per hour
No credit cards

Hot Coffee Internet Cafe
275 meters north of National Theater • tel: +506 258 0303 •
fax: +506 258 0606 • hotcoffee@kitcom.net • www.kitcom.net/hotcoffee

Location and Access
Located near Automercado.
Nearest cross streets are
   Third Avenue and Third
   Street.

Hours
Mon-Fri   8:30am-5pm
Sat   9am-5pm

Prices
US$2 per half hour
US$4 per hour
No credit cards

Nearby Places to Visit
National Theater, National
   Museum, Gold Museum,
   Zoo, Serpentary

COSTA RICA, SAN JOSE (SAN JOSE)

Y2K netcafe—100 meters east of the Universidad Latina,
Lourdes • tel: +506 283 4829 • fax: +506 283 4829 •
info@y2knetcafe.com • www.y2knetcafe.com

Location and Access
Located near the Church of
Lourdes.
Bus: Ask for Parada de
Lourdes.
Nearest cross street is
Avenida Principal de
Lourdes.

Hours
Mon-Fri   8am-8pm
Sat-Sun   9am-8pm

Prices
US$1 per half hour
US$2 per hour
V, MC, AmEx
Student discount available

Nearby Places to Visit
Souvenir places, university
campus, bars

DOMINICA, COMMONWEALTH OF, ROSEAU

Cornerhouse: Dominica's Information Cafe
6 King George V Street • tel: +767 449-9000 • fax: +767 449-9003 •
cornerhoused@hotmail.com • www.delphis.com/cornerhouse

Location and Access
Located near Old Market,
directly in front of Cruise
Ship Berth.
Bus: All buses, ask for main
bus stop/Soufriere bus
stop.
Nearest cross street is Old
Market Square.

Hours
Mon-Thu   7:30am-10am
Fri   7:30am-1am
Sat   8am-1am

Prices
US$4 per half hour
US$8 per hour
No credit cards

Nearby Places to Visit
Trafalgar Falls, Boiling Lake,
Sulphur Springs

ECUADOR, CUENCA (AZUAY)

Cuenc@net Cafe—Calle Larga 6-02 y Hermano Miguel Esquina •
tel: +593 (0)7 826 364/837 347 • fax: +593 (0)7 837 347 •
jcarrasc@etapa.com.ec or mbermeo@hotmail.com • No website

Location and Access
Located near Wunder bar.
Bus: Toward the Escalinatas,
  ask for downtown.

Hours
Mon-Fri   9am-11pm
Sat   11am-11pm
Sun   10am-9pm

Prices
Sucres9.000 per half hour
Sucres15.000 per hour
No credit cards
Student discount available

Nearby Places to Visit
Downtown, churches,
  museums, parks

ECUADOR, QUITO (PICHINCHA)

Cafe Net Cybercafe—Reina Victoria y Cordero, Local 14 •
tel: +593 (0)2 554 005 • fax: +593 (0)2 523 297 (remote) •
cafenet@accessinter.net • www.cafenet.com.ec

Location and Access
Located near the El Cafecito
  hostel.
Bus: 2 (Colon-Camal), any
  bus on Avenida 6 de
  Diciembre that has "La
  Marin" in the window, ask
  for Victoria and Cordero.
Trolley: Ask for Colon.
Located one block from the
  corner of Reina Victoria
  and Colon.

Hours
Mon-Fri   8am-2am
Sat-Sun   10am-midnight

Prices
Sucres12.000 per half hour
Sucres24.000 per hour
No credit cards

Nearby Places to Visit
Colonial Quito, Mariscal
  Sucre tourist district, El
  Ejido Park

C@feWeb

333 Avenida Amazonas • tel: +593 (0)2 553 725 • No fax •
info@cafeweb.com.ec • www.cafeweb.com.ec

Location and Access
Located near Hilton Colon
  Hotel.
Bus: All buses crossing
  Amazonas Avenida, ask for
  Amazonas & Jorge
  Washington.
Trolebus: Ask for Mariscal.
Nearest cross street is Jorge
  Washington.

Hours
Mon-Fri   8:30am-8:30pm

Sat-Sun   9:30am-7:30pm

Prices
Sucres9.000 per half hour
Sucres18.000 per hour
No credit cards
Student discount available

Nearby Places to Visit
Night life, hostels, hotels,
  National Culture House,
  old town

Cybercafe-Cultural

Juan Rodriguez #228A and Reina Victoria • tel: +593 (0)2 231 656 •
fax: +593 (0)2 250 678 • cybercafe@cenfei1.org • www.cenfei1.org

Location and Access
Bus: Many.

Hours
Mon-Sun   8am-10pm

Prices
US$1.25 per half hour
US$2.50 per hour
No credit cards
Student discount available

Gateway to Britain—Information Center

1646 Avenida Amazonas • tel: +593 (0)2 540 225/508 282/508 284 •
fax: +593 (0)2 540 225/508 282/508 283 • erey@britcoun.org.ec
or gateway@britcoun.org.ec • www.britcoun.org/ecuador

Location and Access
Bus: Colon-Camal, ask for
  Colon and Amazonas.
Nearest cross street is
  Orellana.

Nearby Places to Visit
Mitad del Mundo (Equatorial
  Line Monument)

Hours
Mon-Fri   9am-7pm

Prices
Sucres8.000 per half hour
Sucres15.000 per hour
No credit cards

Monkey on line—Virtual Office Cafe—Juan Leon Mera

N 2110 y J. Washington Local 1 • tel: +593 (0)2 500 979 •
fax: +593 (0)2 500 979 • info@altesa.net •
www.altesa.net/monkeyonline

Location and Access
Located near South
  American Explorers Club
  and Hilton Colon.
Bus: Tejar el Inca,
  Amazonas, ask for Carrion.
Trolebus: Ask for Marsical.
Nearest cross street is
  Patria.

Prices
Sucres7.000 per half hour
Sucres15.600 per hour
No credit cards
Student discount available

Nearby Places to Visit
The surrounding area of
  Mariscal

Hours
Mon-Sat   8am-10pm
Sun   noon-8pm

ECUADOR, QUITO (PICHINCHA)

Netzone Cafe Internet
100 Reina Victoria • tel: +593 (0)9 492 801 • No fax •
netzonecafe@netzone.com.ec • www.netzone.com.ec

Location and Access
Located near Hilton Colon
   Hotel.
Bus: All buses passing
   through the center of
   town by asking for Patria
   y 6 de Diciembre.
Nearest cross street is
   Avenida Patria.

Hours
Mon-Fri	9am-9pm
Sat	10am-9pm

Prices
Sucres10.000 per half hour
Sucres20.000 per hour
No credit cards

Nearby Places to Visit
Casa de la Cultura, Museo
   Arqueologico del Barco
   Central

EL SALVADOR, JARDINES DE GUADALUPE
(ANTIGUO CUSCATLAN)

CyberCafe de El Salvador—18 Avenida Rio Lempa (Esq. C.
Marmara) • tel: +503 2430673 • fax: +503 2430673 •
flara@enlinea.com.sv • www.cybercafe.com.sv

Location and Access
Located behind the UCA.
Bus: 27, 42, 44, 101C, ask
   for UCA.

Hours
Mon-Thu	9am-10pm
Fri-Sat	9am-midnight
Sun	10am-6pm

Prices
Colones22.60 per half hour
Colones33.90 per hour
V

Nearby Places to Visit
Antiguo Cuscatlan

FALKLAND ISLANDS, STANLEY

Hard Disk Internet Cafe

Fitzroy Road • tel: +500 2589 • fax: +500 22590 •
hard.disk@horizon.co.fk • No website

Location and Access
Nearest cross street is John
  Street.

Hours
Mon-Sat   noon-8pm
Mon-Fri   4pm-8pm
           (winter)
Sat   noon-8pm
           (winter)

Prices
£5.50 per half hour
£10 per hour
No credit cards

Nearby Places to Visit
Penguin Express, Victory
  Public Bar, KMR Knitwear,
  Pinksho

GUATEMALA, ANTIGUA (SACATEPEQUEZ)

Conexion, Correos Electronicos S.A.

4ta Calle Oriente #14 • tel: +502 832-3768 • fax: +502 832-0082 •
admin@conexion.com • www.conexion.com

Location and Access
Next door to Doña Luisa's
  Cafe.

Hours
Mon-Fri   8:30am-7pm
Sat-Sun   9:30am-5:30pm

Prices
US$0.80 per half hour
US$1.60 per hour
V, MC, AmEx

Nearby Places to Visit
Town of Antigua

CyberMannia La Antigua

5 Avenida Norte No 35 B • tel: +502 832-6556 • fax: +502 337-4004 •
cybermanniaan@centramerica.com • www.centramerica.com/cafeinternet

Location and Access
Located near the Arc.
Bus: La Antigua Guatemala
    routes, ask for the Arc.

Nearby Places to Visit
Colonial ruins, cafes, restau-
    rants, museums, Central
    Park, Volcan de Agua

Hours
Mon-Sat   9am-9pm
Sun   10am-7pm

Prices
Q6 per half hour
Q12 per hour
V, MC, AmEx, DC

Cafe InterNet—5 Avenida & 16 Calle Zona 10 •

tel: +502 337-4060 • fax: +502 337-4004 •
cafeinternet@centramerica.com • www.centramerica.com/cafeinternet

Location and Access
Bus: 20, 63, 101.
Nearest cross street is Los
    Proceres Boulevard.

Nearby Places to Visit
Restaurants, movie theaters,
    bowling, discotheque,
    arcade

Hours
Mon-Sat   9am-9pm
Sun   10am-7pm

Prices
Q6 per half hour
Q12 per hour
V, MC, AmEx, DC

GUATEMALA, GUATEMALA CITY (GUATEMALA)

Cyberi@—Boulevard Los Proceres 26-53 Z10 Centro Comercial
Praderas del Sol, Locales 1 y 2 • tel: +502 367-3861/62/63/64/65 •
fax: +502 367-3868 • cyberia@cyberia.com.gt • www.cyberia.com.gt

Location and Access
Located near Boliches de
  Fun Plaza.

Hours
Mon-Sat   8am-midnight
Sun   noon-10pm

Prices
Q10 per half hour
Q20 per hour
V, MC, AmEx, DC
Student discount available
  for members

GUATEMALA, GUATEMALA CITY (GUATEMALA)

CyberMannia Tikal Futura
Tikal Futura Mall 2nd Level • tel: +502 440-2739 • fax: +502 337-4004 •
cybermanniatf@centramerica.com • www.centramerica.com/cafeinternet

Location and Access
Located inside Tikal Futura
  Mall.
Bus: 40, 40R, 70, 71.

Hours
Mon-Sat   9am-9pm
Sun   10am-7pm

Prices
Q6 per half hour
Q12 per hour
V, MC, AmEx, DC

Nearby Places to Visit
Movie theaters, bowling,
  shopping, restaurants,
  arcade

GUATEMALA, GUATEMALA CITY (GUATEMALA)

CyberMannia USAC-AEU—Edificio AEU, Campus USAC Z12 •
tel: +502 337-4060 • fax: +502 337-4004 •
cybermanniaaeu@centramerica.com • www.centramerica.com/cafeinternet

Location and Access
Located at San Carlos
  University.
Bus: USAC-AEU Routes 4,
  76, 90, 92, 96, 203, ask
  for San Carlos University.

Hours
Mon-Fri 8:30am-8pm
Sat   8:30am-2pm
Sun   10am-7pm

Prices
Q6 per half hour
Q12 per hour
V, MC, AmEx, DC

Nearby Places to Visit
Guatemala City, libraries

HONDURAS, COXEN HOLE (ROATAN, BAY ISLANDS)

The Internet Cafe—Thicket Mouth Road, J.C. Commercial
Center • tel: +504 445-1241 • fax: +504 445-1241 •
internetcafe@roatanet.com • www.roatanet.com/paradise/cafe.html

Location and Access
Located near Nazareno Wood
  Shop.
Bus: Coxen Hole minibuses,
  ask for J.C. Commercial
  Center or Paradise
  Computers.
Nearest cross street is Main
  Highway.

Hours
Mon-Sat 7:30am-6:30pm

Prices
US$7.50 per half hour
US$15 per hour
No credit cards

Nearby Places to Visit
Many diving and snorkeling
  spots, dolphin show, igua-
  na preserve, Carambola
  Gardens

HONDURAS, COXEN HOLE (ROATAN, BAY ISLANDS)

Que tal Cafe
Coxen Hole • tel: +504 445-0354 • No fax •
quetal@globalnet.hn • No website

Location and Access
Located at main entrance
  into town.
Bus: All buses, ask for main
  entrance into town.

Hours
Mon &
  Wed-Fri 7:30am-4pm
Tue 7:30am-9pm
Sat 7:30am-2pm

Prices
US$7.50 per half hour
US$15 per hour
No credit cards

Nearby Places to Visit
Roatan is a tourist destination for diving.

HONDURAS, TEGUCIGALPA (FRANCISCO MORAZON)

Tobacco Road Tavern
1120 Avenida Paz Barahona, La Plazuela •
tel: +504 237-3909 • No fax • tobacord@hondutel.hn • No website

Location and Access
Located near Parque Valle.
Nearest cross street is Las
  Damas.

Hours
Mon-Sat 8:30am-11pm
Sun 8:30am-noon

Prices
L50 per half hour
L80 per hour
No credit cards

HONDURAS, UTILA (BAY ISLANDS)

Bay Island Computer Services

Cola de Mico, 34201 • tel: +504 425-3124 • fax: +602 532-7052 •
bicomput@hondutel.hn • No website

Location and Access
Located between the Mango
Inn and Thompson's
Bakery.
Small island with maybe 5
miles of road. You can get
anywhere on the island by
walking or biking.

Hours
Mon-Sat   9am-5pm

Prices
L95 per half hour
L180 per hour
No credit cards

Nearby Places to Visit
Three minute walk from
Town Dock. Utila is a dive
paradise, also snorkeling,
horseback riding, hiking,
kayaking, and fishing.

JAMIACA, NEGRIL (WESTMORELAND)

Cyber Up Internet Cafe—The Beach House Villas, Norman
Manley Boulevard (Beach Road) • tel: +(876) 957-4472/957-3997 •
fax: +(876) 957-9885 • cyberup@wtjam.net • www.irievibes.com

Location and Access
Located near Negril
Roundabout, on 7-Mile
Beach.

Hours
Mon-Sun   10am-midnight

Prices
J$150 per half hour
J$300 per hour
V, MC, AmEx

Patio de Luz

México 650 c. Azara • tel: +59521 449 741 • fax: +59521 449 741 •
pluz66@hotmail.com • No website

Location and Access
Located near Plaza
  Uruguaya.
Bus: All downtown buses,
  ask for Plaza Uruguaya.

Hours
Mon-Thu   10am-11pm
Fri-Sat   10am-midnight
Sun   4pm-10pm

Prices
Gs6.000 per half hour
Gs12.000 per hour
V, MC, AmEx, DC

Nearby Places to Visit
Train station

Café Cultural La Tertulia—44-50 Procuradores •

tel: +51 (0)84 241422/262345 • fax: +51 (0)84 241422 •
amautaa@mail.cosapidata.com.pe • www.telser.com.pe/amauta

Location and Access
Located near Cusco
  Cathedral.
Bus: Ask for the Cathedral.
Train: Ask for Estacion San
  Pedro.
Nearest cross street is Plaza
  de Armas.

Hours
Mon-Fri   8am-1pm &
    3pm-6pm
Sat   8am-1pm

Prices
US$1 per half hour
US$2 per hour
No credit cards

Nearby Places to Visit
The Cathedral, the Plaza,
  churches, El Casco
  Momunental, ruins

Snooty Agouti

Rodney Bay • tel: +758 4520321 • fax: +758 4529117 •
snooty@candw.lc • www.snooty.com

Location and Access
Located near The Lime.
Bus: 1A, ask for Reduit Gap.
Nearest cross street is
    Reduit Avenue.

Hours
Mon-Sat   9am-12:30am
Sun   3pm-12:30am

Prices
EC$20 per half hour
EC$40 per hour
V, MC, AmEx, D

Nearby Places to Visit
Rodney Bay Lagoon, Reduit
    Beach, Pigeon Island

Banana Boat Cyber Cafe

7 Harbour Walk, Turtle Cove • tel: +649-941-3615 • No fax •
cybercafe@tciway.tc • www.tcimall.tc

Location and Access
Located near the Banana
    Boat Restaurant.
Nearest cross street is Turtle
    Cove Marina.

Hours
Mon-Thu   8:30am-5:30pm
Fri   8:40am-5:30pm

Prices
US$15 per half hour
US$30 per hour
V, MC, AmEx

Nearby Places to Visit
Banana Boat Restaurant

URUGUAY, MONTEVIDEO (MONTEVIDEO)

El Cyberc@fe
25 de Mayo 568 • tel: +598 (0)2 915-4816 • fax: +598 (0)2 915-4816 •
cybercafe@intersys.com.uy • www.cybercafe.com.uy

Location and Access
Located near Plaza Matriz in
  the Old City.
Bus: 102, 103, 104, 105,
  106, 116, 117, 121, 124,
  125, 126, 127, 131, 133,
  140, 141, 142, 148, 155,
  ask for 25 de Mayo and
  Ituzaingo.
Nearest cross street is
  Ituzaingo.

Hours
Mon-Fri   9am-6pm

Prices
US$2.50 per half hour
US$5 per hour
V, MC, DC
Student discount available

Nearby Places to Visit
The Old City, the Cathedral,
  the Solis Theatre

VENEZUELA, MERIDA (MERIDA)

Natoura Adventure Tours
Final Calle 24 • tel: +58 74 524216/524075 • fax: +58 74 524216/
524075 • natoura@telcel.net.ve • www.natoura.com

Location and Access
Located near highest and
  longest cable car in the
  world.
Bus: Los Chorros route, ask
  for Ave 5, St 24.

Hours
Mon-Sat   8am-8pm

Prices
Bs2400 per half hour
Bs4800 per hour
V, MC
Student discount available

Nearby Places to Visit
Downtown Plaza Bolivar,
  Cathedral

Cafe Caltec

8 Km Carratera Panamericana–Entrando IUT • tel: +58 32 727723 • fax: +58 32 727723 • mrcaltec@cantv.net • www.internet.ve/caltec

Location and Access
Located near Instituto Universitario Technologico (IUT).
Bus: Ask for IUT.

Hours
Mon-Fri   8am-6pm
Sat   8am-4pm

Prices
US$10 per half hour
US$15 per hour
V, MC, AmEx, DC
Student discount available

Nearby Places to Visit
Cristalart, La Cascada, La Casona

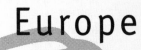

Europe

Cybercafe—27 Gstättengasse •
tel: +43 (0)662 84 26 16 22 • fax: +43 (0)662 84 26 16 15 •
cybercafe@arch.co.at • www.arch.co.at

Location and Access
Located near Stadtkino.
Bus: Ask for Hanuschplat.
Nearest cross street is
Getreidegasse.

Hours
Mon-Sun   2pm-11pm

Prices
ATS35 per half hour
ATS70 per hour
No credit cards

Nearby Places to Visit
Museum of Nature, Mozart's
birthplace

Das Computerhaus—3A Rainbergstrasse •
tel: +43 (0)662 844 377 • fax: +43 (0)662 844 377 23 •
computerhaus@dascom.or.at • www.dascom.or.at

Location and Access
Bus: 1, 2, 15, 29, ask for
Reichenhallerstrasse or
Moosstrasse.
Nearest cross street is
Neutorstrasse.

Hours
Mon-Sun   9am-midnight

Prices
ATS50 per half hour
ATS100 per hour
V, MC, DC

Nearby Places to Visit
The old town of Salzburg

Cafe Bierbeisl Einstein

4 Rathausplatz • tel: +43 (0)1 405 26 26 •
fax: +43 (0)1 405 26 26 24 • albert@einstein.at • www.einstein.at

Location and Access
Located near Town Hall.
Underground: U2, ask for
  Rathaus.
Tram: 1, 2, ask for Rathaus
  or Schottentor.

Hours

Mon-Fri	7am-2am
Sat	9am-2am
Sun	9am-midnight

Prices
ATS54 per half hour
ATS108 per hour
V, MC, AmEx, DC

Nearby Places to Visit
Town Hall

Cafe Stein—6-8 Wahringer Strasse •

tel: +43 (0)1 319 72 41 • fax: +43 (0)1 319 72 412 •
c.stein@magnet.at • www.cafe-stein.co.at/cafe-stein

Location and Access
Located near University of
  Vienna, Votivchurch.
Bus: 1A, ask for
  Schottentor.
Underground: U4, ask for
  Schottentor.
Tram/Trolley: D, 1, 2, 37,
  38, 40, 41, 42, 43, 44,
  ask for Schottentor.
Nearest cross street is
  Schottenring.

Hours
Mon-Sun   10am-11pm

Prices
ATS65 per half hour
ATS130 per hour
No credit cards

Nearby Places to Visit
Votivchurch, Sigmund
  Freud's House

AUSTRIA, VIENNA (WIEN)

Libromania—Internet Cafe—94 Wagramerstrasse •
tel: +43 (0)1 202 52 55 • fax: +43 (0)1 202 52 55 99 •
libromania@libromania.co.at • www.libromania.co.at

Location and Access
Located near Donauzentrum
    (shopping center).
Underground: U1 (red line),
    ask for Zentrum Kagran.
Nearest cross street is
    Donaustadtstrasse.

Hours
Mon-Sat   9am-7pm

Prices
Free

Nearby Places to Visit
Danube Island, Vienna
    International Centre,
    banks of Old Danube

BELGIUM, BRUSSELS (BRABANT)

Cybercafe Internem
68 Boulevard Général Jacques • tel: +32 (0)2 649 45 09 •
fax: +32 (0)2 649 45 09 • info@internem.be • www.internem.be

Location and Access
Located near Université de
    Bruxelles.

Hours
Mon, Wed-Fri &
    Sun   noon-midnight
Sat   6pm-midnight

Prices
BF180 per half hour
BF350 per hour
No credit cards

Nearby Places to Visit
Bois de la Cambre

BELGIUM, BRUSSELS (BRABANT)

CyberTheatre—a Global Theatre Network Product
4/5 Avenue de la Toison d'Or • tel: +32 (0)2 500 78 78 •
fax: +32 (0)2 500 78 45 • infos@nirvanet.net • www.nirvanet.com

Location and Access
Located near Cinema
  Acropole.
Bus: 34, 54, 71, 80, ask for
  Porte de Namur.
Tram: 91, 92, 93, 94, ask
  for Porte de Namur.
Underground: Ligne 2-
  Simonis-Clémenceau, ask
  for Porte de Namur.
Nearest cross street is
  Avenue Louise.

Hours
Mon-Sat   10am-1am

Prices
Free with a drink per 15
  minutes or BF250 per hour
V, MC, AmEx
Student discount available

Nearby Places to Visit
The Sablon

BELGIUM, BRUSSELS (BRABANT)

LFT
215A Avenue Louise • tel: +32 (0)2 627 87 87 •
fax: +32 (0)2 627 87 88 • jcm@dba.be • www.lft.be

Location and Access
Bus: 54, ask for Bailli.
Tram/Trolley: 81, 93, 94,
  ask for Bailli.

Hours
Mon-Thu   10am-9pm
Fri-Sat   10am-1am

Prices
BF75 per half hour
BF150 per hour
V

119

BELGIUM, EUPEN (LIEGE)

Euregio.Net Cybertreff
11, Kehrweg • tel: +32 (0)87 56 11 77 • fax: +32 (0)87 56 11 22 •
hubert@euregio.net • www.euregio.net

Location and Access
Nearest big towns are
  Aachen (Germany) and
  Liège.
Located in the BRF
  Funkhaus, opposite the
  football stadium.

Hours
Mon-Fri   9am-5pm

Prices
BF125 per half hour
BF250 per hour
V, MC, AmEx

Nearby Places to Visit
Ardennes, nature

BELGIUM, GHENT (EAST FLANDERS)

Internetclub "The Globetrotter"
180 Kortrijksepoortstraat • tel: +32 (0)9 269 08 60 • No fax •
club-g@online.be • www.online.be

Location and Access
Located near St-
  Pieterstation.
Tram: 1, 10, 11, 12, 13, ask
  for Kortrijksepoortstraat.
Train: Ghent, ask for St-
  Pieterstation.
Nearest cross street is
  Kortrijksesteenweg.

Hours
Tue-Sat   3pm-11pm

Prices
BF100 per half hour
BF200 per hour
No credit cards

Nearby Places to Visit
s'Gravensteen, St-
  Baafscathedral, Belfort,
  St-Niklaaschurch,
  Vrijdagsmarkt (Stadhuis)

BELGIUM, LIEGE (LIEGE)

II-Mel

77 rue Grètry • tel: +32 (0)4 342 00 77 • fax: +32 (0)4 344 20 59 •
info@ii-mel.com • www.ii-mel.com

Location and Access
Located near Centre
  Commercial Longdoz.
Bus: 4, 29, ask for Longdoz.

Hours
Mon &
  Wed-Sun noon-5am

Prices
BF50 per half hour
BF100 per hour
No credit cards

BELGIUM, MONS (HAINAULT)

Cybercity

7 rue des Capucins • tel: +32 (0)6 540 18 10 •
fax: +32 (0)6 540 18 19 • delfosse@ugr.be or cybercity.ugr.be

Location and Access
Located near a tavern and
  laser game place.
Train: Ask for Mons Station.
Nearest cross street is the
  street from the station to
  the town center.

Hours

Mon-Thu	11am-11pm
Fri	11am-2am
Sat	3pm-2am
Sun	3pm-11pm

Prices
BF100 per half hour
BF200 per hour
No credit cards

Nearby Places to Visit
Mons

BELGIUM, NIVELLES (BRABANT WALLON)

Cyber Café Filink
5 Place de L'Abreuvoir • tel: +32 (0)67 84 09 03 •
fax: +32 (0)67 84 09 03 • filink@ping.be • www.ping.be/filink

Location and Access
Located near Grand Place
(center of city).
Bus: Ask for Esplanade du
Souvenir.
Train: From Brussels, ask for
Nivelles.
Nearest cross street is rue
de Saintes.

Hours
Wed-Sun   2pm-10pm

Prices
BF250 per half hour
BF500 per hour
No credit cards

Nearby Places to Visit
Collegiale de Nivelles, Lion
of Waterloo

BELGIUM, TURNHOUT (ANTWERP)

Forum Internet-Ca-Verne
36 Herentalsstraat • tel: +32 (0)14 47 93 00 •
fax: +32 (0)14 42 42 83 • info@forum.be • www.forum.be

Location and Access
Located near the Market
Place.
Bus: All town buses, ask for
the Market Place.
Train: Main line into
Antwerp, ask for Turnhout
Station.
Nearest cross street is Grote
Market.

Hours
Tue-Thu   10am-midnight
Fri-Sat   10am-1am
Sun   1pm-midnight

Prices
BF90 per half hour
BF175 per hour
No credit cards
Student discount available

Nearby Places to Visit
Tourist Information Office

BULGARIA, SOFIA (SOFIA)

CyberNet Ltd., Internet Club

4A Sveti Naum Str. • tel: +359 (0)2 963 37 50 • No fax •
office@iclub.cybernet.bg • www.iclub.cybernet.bg

Location and Access
Located near Hemus Hotel,
the Museum of Land and
People, Hotel Kempinski-
Zographski.
Bus: 94, 102, ask for Hemus
Hotel.
Tram/Trolley: 6, 9, ask for
Hemus Hotel.
Nearest cross street is
Cherni Vrah Boulevard.

Hours
Mon-Sat   10am-9pm

Prices
leva1,500 per half hour
leva3,000 per hour
No credit cards

CROATIA, ZAGREB

Sublink CyberCafé

12 Teslina • tel: +385 1 4811329 • No fax •
sublink@sublink.hr • www.sublink.hr

Location and Access
Located near main square.
Tram/Trolley: 1, 6, 11, 12,
14, 17, ask for Trg Bana J.
Jelacica.
Nearest cross street is
Gajeva Street.

Hours
Mon-Fri   10am-10pm
Sat-Sun   3pm-10pm

Prices
kn9,60 per half hour
kn19,20 per hour
No credit cards

Nearby Places to Visit
Zagreb Cathedral, parks

CYPRUS, LARNACA (LARNACA)

Web Internet Cafe
54 Lord Byron • tel: +357 (0)4 654954 • No fax •
webcafe@webcafe.com.cy • www.webcafe.com.cy

Location and Access
Located near Larnacas
  Promenade.
Nearest cross street is
  Grigori Afxentiou Avenue.

Hours
Mon-Sat   11am-2am
Sun   1pm-2am

Prices
cyp1 per half hour
cyp2 per hour
No credit cards

Nearby Places to Visit
Zinonos Pieridi Museum,
  Larnacas Museum

CZECH REPUBLIC, DECIN (SEVEROCESKY)

Internet Centrum New Space Decin—664/1 Hudeckova •
tel: +420 (0)412 512 961 • fax: +420 (0)412 511 626 •
centrum@space.cz • www.space.cz/centrum.htm

Location and Access
Located near post office,
  grammar school, business
  academy.

Bus: 1, 2, 3, 4, 5, 6, 7, 8,
  9, 10, 11, 12, 13, ask for
  Myslbekova.

Nearest cross streets are
  Pohranicni Street,
  Myslbekova Street, and
  Komenskeho Square.

Hours
Mon-Thu   9am-5:30pm
Fri   noon-7:30pm

Prices
Czk20 per half hour
Czk40 per hour
No credit cards

Nearby Places to Visit
Labske Piskovce, Hrensko,
  Mezna, Jetrichovice,
  Benesov, Ploucnici

CZECH REPUBLIC, MOST (SEVEROCESKY)

Internet Cafe North Bohemia
1407 Ruzova • tel: +420 (0)35 28533/41215 •
fax: +420 (0)35 29032 • janda@softex.cz • www.softex.cz

Location and Access
Located near the thermal
  swimming pool.
Bus: 15, 30, ask for
  Koupaliste Street.
Nearest cross street is
  Topolova.

Prices
Czk30 per half hour
Czk60 per hour
No credit cards

Nearby Places to Visit
Moved church

Hours
Mon-Thu	3pm-10pm
Fri	3pm-midnight
Sat	2pm-6pm

CZECH REPUBLIC, OSTRAVA (SOUTHERN MORAVIA)

Internet Cafe
38 Havlickovo Nabrezi • tel: +420 (0)69 6164 148 •
fax: +420 (0)69 6164 361 • info@grendel.cz • www.grendel.cz/cafe

Location and Access
Bus: 104, 109, ask for Most
  Pionyru.
Underground: 2, 4, 8, 12,
  14, ask for Kino Vesmir.
Nearest cross street is
  Ceskobratrska, Sokolovska.

Prices
Czk45 per half hour
Czk90 per hour
No credit cards
Student discount available

Nearby Places to Visit
Museum, zoo, shopping cen-
  ters, historical monuments

Hours
Mon-Fri   9am-6pm

Cybeteria—Internet Café

18, Stepanska • tel: +420 (0)2 2223 0707 •
fax: +420 (0)2 2223 2227 • info@cybeteria.cz • www.cybeteria.cz

Location and Access
Located near Wenceslas
   Square.
Underground: Lines A and B,
   ask for Mustek.
Nearest cross street is
   Wenceslas Square.

Hours
Mon-Fri   10am-8pm
Sat   noon-6pm
Sun (July-Sept.)
            noon-6pm

Prices
Czk50 per half hour
Czk100 per hour
No credit cards
Student discount available
   10am-11am and 4pm-6pm

Nearby Places to Visit
Prague, National Museum

Internet Cafe Highland—25 Narodni Trida (25 National

Street) • tel: +420 (0)2 2108 5284 • fax: +420 (0)2 2124 2106 55 •
internetcafe@highland.cz • www.internetcafe.cz

Location and Access
Located across the street
   from Rock Cafe Club and
   Tesco Department Store on
   the main street in town.
Underground: Metro line B,
   ask for Narodni Trida.
Tram: 3, 6, 9, 22, 24, ask
   for Narodni Trida.

Hours
Mon-Fri   9am-10pm
Sat-Sun   2pm-10pm

Prices
Czk60 per half hour
Czk120 per hour
No credit cards

Nearby Places to Visit
Center of town sites, Charles
   Bridge

NetWave Internet Bar

8 Na Bojisti • tel: +420 (0)2 9618 6600 • fax: + 420 (0)2 9618 6601 •
kavarna@netwave.cz • www.netwave.cz

Location and Access

Located near Svejk and
Restaurant U Kalicha near
subway station I.P.
Pavlova.
Underground: Line C (red),
ask for I.P. Pavlova.
Tram: 4, 6, 11, 22, 34, ask
for I.P. Pavlova.

Prices

Czk30-40 per half hour
Czk60-80 per hour
No credit cards
Student discount available

Nearby Places to Visit

Prague

Hours

Mon-Fri   11am-11pm
Sat   3pm-11pm

Pl@neta

102 Vinohradska Street • tel: +420 (0)2 6731 1182 •
fax: +420 (0)2 6731 5789 • info@planeta.cz • www.planeta.cz

Location and Access

Located near
Telecommunication Tower
and the square of Jiriho z
Podebrad.
Underground: Line A, ask
for Jiriho z Podebrad.
Tram: 11, ask for Jiriho z
Podebrad.

Prices

Czk45 per half hour
Czk90 per hour
V

Hours

Mon-Sun   8am-10pm

The Terminal Bar

6 Soukenicka • tel: +420 (0)2 2187 1115 •
fax: +420 (0)2 2187 1118 • kavarna@terminal.cz • www.terminal.cz

Location and Access
Located near Obecni Dum, Powder Tower.
Underground: Line B (yellow), ask for Namesti Republiky.
Tram: 5, 8, 14, ask for Dlouha Trida.
Nearest cross streets are Revolucni, Dlouha Soukenicka.

Hours
Mon-Sun   11am-1am

Prices
Czk60 per half hour
Czk120 per hour
V, AmEx
Student discount available evenings and weekends

Nearby Places to Visit
Old Town Square

NetPoint Games

40 Langelinie Allé • tel: +45 70221008 • fax: +45 70221007 •
mail@netpoint.dk • www.netpoint.dk

Location and Access
Located near the Little Mermaid.
Bus: 29, ask for Langelinie.
Underground: Ask for Österport Station.
Train: Österport line, ask for Österport Station.
Nearest cross street is Langelinie.

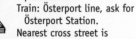

Hours
Mon-Fri   3pm-1am
Sat   noon-1am
Sun   noon-midnight

Prices
Dkr30 per hour (minimum)
V, MC, AmEx, DC

FRANCE, ANNECY (HAUTE SAVOIE)

Syndrome Cybercafe
3, bis ave de Chevene • tel: +33 (0)4 50 45 39 75 •
fax: +33 (0)4 50 45 85 65 • infos@syndrome.com • www.syndrome.com

Location and Access
Located right next to the
  SNCF train station.
Bus: All buses to the SNCF
  station.
Train: Intercity trains, ask
  for Annecy.

Hours
Mon-Sun   noon-midnight

Prices
FF20 per half hour
FF40 per hour
V, MC

Nearby Places to Visit
Old town of Annecy, the
  lake

FRANCE, AVIGNON (VAUCLUSE)

Cyberdrome—68, rue Guillaume Puy •
tel: +33 (0)4 90 16 05 15 • fax: +33 (0)4 90 16 05 14 •
webmaster@cyberdrome.fr • www.cyberdrome.fr

Location and Access
Located near rue des
  Teinturiers, la Chapelle, la
  Maison Quatre Deux
  Chiffre.
Bus: Ask for Porte Limbert.
Train: SNCF, ask for Avignon
  Station.

Hours
Mon-Sun   7am-1am

Prices
FF25 per half hour
FF50 per hour
No credit cards
Student discount available

Nearby Places to Visit
La Cité Papale (Papal City)

FRANCE, BORDEAUX (GIRONDE)

Cyberstation
23, Cours Pasteur • tel: +33 (0)556 01 15 15 •
fax: +33 (0)556 79 07 59 • info@cyberstation.fr • www.cyberstation.fr

Location and Access
Located opposite the Musée
d'Aquitaine.
Bus: B, F, G, L, U, 2, 3, 4,
5, 6, 12, 20, 21, ask for
Cours Pasteur.
Nearest cross street is Cours
Victor Hugo.

Hours
Mon-Sat   11am-2am
Sun   2pm-midnight

Prices
FF25 per half hour
FF40 per hour
V, MC

Nearby Places to Visit
Musée d'Aquitaine

FRANCE, CAGNES SUR MER (ALPES MARITIMES)

Planete Web
56, avenue de Nice • tel: +33 (0)492 07 55 44 • No fax •
praynaud@dial-up.com • www.competences.com/planete

Location and Access
Nearest big city is Nice.
Located in the School
Pinëde.
Bus: Cros de Cagnes, ask for
Avenue de Nice.

Hours
Fri   5pm-10pm

Prices
FF100 for 3 months (only
price offered)
No credit cards

Asher, la Boutique de l'Internet

44, boulevard Carnot • tel: +33 (0)492 99 03 01 •
fax: +33 (0)492 99 09 04 • asher@riviera.net • No website

Location and Access
Boulevard Carnot is a main
   street.

Hours
Mon-Thu   9:30am-7pm
Fri & Sun 9:30am-12:30pm

Prices
FF23 per half hour
FF45 per hour
No credit cards
Student discount available

Cyber-restaurant La Creperie

2, rue Raspail • tel: +33 (0)490 63 43 08 • No fax •
lacreperie@infonie.fr • www.chez.com/lacreperie

Location and Access
Nearest cross street is Porte
   de Monteux.

Hours
Mon-Sat   11am-2pm &
               7pm-10pm

Prices
Call for prices
No credit cards

FRANCE, COLMAR (HAUT-RHIN)

La Maison des 6 Ours (House of the 6 Bears)
37, Route de Neuf-Brisach • tel: +33 (0)389 24 10 00 • No fax •
invites@6-ours.com or reserve@6-ours.com • www.6-ours.com

Location and Access
Located near Ambassade des Vins.
Nearest cross street is Avenue d'Alsace.

Hours
Mon-Fri   11am-midnight
Sat   4pm-1:30am

Prices
FF30 per half hour
FF40-50 per hour
V, MC
Student discount available

Nearby Places to Visit
Old Town of Colmar, museums

FRANCE, GRENOBLE (ISERE)

CyberNet Cafe—3, rue Bayard •
tel: +33 (0)476 51 73 18/63 94 18 • fax: +33 (0)476 03 20 33 •
services@neptune.fr • www.neptune.fr/cybernetcafe

Location and Access
Located near the Cathedral Notre-Dame and the Musée de Grenoble.
Bus: TAG 32, ask for opposite the Musée de Grenoble.
Tram: TAG B, ask for Ste-Claire.
Train: From the railway station, take tramway line B, ask for Sus-Cité.

Hours
Mon-Sat   noon-1am

Prices
FF30 per half hour
FF47 per hour
V
Student discount available after 2pm

Nearby Places to Visit
Museum of Modern Arts of Grenoble, Medieval Cathedral

FRANCE, LA GAUDE (ALPES-MARITIMES)

Espace Internet—Salle Louis Feraud, Avenue de l'Hotel de Ville • tel: +33 (0)492 07 55 44 • No fax • praynaud@dial-up.com • www.mairie-lagaude.fr/espace

Location and Access
Nearest big city is Nice.
Located near the Mairie (Town Hall).
Bus: From Saint-Laurent (du Var) to La Gaude, ask for the Mairie.

Prices
FF20 per half hour
FF30 per hour
No credit cards
Student discount available with 3 month prepayment

Hours
Tue & Fri   5:30pm-8:30pm
Sat   8pm-midnight

FRANCE, LES GETS (HAUTE-SAVOIE)

CyberStella Hotel Stella
rue Centrale • tel: +33 (0)450 75 80 40 • fax: +33 (0)450 75 89 25 • cybercafe@stella-galaxy.com • www.stella-galaxy.com

Location and Access
Located near the center of the ski resort.

Nearby Places to Visit
Ski resort in Portes du Soleil ski area

Hours
Mon-Sun   10am-10pm

Prices
FF30 per half hour
FF60 per hour
V, MC, AmEx
Student discount available

FRANCE, LISIEUX (NORMANDY)

Cyber Station—3, Place Pierre Sëmard (Place de la Gare) •
tel: +33 (0)231 62 10 22 • No fax •
station3@mail.cpod.fr • www.cpod.monoweb.cybersta

Location and Access
Located opposite the
    station.
Train: Main lines, ask for
    Lisieux Station.

Hours
Mon-Fri   9am-12:15pm &
            2pm-7:30pm

Prices
Call for prices
No credit cards

FRANCE, LOMME (NORD)

Planet Bowling
ZA du Grand But • tel: +33 (0)320 08 10 50 •
fax: +33 (0)320 08 10 52 • jerome@etnet.fr • www.planetbowling.com

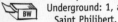

Location and Access
Nearest big city is Lille.
Located opposite Kinepolis
    multiplex cinema.
Underground: 1, ask for
    Saint Philibert.

Prices
FF25 per half hour
FF50 per hour
V, MC

Hours
Mon-Thu   11am-2am
Fri-Sat   11am-4am
Sun   10am-2am

Cyber Concept

16, rue Julia • tel: +33 (0)491 78 08 78 • fax: +33 (0)491 78 07 72 • contact@cyberconcept.fr • www.cyberconcept.fr

Location and Access
Located near Place
 Castellane.
Bus: Ask for Baille-Vertus.
Underground: Ask for Baille.
Nearest cross street is
 Boulevard Baille.

Prices
FF30 per half hour
FF50 per hour
No credit cards
Student discount available

Hours
Mon-Fri   9am-7pm
Sat   10am-7pm

Oxygène

32, rue Frederic Bastiat • tel: +33 (0)558 46 47 46 • fax: +33 (0)558 06 39 70 • oxygene@oxygene.fr • www.oxygene.fr

Location and Access
Located near the
 Commissariat.
Bus: Ask for rue Gambetta.
Nearest cross street is rue
 Gambetta.

Prices
FF25 per half hour
FF45 per hour
No credit cards

Nearby Places to Visit
Despiau-Wlérick Museum

Hours
Tue-Sat   2pm-7pm

FRANCE, MORLAIX (FINISTERE)

Pub Le Macao
4, rue Basse • tel: +33 (0)298 88 47 26 • fax: +33 (0)298 88 47 26 •
flutes.celtes@wanadoo.fr • http://perso.wanadoo.fr/moa

Location and Access
Located near Church of St. Mathieu.

Hours
| Tue-Sat | 3pm-1am (winter) |
| Tue-Sat | 8pm-1am (summer) |

Prices
FF40 per half hour
FF70 per hour
No credit cards

FRANCE, NICE (ALPES-MARITIMES)

Webstore
12, rue de Russie • tel: +33 (0)493 87 87 99 •
fax: +33 (0)493 87 14 14 • info@webstore.fr • www.webstore.fr

Location and Access
Located near the Cathedral.
Bus: Ask for avenue Jean Medecin and rue de Russie.
Nearest cross street is Avenue Jean Medecin.

Hours
Mon-Sat 10am-7pm

Prices
FF30 per half hour
FF50 per hour
V, MC, AmEx

Café Orbital

13, rue de Medicis • tel: +33 (0)143 25 76 77 •
fax: +33 (0)156 24 09 04 • info@orbital.fr • www.orbital.fr

Location and Access
Located near La Sorbonne.
Bus: 21, 27, 38, 82, 84, 85,
  86, 89, ask for
  Luxembourg.
Underground: Odéon, ask for
  Luxembourg.
Nearest cross street is
  Boulevard Saint Michel.

Prices
FF30 per half hour
FF55 per hour
V, MC
Student discount available

Nearby Places to Visit
Les Jardins du Luxembourg,
  Quartier Latin

Hours
Mon-Sat   10am-11pm
Sun   noon-8pm

Le Jardin de l'Internet—79, boulevard Saint-Michel •
tel: +33 (0)144 07 22 20 • fax: +33 (0)144 07 22 20 •
cybercafe@jardin-internet.com • www.jardin-internet.com

Location and Access
Located in front of
  Luxembourg Garden.
Bus: 21, 27, 38, 82, 84, 85,
  89, ask for Luxembourg.
Subway: RER B Luxembourg
  station.

Prices
FF25 per half hour
FF48 per hour
No credit cards

Nearby Places to Visit
Latin Quarter, Panthéon, Le
  Sénat (Senate)

Hours
Mon-Sat   9am-11pm
Sun   11am-10pm

FRANCE, PARIS (ILE DE FRANCE)

Web bar

32, rue de Picardie • tel: +33 (0)142 72 66 55 •
fax: +33 (0)142 72 66 75 • webbar@webbar.fr • www.webbar.fr

Location and Access
Located near Place de la
  République, Picasso
  Museum, Place des Vosges,
  la Bastille.
Bus: 54, 56, ask for Place
  de la République.
Underground: Ask for
  République or Temple.
Train: SNCF, ask for Gare du
  Nord, Gare de l'Est and
  then take the Métro.

Hours

Mon-Fri	8:30am-2am
Sat	11am-2am
Sun	11am-midnight

Prices
FF25 per half hour
FF40 per hour
V, MC
Student discount available

Nearby Places to Visit
Le Marais, Pompidou Center,

FRANCE, SAINT-ETIENNE (LOIRE)

CyberCafe L'Intern@ute

29, rue du 11 Novembre • tel: +33 (0)477 25 03 57 •
fax: +33 (0)477 42 32 19 • web@internaute.fr • www.internaute.fr

Location and Access
Located near University
  Jean-Monnet in city town.
Tram: There's only one, ask
  for University.
Nearest cross street is the
  biggest street in the city,
  La Grand Rue.

Hours
Mon-Sat   7am-1am

Prices
FF30 per half hour
FF50 per hour
V, MC, AmEx, DC
Student discount available

Cyber Boutic

15, rue de la Nuée Bleue • tel: +33 (0)388 75 80 50
fax: +33 (0)388 23 56 32 • info@sdv.fr • www.sdv.fr

Location and Access
Located near Place Kleber.

Nearby Places to Visit
Petite France

Hours
Mon-Fri   8:30am-5:30pm

Prices
FF29 per half hour (maximum)
No credit cards
Student discount available

Webcontact

35, rue Nericault-Destouches • tel: +33 (0)247 05 57 05 •
fax: +33 (0)247 05 57 05 • contact@centrale.net • No website

Location and Access
Located near Saint-Martin.
Bus: 1, 2, 5, 7, 8, 9, 14, 55, 61, ask for Nericault-Destouches.
Nearest cross street is rue Nationale.

Prices
FF25 per hour
No credit cards

Nearby Places to Visit
Quartier du Vieux Tours, Crypte Saint-Martin

Hours
Mon-Fri   9am-8pm
Sat   2pm-8pm

Smiley

4, rue de la Doua • tel: +33 (0)472 44 06 46 •
fax: +33 (0)472 44 26 01 • smiley@smiley.fr • www.smiley.fr

Location and Access
Nearest big city is Lyon.
Bus: 37, ask for Colin.

Nearby Places to Visit
University of Science

Hours
Mon-Fri   10am-8pm

Prices
FF27-60 per hour
No credit cards
Student discount available

Planet Wipe Out, Raststätte

23-25 Lothringerstrasse • tel: +49 (0)241 26574 • No fax •
wipeout@aachen.heimat.de • heimat.de/wipeout

Location and Access
Located near the main train
     station.
Bus: 1, 3, 13, 14, and
     Interliner (from The
     Netherlands), ask for
     Hauptbahnhof (Main
     Station).
Nearest cross street is the
     Main Station street.

Hours
Tue, Thu, &
     Sun   6pm-10pm

Prices
Free

Nearby Places to Visit
UNESCO Cathedral, theatre,
     Altstadt (Old City)

GERMANY, ANSBACH (BAYERN)

First Internet Café
5 Würzburgerstrasse • tel: +49 (0)981 12955 • fax: +49 (0)981 12966 •
info@first-icafe.de • www.first-icafe.de

Location and Access
Located near the city.
Nearest cross street is
Würzburger Landstrasse.

Nearby Places to Visit
Kaspar Hauser

Hours
Mon-Sat   11am-1am
Sun   2pm-1am

Prices
DM5 per half hour
DM10 per hour
No credit cards

GERMANY, BERGHEIM (NORDRHEIN-WESTFALEN)

iorgio's
6-10 Kölner Strasse • tel: +49 (0)2271 41752 • No fax •
root@surfline.ipos.de • http://surfline.ipos.de

Location and Access
Located next to the main
bus and train station.
Bus: All buses to Bergheim,
ask for main bus station.
Train: All trains to
Bergheim, ask for
Bergheim Main Station.

Prices
DM5 per half hour
DM10 per hour
No credit cards

Hours
Mon-Sun   9am-10:30pm

Internet Café Cyberb@r Zoo—5-6 Joachimstaler Strasse •
tel: +49 (0)30 8802 4198 • fax: +49 (0)30 8802 4180 •
berlinzoo@cyberbar.de • www.mem.de/cyberbar or www.cyberbar.de

Location and Access
Located near Central Rail
  Station and the Zoo.
Bus: 109, 119, 145, 146,
  149, 219, 245, 249, X9,
  ask for Kantstrasse,
  Joachimstaler Strasse, or
  Zoo.
Underground: U2, U9, U12,
  U15, ask for Zoo &
  Kurfürstendamm.
Train: Intercity trains, ask
  for Berlin Central.

Hours
Mon-Thu   10am-8pm
Sat   9am-4pm

Prices
DM5 per half hour
DM10 per hour
No credit cards
Student discount available

Nearby Places to Visit
Theater des Westens,
  Kurfürstendamm

---

surf-inn Internetcafé
Alexanderplatz • tel: +49 (0)30 24743 406 •
fax: +49 (0)30 2424 703 • czube@piro.net • www.surfinn.com

Location and Access
Located near Fernsehturm S
  Bahnhof Alexanderplatz
  Weltzeituhr.
Underground: S3, S5, S7,
  S9, U5, ask for
  Alexanderplatz.
Train: RE 1 to Magdeburg,
  Stralsund, Brandenburg,
  Cottbus, Fürstenwalde,
  Frankfurt-Oder, ask for
  Alexanderplatz.
Nearest cross street is S and

U Bahnhof Berlin
  Alexanderplatz.

Hours
Mon-Fri   9am-8pm
Sat   9am-4pm or
          9am-6pm

Prices
DM3 per half hour
DM6 per hour
No credit cards

Nearby Places to Visit
Palast der Republik

GERMANY, BERLIN (BERLIN)

Website

41 Joachimstaler Strasse • tel: +49 (0)30 8867 9630 •
fax: +49 (0)30 8867 8267 • info@vrcafe.de • www.vrcafe.de

Location and Access

Bus: 34, 100, 109, 119,
129, 146, 149, 219, 249,
ask for Kurfüerstendamm/
Zoologischer Garten.
Underground: U1, U2, U7,
U9, U15, ask for
Kurfüerstendamm/
Zoologischer Garten.
Train: S3, S7, S9, S75, ask
for Zoologischer Garten.

Nearest cross street is
Kurfüerstendamm

Hours

Mon-Thu &
Sun   10am-2am
Fri-Sat   10am-4am

Prices

DM5-7 per half hour
DM10-14 per hour
V

GERMANY, BÖBLINGEN (BADEN-WÜRTTEMBERG)

MedienCafé Böblingen—14 Schafgasse •

tel: +49 (0)7031 23 27 66 • fax: +49 (0)7031 23 27 68 •
info@mediencafe.boeblingen.de • www.mediencafe.boeblingen.de

Location and Access

Located near
Volkshochschule,
Böblingen.
Tram/Trolley: S-Bahn, S1,
ask for Haltestelle
Goldberg oder Böblingen
Hauptbahnhof.
Train: Intercity trains, ask
for Böblingen
Hauptbahnhof.
Nearest cross street is
Postplatz Poststrasse.

Hours

Tue-Sun   10am-11pm

Prices

DM5 per half hour
DM9.50 per hour, DM4 per
additional 30 minutes
No credit cards
Student discount available

Nearby Places to Visit

Gedaechtniskirche,
Zoologischer Garten,
Bahnhof Zoo

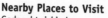

GERMANY, BONN (NORDRHEIN-WESTFALEN)

surf-inn Bonn
6-8 Remigiustrasse • tel: + 49 (0)228 516 513 •
fax: +49 (0)228 516 125 • efries@piro.net • www.surfinn.com

Location and Access
Phone for directions.

Hours
Mon-Sat   9am-2pm

Prices
DM3 per half hour
DM6 per hour
No credit cards

GERMANY, BREMEN (BREMEN)

NetCafé
86 Hohentorsstrasse • tel: +49 (0)421 598 0900 •
fax: +49 (0)421 178 8899 • netcafe@netwave.de • www.netwave.de

Location and Access
Located near Technical High
School and Beck's
Brewery.
Bus: 24, ask for
Hohentorsstrasse.
Tram/Trolley: 1, ask for
Hochschule fuer Technik.

Hours
Mon-Thu &
  Sun   10am-1am
Fri   10am-2am
Sat   10am-3am

Prices
First hour free then DM5 per
  hour
No credit cards

GERMANY, BRUNSWICK (BREMEN NIEDERSACHSEN)

Two Worlds—9 Reichenbergstrasse • tel: +49 (0)531 343 066 •
fax: +49 (0)531 343 067 • derwirt@twoworlds.de • www.twoworlds.de

Location and Access
Bus: 1, 19, ask for
   Hamburgerstrasse.
Nearest cross street is
   Hamburgerstrasse.

Hours
Mon-Thu   3pm-midnight
              (or later)
Fri-Sat   3pm-3am
Sun   3pm-midnight

Prices
DM10 per hour (minimum),
   DM5 per each additional
   hour
No credit cards

Nearby Places to Visit
See homepage

GERMANY, COLOGNE (NORDRHEIN-WESTFALEN)

Future Point
13 Richmodstrasse • tel: +49 (0)221 206 7206 •
fax: +49 (0)221 206 7199 • info@futurepoint.de • www.futurepoint.de

Location and Access
Located near Neumarkt.
Bus: 136, 146, and all buses
   to Neumarkt, ask for
   Neumarkt.
Underground: U-Bahn 1, 3,
   4, 14, 16, 18, ask for
   Neumarkt.
Tram: Strassenbahn 2, 7, 9,
   12, ask for Neumarkt.
Train: Ask for Cologne
   (Köln) Hauptbahnhof.
Located between

Richmodstrasse and
   Wolfsstrasse.

Hours
Mon-Sun   9am-1am

Prices
DM3 per half hour
DM6 per hour
No credit cards

Nearby Places to Visit
Dom (Cologne Cathedral),
   all of Cologne, the Old
   Town (Altstadt), the Rhine

GERMANY, COLOGNE (NORDRHEIN-WESTFALEN)

surf-inn Köln—41-43 Hohestrasse in the Galeria Kaufhof •
tel: +49 (0)221 925 3301 • fax: +49 (0)221 223 4231 •
jzimmerman@piro.net • www.surfinn.com

Location and Access
Located near Marks and
Spencer.
Bus: Ask for Heumarkt.
Underground or Tram: 1, 2,
7, 9, ask for Heumarkt.
Train: Main lines, ask for
Cologne Main Station and
walk 10 mins down
Hohestrasse.
Nearest cross street is
Schildergasse.

Hours
Mon-Sat   9am-8pm

Prices
DM3 per half hour
DM6 per hour
No credit cards

Nearby Places to Visit
Dom (Cologne Cathedral),
all of Cologne, the Old
Town (Altstadt), the Rhine

GERMANY, CONSTANCE (BADEN-WÜRTTEMBERG)

m@yers internet club café—70 Wollmatingerstrasse •
tel: +49 (0)7531 690 016 • fax: +49 (0)7531 690 015 •
info@mayers.de • www.mayers.de

Location and Access
Bus: 2, 3, 12, ask for
Friedhof.
Train: Seehas (regional
train), ask for
Petershausen.
Nearest cross street is
Zähringerplatz.

Hours
Tue-Sun   6pm-1am

Prices
DM5 per half hour
DM10 per hour
No credit cards

g@rden Gastronomie

8 Rathausufer • tel: +49 (0)211 866 160 •
fax: +49 (0)211 866 1611 • gsg@garden.de • www.garden.de

Location and Access
Located near the Rathaus
   (Town Council) of
   Düsseldorf.
Streetcars (Strassenbahnen):
   Ask for the Rathhaus.
Nearest cross streets, are
   Rheinuferpromenade and
   Burgplatz.

Hours
Mon-Fri   3pm-1am
                (winter)

Mon-Fri   11am-1am
                (summer)
Sat-Sun   11am-1am

Prices
DM3 per half hour
DM5 per hour
V, MC, AmEx

Nearby Places to Visit
Altstadt (Old Town)

---

surf-inn Düsseldorf

1 Königsallee • tel: +49 (0)211 139 1213 •
fax: +49 (0)211 454 3710 • mpaulus@piro.net • www.surfinn.com

Location and Access
Phone for directions.

Hours
Mon-Sat   9am-8pm

Prices
DM3 per half hour
DM6 per hour
No credit cards

GERMANY, ERLANGEN (BAVARIA)

Cafe Online—55-57 Hauptstrasse (in Alstadt Market) •
tel: +49 (0)9131 897 630 • fax: +49 (0)9131 897 631 •
info@c-online.de • www.c-online.de

Location and Access
Phone for directions.

Hours
Mon-Thu   10am-11pm
Fri-Sat   10am-1am

Prices
DM5 per half hour
DM10 per hour
No credit cards

Nearby Places to Visit
Northern Bavaria, Nürnberg,
Fürth, Erlangen

GERMANY, FRANKFURT (HESSEN)

CyberRyder Internet-Café
31 Töngesgasse • tel: +49 (0)69 9139 6754 •
fax: +49 (0)69 287 929 • info@cyberyder.de • www.cyberyder.de

Location and Access
Located near the Zeil (Main
    Shopping St.), Römer Sq.
Bus: Strassenbahn 11, ask
    for Römer-Paulskirche.
Underground: U1-U3, U4,
    U6, U7, ask for
    Hauptwache or
    KonstablerWache (U4, U7).
Train: Suburban lines S1-S6,
    S8, ask for Hauptwache.
Nearest cross street is
    Hauptwache/Zeil.

Hours
Mon-Thu   10am-11pm
Fri-Sat   10am-1am
Sun   3pm-11pm (and
               holidays)

Prices
DM6 per half hour
DM12 per hour
V, MC

Nearby Places to Visit
Liebfrauen-Kirche (church)

GERMANY, FREIBURG (BADEN-WÜRTTEMBERG)

Equinoxe Internet Galerie
7 Adlerstrasse • tel: +49 (0)761 382 263 • fax: +49 (0)761 382 265 • info@equinoxe.de • www.equinoxe.de

Location and Access
Located near Hauptbahnhof (Main Station).
Bus: 10, 12, ask for Stadttheater.
Tram/Trolley: 1, 4, 6, ask for Hauptbahnhof or Stadttheater.
Train: Intercity lines, ask for Main Station in Freiburg.
Nearest cross street is Kronenbrücke.

Hours
Mon-Sun   noon-8pm

Prices
DM3 per half hour
DM6 per hour
No credit cards

Nearby Places to Visit
The City Center

GERMANY, FULDA (HESSEN)

Café Online—80-82 Königstrasse •
tel: +49 (0)661 901 2460 • fax: +49 (0)661 32279 • wolfgang@cafeonline.com • www.cafeonline.com

Location and Access
Located near Dom (Cathedral), Hotel Zum Goldenen Karpfen.
Bus: 4, ask for Robert-Kircher-Strasse.
Train: Ask for Hauptbahnhof Fulda.
Nearest cross street is Frankfurter Strasse.

Hours
Tue-Thu &
  Sun   10am-midnight
Fri-Sat   10am-1am

Prices
DM5 per half hour
DM10 per hour
No credit cards

Nearby Places to Visit
Fuldaer Altstadt (Old Town), Stadtschloss (Castle), Michaelskirche, Hexenturm

GERMANY, GESCHER (NORDRHEIN-WESTFALEN)

icafe Login
22 Schuckerstrasse, in Sprung Systemhaus • tel: +49 (0)2542 93160 •
fax: +49 (0)2542 7686 • icafe@sprung.de • www.icafe.sprung.de

Location and Access
Nearest cross street is
   Autobahn A31/Abfahrt
   Gescher.

Hours
Mon-Fri	9am-8pm
Sat	10am-4pm
Sun	4pm-8pm

Prices
DM3 per half hour
DM6 per hour
No credit cards

GERMANY, GÖPPINGEN (BADEN-WÜRTTEMBERG)

Toptron—Flash
46 Vordere Karlstrasse • tel: +49 (0)7161 968 470 •
fax: +49 (0)7161 968 472 • toptron@toptron.de • www.toptron.de

Location and Access
Located near China-
   Restaurant.

Hours
Mon	noon-1am
Tue-Sat	10am-1am
Sun	2pm-1am

Prices
DM5 per half hour
DM10 per hour
No credit cards
Student discount available

GERMANY, HAGEN (NORDRHEIN-WESTFALEN)

surf-inn Hagen
1 Friedrich-Ebert-Platz • tel: +49 (0)233 110 7212 •
fax: +49 (0)233 110 7212 • shollenstein@piro.net • www.surfinn.com

Location and Access
Phone for directions.

Hours
Mon-Sat   9am-8pm

Prices
DM3 per half hour
DM6 per hour
No credit cards

GERMANY, HAMBURG (HAMBURG)

Spiele-Netzwerk—24 Kleiner Schäferkamp •
tel: +49 (0)40 4503 8210 • fax: +49 (0)40 4503 8211 •
Spiele-Netzwerk@mail.hh.provi.de • www.Spiele-Netzwerk.pop.de

Location and Access
Located near Haus des
   Sports.
Bus: 115, 181, 182, ask for
   Schlump Bahnhof.
Underground: U2, U3, ask
   for Schlump.
Nearest cross street is Beim
   Schlump.

Prices
DM5 per half hour
DM9 per hour
No credit cards

Hours
Mon-Sat   11am-midnight

GERMANY, HAMELN (NIERSACHSEN)

Fa. Witte Multimedia and Internet Café
69 Kopmannshof • tel: +49 (0)5151 94440 •
fax: +49 (0)5151 944450 • Info@witte.de • www.witte.de

Location and Access
Located near McDonald's, Halmelner Altstadt (Old Town).
Train: Regional Bahn, StadtEXPRESS, ask for BF Hameln.

Prices
DM5 per half hour
DM10 per hour
No credit cards
Student discount available

Hours
Mon-Fri   9am-6pm
Sat   10am-2pm

GERMANY, HANNOVER (NIERSACHSEN)

surf-inn Hannover
8 Seilwinder Strasse • tel: +49 (0)511 366 6238 •
fax: +49 (0) 511 366 6238 • mkrueger@piro.net • www.surfinn.com

Location and Access
Phone for directions.

Hours
Mon-Sat   9am-8pm

Prices
DM3 per half hour
DM6 per hour
No credit cards

GERMANY, LIMBURG-STAFFEL (HESSEN)

Billard Bistro Staffel
7 Elzer Strasse • tel: +49 (0)643 125 127 • fax: +49 (0)643 151 930 •
micha@billard-bistro.de • www.billard-bistro.de

Location and Access
Located near the Renault
  Dealer, in the Autovorteile
  Bäsch Gebäude.
Bus: Stadtlinie, ask for Elzer
  Strasse.
Nearest cross street is B49.

Hours
Mon-Sun   10:30am-1am

Prices
DM5 per half hour
DM10 per hour
No credit cards

Nearby Places to Visit
Limburger Dom

GERMANY, LIPPSTADT (NORDRHEIN-WESTFALEN)

INI Internet-Café
10 Bahnhofstrasse • tel: +49 (0)2941 59090 •
fax: +49 (0)2941 4026 • cafe@ini.de • www.ini.de

Location and Access
Nearest big town is
  Dortmund.
Located near Bahnhof
  Lippstadt (Station).
Bus: 663, 664, ask for
  Busbahnhof.
Train: Deutsche Bahn, ask
  for Lippstadt.

Hours
Mon-Tue &
  Thu-Fri   4:30pm-8pm
Wed   4:30pm-6pm

Prices
DM1.50 per half hour
DM3 per hour
No credit cards

GERMANY, MANNHEIM (BADEN-WÜRTTEMBERG)

Cyber's Place Internet Bar
F 2, 2 Marktplatz • tel: +49 (0)621 122 1810 •
fax: +49 (0)621 15 1663 • cybers@flip-inn.de • www.flip-inn.de

Location and Access
Located near Marktplatz.
Tram: All numbers stop at
   Marktplatz.
Nearest cross street is
   Marktplatz.

Hours
Mon-Sun   10am-3am

Prices
DM2.50 per half hour
DM5 per hour
No credit cards

Nearby Places to Visit
Watertower, castle

GERMANY, MUNICH (BAYERN)

Internet-Cafe—145 Nymphenburger Strasse •
tel: +49 (0)89 129 1120 • fax: +49 (0)89 2602 6780 •
manager@icafe.spacenet.de • www.icafe.spacenet.de

Location and Access
Bus: 33, ask for Landshuter
   Allee.
Underground: Ask for
   Rotkreuzplatz.
Tram/Trolley: 12, ask for
   Rotkreuzplatz.
Train: Ask for Donnersberger
   Bruecke.
Nearest cross street is
   Landshuter Allee.

Hours
Mon-Sun   11am-4am

Prices
DM5 per half hour
DM10 per hour
V, MC, AmEx, DC, D

Nearby Places to Visit
Nymphenburg Castle

GERMANY, MUNICH (BAYERN)

Internet-Cafe—12 Altheimer Eck •
tel: +49 (0)89 260 7815 • fax: +49 (0)89 2602 6780 •
manager@icafe.spacenet.de • www.icafe.spacenet.de

Location and Access
Located near Michaels
  Church.
Bus: 31, ask for Sendlinger
  Tor.
Underground: All lines, ask
  for Marienplatz,
  Karlsplatz, or Sendlinger
  Tor.
Tram/Trolley: All lines, ask
  for Karlsplatz.
Train: Ask for Karlsplatz or
  Marienplatz.

Nearest cross street is a
  pedestrian zone.

Hours
Mon-Sun   11am-1am

Prices
DM5 per half hour
DM10 per hour (one hour
  free if you buy a meal)
V, MC, AmEx, DC

Nearby Places to Visit
Marienplatz

GERMANY, MUNSTER (NORDRHEIN-WESTFALEN)

surf-inn Münster
1 Ludgerisstrasse • tel: +49 (0)251 5000 2184 •
fax: +49 (0)251 5000 2210 • skueper@piro.net • www.surfinn.com

Location and Access
Nearest cross street is
  Schildergasse.

Hours
Mon-Sat   9am-8pm

Prices
DM3 per half hour
DM6 per hour
No credit cards

GERMANY, NEUSTADT/WEINSTRASSE (RHEINLAND-PFALZ)

netc@fe Neustadt/Weinstrasse

5 Konrad-Adenauerstrasse • tel: +49 (0)632 192 9109 • No fax •
cafe@concept-net.de • www.concept-net.de/cafe/cafe.htm

Location and Access
Located near Hambacher
  Schloss (Hambach Castle),
  Deutsche Weinstrasse
  (German winestreet).
Bus: Ask for main bus sta-
  tion.

Hours
Mon-Sat   11am-midnight
Sun   3pm-midnight

Prices
DM5 per half hour
DM10 per hour
No credit cards
Student discount available

Nearby Places to Visit
Holiday Park (Hassloch),
  Strasbourg (90 km)

GERMANY, NURNBERG (BAYERN)

Stereo Deluxe/Vianet

5 Bahnhofstrasse • tel: +49 (0)911 527 9760 •
fax: +49 (0)911 527 9750 • vianet@vianet.de • www.stereo-deluxe.de

Location and Access
Located near Hauptbahnhof
  (Main Station).
Bus: All buses going to the
  Main Station & 124.
Underground: All U-bahns
  going to the Main Station.
Tram/Trolley: All
  Strassenbahns going to
  the Main Sation.
Train: Intercity Trains, ask
  for Main Station.

Hours
Mon-Wed &
  Sun   10am-7pm
Thu-Sat   10am-3am

Prices
DM5 per half hour
DM10 per hour
No credit cards

Nearby Places to Visit
Nurnberger Altstadt (Old
  Town)

GERMANY, OBERHAUSEN (NORDRHEIN-WESTFALEN)

surf-inn Oberhausen
Centroallee • tel: +49 (0)208 26940 • fax: +49 (0)208 823 0130 •
mgaib@piro.net • www.surfinn.com

Location and Access
Phone for directions.

Hours
Mon-Sat   9am-8pm

Prices
DM3 per half hour
DM6 per hour
No credit cards

GERMANY, REGENSBURG (BAVARIA)

Netzblick Online Cafe
9 Am Roemling • tel: +49 (0)941 599 9702 • No fax •
info@netzblick.de • www.netzblick.de

Location and Access
Located near Haidplatz.
Bus: Old town lines 1, 2, 3,
4, 6, 11, 13, 17, ask for
Haidplatz & Arnulfsplatz.
Train: Main lines from
Frankfurt, Stuttgart, or
Munich, ask for
Regensburg Station.
Nearest cross street is
Haidplatz.

Hours
Tue-Sun   7pm-1am

Prices
DM5 per half hour
DM10 per hour (DM2
discount with a drink)
No credit cards

GERMANY, REGENSBURG (BAYERN)

surf-inn Regensburg

8 Neupfarrplatz • tel: +49 (0)941 583 7258 •
fax: +49 (0)941 583 7111 • jhastreiter@piro.net • www.surfinn.com

Location and Access
Phone for directions.

Hours
Mon-Sat   9am-8pm

Prices
DM3 per half hour
DM6 per hour
No credit cards

GERMANY, ROSTOCK (BRANDENBURG)

surf-inn Rostock

Lange Strasse • tel: +49 (0)381 375 6216 •
fax: +49 (0)381 375 6110 • gberg@piro.net • www.surfinn.com

Location and Access
Phone for directions.

Hours
Mon-Sat   9am-8pm

Prices
DM3 per half hour
DM6 per hour
No credit cards

GERMANY, SCHWERIN (MECKLENBURG-VORPOMMERN)

C@fe "Doktor K."—3 Dr.-Külz-Strasse •
tel: +49 (0)385 764 9738 • fax: +49 (0)385 764 9712 •
cafe@toaster.imv.de • www.toaster.imv.de/doktor.k

Location and Access
Bus: 10, 11, ask for Platz der Freiheit.
Train: Intercity trains, ask for Hauptbahnhof Schwerin.
Nearest cross streets are Lübecker Strasse and Obotritenring.

Prices
DM5 per half hour
DM8.50 per hour
No credit cards

Hours
Mon-Fri   9am-10pm

GERMANY, STUTTGART (BADEN-WÜRTTEMBERG)

surf-inn Stuttgart—8 Kæigstrasse •
tel: +49 (0)711 226 2330 • fax: +49 (0)711 203 6225 •
mvaupotic@piro.net.com • www.surfinn.com

Location and Access
Phone for directions.

Hours
Mon-Sat   9am-8pm

Prices
DM3 per half hour
DM6 per hour
No credit cards

GERMANY, WIESBADEN (HESSEN)

surf-inn Wiesbaden
28 Kirchgasse • tel: +49 (0)611 175 304 • fax: +49 (0)611 175 175 •
jruecker@piro.net • www.surfinn.com

Location and Access
Phone for directions.

Hours
Mon-Sat   9am-8pm

Prices
DM3 per half hour
DM6 per hour
No credit cards

GERMANY, WITTEN (NORDRHEIN-WESTFALEN)

Café InterNezzo
70 Oberstrasse • tel: +49 (0)2302 390 596/83848 • No fax •
mbranscheidt@metronet.de • No website

Location and Access
Bus: 376, ask for
  Oberstrasse and
  Ardeystrasse.
Nearest cross street is
  Ardeystrasse.

Hours
Mon-Thu	3pm-1am
Fri-Sat	3pm-3am
Sun	5pm-1am

Prices
DM4-5 per half hour
DM8-10 per hour
No credit cards
Student discount available

GERMANY, ZWICKAU (BUNDESLAND SACHSEN)

MNC-Net
4 Lessingstrasse • tel: +49 (0)375 541 555/541 682 •
fax: +49 (0)375 541 687 • g.ltg@mnc-net.de • www.mnc-net.de

Location and Access
Located near
   Polizeipraesidium/BIC-
   Stammgebaeude.
Nearest cross street is Platz
   der Voelkerfreunschaft/
   Leipziger Strasse.

Prices
DM5 per half hour
DM10 per hour
No credit cards
Student discount avilable

Hours
Mon-Fri   3pm-6pm and by
           appointment
Sat-Sun   by appointment

GREECE, ATHENS (ATTIKI)

Carousel Cyber Cafe—32 Eftihidou Street, Pagrati •
tel: +30 (0)1 7564305 • fax: +30 (0)1 7564153 •
info@carousel-cafe.com • www.carousel-cafe.com

Location and Access
Located near the old
   Olympic Stadium.
Bus: 204, 211, ask for Alsos
   stop.
Trolley: 2, 11, ask for Alsos
   bus stop.

Hours
Mon-Sun   10am-midnight

Prices
Dr800 per half hour
Dr1,600 per hour
No credit cards

Nearby Places to Visit
The old Olympic Stadium,
   the Acropolis of Athens,
   the Kings Gardens, the old
   Parliament with changing
   of the guards

Cyberspace Hall at "Hellenic Cosmos" Cultural Centre

—254 Pireos Street • tel: +30 (0)1 4835300 • fax: +30 (0)1 4834634 • Cyber_hall@fhw.gr • www.fhw.gr

Location and Access

Located near College of Fine Arts.

Bus: 049 (Piraeus-Omonia), 814 (Omonia Square-downtown Athens). Ask for College of Fine Arts.

Train: Ask for Kallithea Station.

Nearest cross street is Hamosternas Street.

Hours

Mon	9am-6pm
Tue & Thu-Fri	9am-2pm
Wed	9am-8:30pm
Sun	11am-3pm

Prices

Dr550 per half hour
Dr1,100 per hour
V, MC
Student discount available

Hypercorner Internet Cafe

—102, Agiou Ionnou Street, Agia Parakevi • tel: +30 (0)1 6009442/6012256 • fax: +30 (0)1 6015981 • administrator@hypercorner.gr • www.hypercorner.gr

Location and Access

Located near Deree College, the American College of Greece.

Bus: B5, or A5 to B5, ask for Agiou Ionnou Square, Agia Paraskevi (end of the line).

Nearest cross street is Gravia Street.

Hours

Mon-Fri	9:30am-11pm
Sat	noon-10pm
Sun	3pm-10pm

Prices

Dr500 per half hour
Dr1,000 per hour
No credit cards

Nearby Places to Visit

Acropolis, museums

Netoikos Internet-Cafe

14 Kaloheretou • tel: +30 (0)661 47481 • No fax •
netoikos@netoikos.gr • www.netoikos.gr/internet.htm

Location and Access
Located behind Liston.
Bus: Kanoni (blue), ask for
  Liston.

Hours
Mon-Sat   9am-midnight
Sun   5pm-midnight

Prices
US$2 per half hour
US$4 per hour
No credit cards
Student discount available

Nearby Places to Visit
St. Spiridon Church, Royal
  Palace (Museum), Old
  Town Fort

Mykonos Cyber Cafe—M. Axioti 26, Myli •
tel: +30 (0)289 27684 • fax: +30 (0)289 27685 •
info@mykonos-cyber-cafe.com • www.mykonos-cyber-cafe.com

Location and Access
Located near the Windmills.
Bus: 100 meters from the
  bus station, ask for
  Fabrica.

Nearby Places to Visit
Mon-Sat   10am-7pm
           (winter)

Mon-Sat   10am-10pm
           (summer)

Sun   noon-10pm
           (summer)

Prices
Dr4,500 per half hour
Dr9,000 per hour
V, AmEx

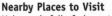

Nearby Places to Visit
Mykonos is full of places to
  visit.

GREECE, RHODES (DODECANESE)

RockStyle Internet Cafe
7 Dimokratias • tel: +30 (0)241 27502 • No fax •
admin@rockstyle.gr • www.rockstyle.gr

Location and Access
Located near the port.
Bus: Ask for Saint Francisko.
Nearest cross street is Saint
  Francisko.

Hours
Mon-Sun   10am-1am

Prices
Dr500 per half hour
Dr1,000 per hour
No credit cards

GREECE, VOLOS (MAGNISIA)

Internet Channel
15 Gallias-Ag. Nikolaou • tel: +30 (0)932 468158 •
No fax • info@ichannel.gr • www.ichannel.gr

Location and Access
Located near the fire
  department.
Bus: 3, 4, ask for Lido
  Cinema.
Nearest cross street is
  Iolkou.

Hours
Mon-Fri   3:30pm-midnight
Sat-Sun   11am-midnight

Prices
Dr500 per half hour
Dr1,000 per hour
V, MC, AmEx

Nearby Places to Visit
Museum

COMFORT-NETshare Ltd.

109/C Ulloi ut • tel: +36 1 216 0050 • fax: +36 1 216 0051 •
comfort@comfort.hu • www.comfort.hu

Location and Access

Located near Internet Rock
Cafe.
Underground: Metro 3, ask
for Klinikak.
Tram/Trolley: 31, ask for
Nagyvarad ter.
Nearest cross street is
Ferenc korut.

Hours

Mon-Fri   9am-4pm

Prices

HUF500 per half hour
HUF800 per hour
V, MC

Nearby Places to Visit

Museum

Different's Brain-Store Internet Cafe & Club

20. Liszt Ferenc u. • tel: +36 96 516 810 • fax: +36 96 317 675 •
brain-store@different.hu • www.different.hu/brain-store

Location and Access

Located near the theatre.
Bus: 11, ask for the theatre,
or walk from the bus sta-
tion.
Nearest cross street is
Palffy u.

Hours

Mon-Fri   10am-9pm
Sat   3pm-9pm

Prices

HUF250 per half hour
HUF500 per hour
No credit cards

Nearby Places to Visit

Zichy-palace, Castle of Gyor,
Szechenyi Square, Baroque
Square, Cathedral of Gyor,
museums

HUNGARY, NYIREGYHAZA (SZABOLCS-SZATMAR-BEREG)

Cyber Cafe—1-3 Szarvas • tel: +36 (06) 42 420 633/228 • fax: +36 (06) 42 420 633/228 • oktaneti@szabinet.hu • http://stg.szabinet.hu/cybercafe

Location and Access
Bus: 7A, 8, ask for Omnia.
Nearest cross street is Gabor
  Bethlen Street.

Prices
HUF400 per half hour
HUF600 per hour
No credit cards

Hours
Mon-Fri   2pm-5pm

IRELAND, CARRICK-ON-SHANNON (COUNTY LEITRIM)

Gartlan's Cybercafe
Bridge Street • tel: +353 (0)78 21735 • fax: +353 (0)78 21735 • gartlan@iol.ie • www.iol.ie/~gartlan/index.htm

Location and Access
Located near Gartlan's
  Newsagents.
Bus: Dublin to Sligo route,
  ask for Carrick-on-
  Shannon.

Hours
Mon-Sat   10am-9pm
Sun   10am-7pm

Prices
Ir£4.50 per hour (half hour
  minimum)

MC, AmEx, DC, D

Nearby Places to Visit
Costello Memorial Chapel,
  Moon River pleasure
  cruiser, Lough Rynn,
  House and Gardens
  (Mohill), Parkes Castle
  (Drumkeerin), King House
  (Boyle), Famine Museum
  (Strokestown), Drumcoura
  City, Ballinamore, Lough
  Key (Forest Park)

IRELAND, DINGLE (COUNTY KERRY)

DingleWeb
Lower Main Street • tel: +353 (0)66 915 2477 •
fax: +353 (0)66 915 2479 • info@dingleweb.com • www.dingleweb.com

Location and Access
Located opposite the Small
 Bridge (An Droichead
 Beag) Pub.
Bus: Only one bus to
 Dingle, ask for Dingle.

Hours
Mon-Sat 9:30am-9:30pm
Mon-Sat 10am-6:30pm
             (winter)

Prices
Ir£3 per half hour
Ir£5 per hour
V, MC, AmEx, DC

Nearby Places to Visit
The Dingle Peninsula is a
 popular tourist site.

IRELAND, DUBLIN (COUNTY DUBLIN)

The Planet Cyber Cafe
23 South Great Georges Street • tel: +353 (0)67 90583 •
fax: +353 (0)67 71463 • info@irelands-web.ie • www.irelands-web.ie

Location and Access
Located near Georges Street
 Arcade.
Bus: All city buses, ask for
 South Great Georges
 Street.
Nearest cross street is Dame
 Street.

Hours
Mon-Wed &
 Sun   10am-10pm
Thu-Sat 10am-midnight

Prices
Ir£2.75 per half hour
Ir£4.50 per hour
No credit cards

Nearby Places to Visit
Dublin Castle, Temple-Bar

IRELAND, ENNIS (COUNTY CLARE)

MacCools Internet Cafe
Brewery Lane • tel: +353 (0)65 21988 • No fax •
maccools@clarenet.ie • www.clarenet.ie/maccools

Location and Access
Located near O'Connell's Statue, follow the lane down to the Abbey Street carpark.
Nearest cross street is the Square, Abbey Street.

Hours
Mon-Sat   11am-10pm
Sun   noon-6pm

Prices
Ir£3 per half hour
Ir£6 per hour
No credit cards

Nearby Places to Visit
The Burren, the Cliffs of Moher, Lahinch Golf Course, Bunratty Castle

---

IRELAND, GALWAY (COUNTY GALWAY)

NetAccess
Olde Malte Arcade, High Street • tel: +353 (0)91 569772 •
fax: +353 (0)91 568633 • info@netaccess.ie • www.netaccess.ie

Location and Access
Located near Kings Head Pub.
Bus: From Eyre Square and the surrounds, or intercity lines to Galway, ask for Olde Malte, High Street.
Train: Mainline trains, ask for Ceannt Station just off Eyre Square.
Nearest cross street is Shop Street.

Hours
Mon-Sat   10am-7pm
Sun   noon-6pm

Prices
Ir£3 per half hour
Ir£5 per hour
No credit cards
Student discount available

Nearby Places to Visit
Connemara, Ailwee Caves, the Burren

PC Assist

High Street • tel: +353 (0)64 37288 • fax: +353 (0)64 37281 •
pca@tinet.ie • No website

Location and Access
Located near police station
and public library.
Bus: Ask for Main Bus
Station (8 min. walk).
Train: Cork or Dublin to
Killarney train, ask for
Killarney Train Station.

Hours
Mon-Sat   9am-5:30pm

Prices
Ir£3 per half hour
Ir£5 per hour
V
Student discount available

Nearby Places to Visit
The National Park, horse riding, the Cathedral

Websters Internet Cafe

44 Thomas Street • tel: +353 (0)61 312066 •
fax: +353 (0)61 312066 • info@websters.ie • www.websters.ie

Location and Access
Bus: 1, 2, 4, 8, 11, ask for
Todds, Boyds.
Nearest cross street is
O'Connell Street.

Hours
Mon-Sat   9am-9pm
Sun   2pm-9pm

Prices
Ir£3 per half hour
Ir£6 per hour

V, MC
Student discount available

Nearby Places to Visit
King John's Castle, Bunratty
Folk Park and Castle,
Adare, Angela's Ashes
walking tour of Limerick,
Galway, Gateway to the
southwest, Killarney, Kerry

IRELAND, MAYNOOTH (COUNTY KILDARE)

Cyber X Internet Cafe

Unit 5 Glenroyal Centre Maynooth • tel: +353 (0)16 291747 • fax: +353 (0)16 291020 • enquiries@CyberX.ie • www.CyberX.ie

Location and Access
Located opposite Glenroyal Hotel.
Bus: 67, 67A, ask for Glenroyal Hotel.
Train: From Sligo, ask for Maynooth.
Nearest cross street is Main Centre in town.

Hours
Mon-Sun   noon-midnight

Prices
Ir£2 per half hour
Ir£4 per hour
V, MC, AmEx
Student discount available

Nearby Places to Visit
Maynooth College & Seminary

IRELAND, SLIGO (COUNTY SLIGO)

Futurenet Internet Cafe

Pearse Road • tel: +353 (0)71 50345 • fax: +353 (0)71 50346 • info@futurenet.ie • www.futurenet.ie

Location and Access
Located near Garda Barracks.
Bus: City Centre buses, ask for St. Bridgets Place.
Train: From Dublin, ask for Sligo Station.
Nearest cross street is Mail Coach Road.

Hours
Mon-Sat   10am-6:30pm

Prices
Ir£3 per half hour
Ir£6 per hour
V, MC
Student discount available

Nearby Places to Visit
Too many to mention—Sligo is such a beautiful place!

IRELAND, TULLAMORE (COUNTY OFFALY)

MidNet Café
5 Bridge Street • tel: +353 (0)506 22292 • fax: +353 (0)506 22899 •
pauline@midnet.ie • www.midnet-cafe.net

Location and Access
Located near Bridge House.
Bus: Regular buses from
  Dublin, ask for Tullamore.
Train: Dublin to Galway
  route, ask for Tullamore.
Nearest cross street is
  Bridge Centre.

Hours
Mon-Sat   10am-6pm

Prices
Ir£3 per half hour
Ir£6 per hour
V, MC
Student discount available

Nearby Places to Visit
Two 4-star hotels, good
  point for touring the
  Midlands of Ireland,
  Clonmacnoise

IRELAND, WATERFORD CITY (COUNTY MUNSTER)

Voyager Internet Cafe
Parnell Street • tel: +353 (0)51 843843 • fax: +353 (0)51 843900 •
webmaster@voyager.ie • www.voyager.ie

Location and Access
Located near Muldoons Bar,
  Saint John's Church.

Hours
Mon-Sat   11am-11pm
Sun   3pm-11pm

Prices
Ir£3 per half hour
Ir£6 per hour
No credit cards
Student discount available

Nearby Places to Visit
Waterford Crystal Factory
tour, John F. Kennedy
Memorial Park and
Arboretum, walking tours
of medieval city and of
Kilkenny city and castle
(45 min. drive), Tramore &
Dunmore East beaches,
Mount Juliet golf course,
heritage center, riding,
polo

ITALY, BROCCOSTELLA (FROSINONE)

Cyberpub New York Express
96 Via Stella • tel: +39 (0)77 6891336 • fax: +39 (0)77 6871786 •
cyberpub@cyberpub.it • www.cyberpub.it

Location and Access
Located in a town between
   Rome and Naples.
Bus: Sora to Cassino bus,
   ask for Via Stella.
Nearest cross street is Via
   Sora.

Hours
Mon-Sun   6pm-3am

Prices
L5,000 per half hour
L10,000 per hour
No credit cards
Student discount available

Nearby Places to Visit
Montecassino

ITALY, FLORENCE (TUSCANY)

CyberOffice
4/R Via San Gallo • tel: +39 (0)55 211103 • fax: +39 (0)55 211103 •
gheri.fiers@dada.it • www.dada.it/gheri.fiers/cyber_english.htm

Location and Access
Located near McDonald's Via
   Cavour.
Bus: 1, 6, 7, 10, 17, ask for
   San Marco.
Nearest cross street is Via
   Cavour/Via Guelfa.

Hours
Mon-Sat   10:30am-7:30pm

Prices
L5,000-6,000 per half hour
L10,000 per hour
V, MC
Student discount available

Nearby Places to Visit
Museo dell'Academia
   (David), San Lorenzo, San
   Marco

Internet Train 1—25/R Via dell'Oriuolo •
tel: +39 (0)55 9638968 • fax: +39 (0)55 9638968 •
oriolo@fionline.it • www.fionline.it/internet_train

Location and Access
Located one block from the
  Duomo on the way to
  Piazza S. Croce.
Bus: 14, 23, ask for
  Proconsolo.

Prices
L6,000 per half hour
L12,000 per hour
V, MC, AmEx, DC
Student discount available
  for long term residents

Hours
Mon-Thu 10am-10:30pm
Fri-Sat 10am-8pm
Sun 3pm-7pm

Nearby Places to Visit
S. Croce Church

Internet Train 2
24A Via Guelfa • tel: +39 (0)55 214794 • fax: +39 (0)55 214794 •
info@fionline.it • www.fionline.it/internet_train

Location and Access
Located near S. Lorenzo
  Market.
Bus: Most lines, ask for
  Central Station.
Nearest cross street is Via
  Cavour at McDonald's.

Prices
L6,000 per half hour
L12,000 per hour
V, MC
Student discount available
  for long term residents

Nearby Places to Visit
Medici's Chapel

Hours
Mon-Fri 10am-11pm
Sat 10am-8pm
Sun noon-7pm

ITALY, FLORENCE (TUSCANY)

The Netgate—Your Internet Point
10/R Via Sant'Egidio • tel: +39 (0)55 2347967 •
fax: +39 (0)55 2638527 • netgate@aspide.it • www.thenetgate.it

Location and Access
Located near the Duomo.
Bus: 14.
Nearest cross streets are
  Borgo Pinti, Piazza Santa
  Croce, Piazza Duomo.

Hours
Mon-Sun   10:30am-8:30pm

Prices
L5,000 per 20 minutes
L10,000 per hour
V, MC, AmEx
Student discount available

Nearby Places to Visit
Piazza Santa Croce

ITALY, L'AQUILA (ABRUZZO)

Gli Internauti—Centro Multimediale e Pub
51 Via Cimino • tel: +39 (0)86 2404338 • No fax •
internauti@internauti.it • No website

Location and Access
Located near Costa
  Masciarelli-Porta Bazzano.
Bus: 3, 4, 4D, 11, 77, 77A,
  78, 79, 79A, 79B, 79C,
  ask for La Standa.
Nearest cross street is
  Piazza Duomo.

Hours
Thu & Sun 5pm-8pm &
          9:30pm-2am

Prices
L5,000 per half hour
L10,000 per hour
No credit cards
Student discount available

Nearby Places to Visit
Duomo, Chiesa S. Giusta

ITALY, LIGNANO SABBIADORO (UDINE)

Netcafe
11 Corso Alisei • tel: +39 (0)431 427209 • fax: +39 (0)431 423005 •
netcafe@netanday.it • www.lignano.it

Location and Access
Bus: Lignano line, ask for La
    Botte.
Nearest cross street is Via
    dei Fiori.

Prices
L5,000 per half hour
L7,000 per hour
No credit cards
Student discount available

Hours
Mon-Sun   8am-3am
(Wed closed Sept.-April)

Nearby Places to Visit
Venice, Trieste, Aquileia

ITALY, MILAN (LOMBARDIA)

Relax Bar—7 Via Cellini, Garbagnate Milanese •
tel: +39 (0)2 9954334 • fax: +39 (0)2 99010773 •
relax@maganet.net • www.maganet.net/cyber/relax.htm

Location and Access
Nearest cross street is SS
    Varesina.

Nearby Places to Visit
Milan

Hours
Mon &
    Wed-Sun 7am-11:30pm

Prices
L6,000 per half hour
L10,000 per hour
No credit cards

ITALY, MILAN (LOMBARDIA)

TerzoMillennio

2 Via Lazzaretto • tel: +39 (0)2 2052121 • fax: +39 (0)2 20521299 •
info@abc2000.it • www.abc2000.it

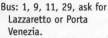

Location and Access
Located near Central
   Station.
Bus: 1, 9, 11, 29, ask for
   Lazzaretto or Porta
   Venezia.
Underground: MM1, MM3,
   Passante-ferroviario, ask
   for Repubblica, Venezia.
Nearest cross street is Corso
   Buenos Aires.

Hours
Mon-Sat   9am-10pm
Sun   9am-6pm

Prices
L8,000 per hour (minimum)
V, MC, AmEx
Student discount available

Nearby Places to Visit
Venice's Gate

ITALY, NAPLES (NAPOLI)

Internetbar

74 Piazza V. Bellini • tel: +39 (0)81 295237 • fax: +39 (0)81 295035 •
info@tightrope.it • www.tightrope.it

Location and Access
Located near Piazza Dante-
   Port' Alba.
Bus: R1, R2, R3, ask for
   Piazza Dante.
Underground: F.S. train, ask
   for Piazza Cavour.
Nearest cross street is Port'
   Alba.

Hours
Mon-Fri   9am-3am

Sat   9am-3pm &
               9pm-3am
Sun   9pm-3am

Prices
L5,000 per half hour
L10,000 per hour
No credit cards

Nearby Places to Visit
Naples City Center

ITALY, PALERMO (SICILY)

Malox Internet Cafe
Piazzetta della Canna 8/9 • tel: +39 (0)91 6118766 •
fax: +39 (0)91 6121994 • boiler@malox.com • www.malox.com

Location and Access
Located near Arabian
   Mosque.
Bus: 101, ask for Quattro
   Canti di città.
Nearest cross street is Via
   Vittorio Emanuele.

Hours
Mon-Fri   4pm-2am
Sat   6pm-2am

Prices
L4,000 per half hour
L8,000 per hour
No credit cards
Student discount available

Nearby Places to Visit
Palermo Cathedral, Palermo
   City Hall

ITALY, ROME (ROMA-LAZIO)

Internet Café
170 Via Salaria • tel: +39 (0)6 8411977 • fax: +39 (0)6 8411977 •
clienti@internet-cafe.it • www.internet-cafe.it

Location and Access
Located near Piazza Fiume.
Bus: 56, 319, ask for Via
   Salaria.
Train: 19, ask for Via
   Salaria.

Hours
Mon-Fri   10am-2am
Sat-Sun   4pm-2am

Prices
L2,500 10am-4pm & L5,000

4pm-2am per half hour
L5,000 10am-4pm &
   L10,000 4pm-2am per
   hour
No credit cards
Student discount available

Nearby Places to Visit
Modern Art Museum, Villa
   Borghese Art Gallery, Villa
   Borghese gardens, St.
   Agnes Catacombs and
   Basilica, Villa Torlonia

Internet Café

12 Via dei Marrucini • tel: +39 (0)6 4454953 •
fax: +39 (0)6 4454953 • info@internetcafe.it • www.internetcafe.it

Location and Access
Located in San Lorenzo District near Termini Station (Train Station).
Bus: 11, 71, 204, 492, and 29 night bus, ask for Via Cesare de Lollis.
Underground: A, B, ask for Termini Station (line A) and Policlinico (line B).
Nearest cross street is Tiburtina Street.

Hours
Mon-Fri   9am-2am
Sat-Sun   5pm-2am

Prices
L5,000 until 9pm, L6,000 after 9pm per half hour
L8,000 until 9pm, L10,000 after 9pm per hour
V, MC

Nearby Places to Visit
S. Maria Maggiore

The Netgate—Your Internet Point

25 Piazza Firenze • tel: +39 (0)6 6893445 • fax: +39 (0)6 6893445 •
netgate@aspide.it • www.thenetgate.it

Location and Access
Located near Pantheon.
Bus: 116, ask for Piazza Firenze.
Underground: Metro, ask for Piazza di Spagna.
Nearest cross streets are Pantheon, Piazza Navona, Piazza di Spagna.

Prices
L5,000 per 20 minutes
L10,000 per hour
V, MC, AmEx
Student discount available

Hours
Mon-Sun   10:30am-8:30pm

ITALY, SALERNO (SALERNO)

Attendere Prego...
26 Via Roma • tel: +39 (0)89 221506 • fax: +39 (0)89 231041 •
mail@attendereprego.com • www.attendereprego.com

Location and Access
Located near Chamber of
Commerce.
Bus: All buses, ask for
Chamber of Commerce.

Hours
Mon-Sun   10am-1pm &
          5pm-1:30am

Prices
L7,500 per half hour
L13,000 per hour
No credit cards

Nearby Places to Visit
Salerno Dome

ITALY, TURIN (TORINO)

Interlink—108 bis, Via Ormea •
tel: +39 (0)11 6693751 • fax: +39 (0)11 6695403 •
postmaster@interlink.it • www.interlink.it

Location and Access
Located near Torino
Esposizioni (City
Exhibition Hall).
Bus: 42, 45, 67, ask for Via
Madama Cristina.
Tram/Trolley: 18, ask for
Corso Dante.
Nearest cross street is c.so
Massimo d'Azeglio.

Hours
Mon-Fri   9:30am-6:30pm
Sat   by appointment
          only

Prices
L7,500 per half hour
L15,000 per hour
No credit cards

Nearby Places to Visit
Museo dell'Automobile (Car
Museum)

Bilteks Internet Cafe

20/22 Jekaba Street, Old Town • tel: +371 7 32 22 08 •
fax: +371 7 33 81 73 • cafe.operator@binet.lv • www.binet.lv

Location and Access
Located near Dome Square.
Tram/Trolley: 6, 9, 21, ask
  for Valdemara Street and
  Jekaba Street.

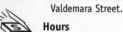

Nearest cross street is
  Valdemara Street.

Hours
Mon-Sun   10am-9pm

Prices
US$2 per half hour
US$3.50 per hour
No credit cards
Student discount available
  with special discount
  cards

Nearby Places to Visit
Old Riga

Astoria Internet Cafe—27A Partizanska •

tel: +389 (0)91 124856/109694 • fax: +389 (0)91 124857 •
astoria@astoria.com.mk • www.astoria.com.mk

Location and Access
Located on one of the major
  city roads near the
  biggest church in the
  country, St. Kliment.

Bus: 2, 4, 7, 12, 15, 21, 64,
  ask for Kim or Bunjakovec
  (cafe is between these
  stops).

Hours
Mon-Sun   10am-10pm

Prices
denars60 per half hour
denars100 per hour
V, MC, DC

Nearby Places to Visit
St. Kliment Orthodox Church

Waves Internet C@fe & Cocktail Bar Malta

139/1C Tower Road • tel: +356 342242 • No fax •
waves@waldonet.net.mt • www.waldonet.net.mt/waves

Location and Access

Located near TGIF and the Europa Hotel.

Bus: 62, ask for Chalet Hotel.

Nearest cross street is the seafront, which is the main road.

Hours

Mon-Sun   11:30am-2am

Prices

Lm1 per half hour
Lm2 per hour
No credit cards
Student discount available sometimes, ask at the bar.

Nearby Places to Visit

Malta is very small so everything is close, plenty of places to see and the bar is opposite the beach.

The Cyberc@fe Amsterdam—19hs Nieuwendijk •

tel: +31 (0)20 6235146 • fax: +31 (0)20 4203113 •
cyber@cybercafe.euronet.nl or info@cybercafe.euronet.nl •
www.cybercafe.euronet.nl

Location and Access

Located near Centraal Station.

Bus, Train, and Underground: Ask for Centraal Station.

Tram/Trolley: 1, 2, 5, 13, 17, ask for Centraal Station or Nieuwezijds Voorburgwal.

Hours

Mon-Thu &
Sun   10am-1am

Fri-Sat   10am-3am

Prices

fl3 per twenty minutes (compulsory drink order)
fl9 per hour (compulsory drink order)
V, MC

Nearby Places to Visit

Sex Museum, Hash Museum, Anne Frank's House

THE NETHERLANDS, HAARLEM (NOORD-HOLLAND)

Cybercafé Amadeus—10 Grote Markt, 2nd Floor •
tel: +31 (0)23 5324530 • fax: +31 (0)23 5322328 •
cybercafe@amadeus-hotel.com • www.amadeus-hotel.com/cybercafe.html

Location and Access
Located near the St. Bavo
  Cathedral.
Bus: 2, ask for Grote Markt.
Train: From station, 10 min.
  walk to Grote Markt.

Hours
Mon-Sun   10:30am-10pm

Prices
fl7.50 per half hour
fl15 per hour
MC

Nearby Places to Visit
Frans Hals Museum, Corrie
  Ten Boom House, Red
  lights

THE NETHERLANDS, THE HAGUE (ZUID-HOLLAND)

Internetcafe Den Haag—48 Elandstraat •
tel: +31 (0)70 3636286 • No fax •
info@internetcafe-dh.demon.nl • www.internetcafe-dh.demon.nl

Location and Access
Located near the Royal
  Stables.
Tram: 3, ask for Elandstraat.

Hours
Mon-Sat   5pm-1am

Prices
fl6 per half hour
fl12 per hour
No credit cards

Nearby Places to Visit
International Peace Palace,
  Postmuseum, Panorama
  Mesdag, Royal Palaces

THE NETHERLANDS, HILVERSUM (NOORD-HOLLAND)

Cytag Cyberbar
44 Koninginneweg • tel: +31 (0)35 6215841 •
fax: +31 (0)35 6241819 • info@cytag.nl • www.cytag.nl

Location and Access
Located near Hilversum
 Centraal Station.
Train: All lines, ask for
 Hilversum Centraal
 Station.

Hours
Wed   6pm-midnight
Sat   10pm-3am

Prices
Free

THE NETHERLANDS, TILBURG (NOORD-BRABANT)

CyberGate
22 Fabriekstraat • tel: +31 (0)13 5420604 • fax: +31 (0)13 5442080 •
cybergate@cybergate.nl • www.cybergate.nl

Location and Access
Located near Centraal
 Station.
Bus: Ask for Centraal
 Station.
Train: Ask for Centraal
 Station Tilburg.
Nearest cross street is
 Stationsstraat.

Hours
Mon-Thu &
 Sun   2pm-1am
Fri-Sat   2pm-3am

Prices
fl9 per half hour
fl12.50 per hour
No credit cards

Nearby Places to Visit
Museum the Pont, Museum
 Scription

NORWAY, JOSTEDAL (FJORDANE)

Breheimsenteret
Jostedal • tel: +47 57683250 • fax: +47 57683240 •
jostedal@jostedal.com • www.jostedal.com

Location and Access
Located near Nigard Glacier.
Bus: Ask for
  Breheimsenteret.
Nearest cross street is
  Sogndal.

Hours
Mon-Sun   9am-7pm
          (May-Sept.
          only)

Prices
Included in museum ticket.
V, MC, AmEx, DC
Student discount available

Nearby Places to Visit
The computer is inside our
  glacier museum, which is
  at the foot of the Nigard
  Glacier, so there are plenty
  of opportunities to sight-
  see.

NORWAY, KRISTIANSAND (WEST AGDER)

Kafe Natmanden—Samsen Allaktivitetshus, 2nd West Road
(Vesterveien 2) • tel: +47 38025570 • fax: +47 38027166 •
tore@samsen.com • www.samsen.com

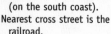

Location and Access
Located near signs beside
  the road.
Bus: All the west-going
  buses, ask for Samsen.
Train: Ask for Kristiansand
  (on the south coast).
Nearest cross street is the
  railroad.

Hours
Mon-Thu   10am-10pm
Fri   10am-7pm
Sat   3pm-midnight
Sun   2pm-9pm

Prices
Nkr10 per half hour
Nkr20 per hour
V, MC, AmEx

Nearby Places to Visit
The Zoo and more

POLAND, BOCHNIA (TARNOWSKIE)

Kawiarnia Internetowa Igloonet
ul. Regis 1 • tel: +48 (0)14 611 75 30 • No fax •
info@igloonet.bochnia.pl • www.igloonet.bochnia.pl

Location and Access
Located at Miejski Dom
  Kultury w Bochni.
Bus: 2, 3, 5, 7, 8, 10, 11,
  12, ask for Miejski Dom
  Kultury w Bochni.
Train: 120, ask for Bochnia.
Nearest cross street is E4.

Prices
Zl3 per half hour
Zl5 per hour
No credit cards

Nearby Places to Visit
Kopalnia Soli, Zamek w
  Nowy Wisnicz

Hours
Mon-Fri   8am-9pm

POLAND, BYDGOSZCZ (BYDGOSZCZ)

Publiczny Dostep do Internetu Cybercafe
47 Dworcowa • tel: +48 (0)52 221 567 • fax: +48 (0)42 630 21 94 •
helpdesk@pdi.net • www.pdi.net

Location and Access
Located near railway
  station.
Train: From Warsaw, ask for
  Bydgoszcz Station.

Nearby Places to Visit
The town itself

Hours
Mon-Fri   10am-6pm

Prices
US$0.70 per half hour
US$1 per hour
V, MC

Global Village Schools

27 Zlota • tel: +48 (0)602 656 418 • fax: +48 (0)41 362 1393 •
office@gv.edu.pl • www.gv.edu.pl

Location and Access
Located near railway sta-
tion.
Bus: 1, 2, 20, 44, ask for
sports hall and railway
station.
Nearest cross street is
Zelazna.

Hours
Mon-Fri   noon-7pm
Sat   9am-2pm

Prices
Zl2.50 per half hour
Zl5 per hour
No credit cards
Student discount available

Nearby Places to Visit
Bishop's Palace

C@fe Internet

Batorego 20 • tel: +48 (0)12 632 18 96 • No fax •
cafe@kompit.com.pl • www.kompit.com.pl

Location and Access
Tram: 4, 8, 12, 13, 14, ask
for Batorego and
Karmelicka.
Nearest cross street is
Karmelicka.

Hours
Mon-Sun   11am-10pm

Prices
Zl2.50 per half hour
Zl5 per hour
No credit cards

Internet Cafe LOOZ—13 Mikolajska Street •
tel: +48 (0)12 428 42 10 • fax: +48 (0)12 428 42 10 •
looz@looz.com.pl • www.looz.com.pl

Location and Access
Located between Main
Market Square and Dom
Turysty Hotel.
Bus: C, ask for Kino Wanda;
502, 511, ask for Railway
Station.
Tram/Trolley: 1, 2, 3, 6, 7,
8, 10, 13, 18, 19, ask for
Poczta Glüwna (main post
office).
Nearest cross street is Main
Market Square.

Hours
Mon-Sun   10am-10pm

Prices
Zl4 per half hour
Zl7 per hour
V, MC, AmEx, DC

Nearby Places to Visit
Old City of Krakow

Klub Internetowy—6 Budryka Street, in Unimarket Building •
tel: +48 (0)12 636 00 60/637 38 25/636 37 99 ext 36 or 44 •
fax: +48 (0)12 637 88 77 • biuro@cybernet.krakow.pl or
cafe@cybernet.krakow.pl • www.cybernet.krakow.pl

Location and Access
Located near the Piast Hotel
and the Continental Hotel.
Bus: 103, 139, 144, 173,
208, ask for Czarnowiejska
Street.
Nearest cross street is
Czarnowiejska Street.

Prices
Zl1-2 per half hour
Zl2-3 per hour
V, MC, AmEx, DC

Hours
Mon-Sun   10am-2am

POLAND, KRAKOW (KRAKOW)

U Louis'a Cyber Cafe—13 Rynek Glowny •
tel: +48 (0)12 421 80 92 • fax: +48 (0)12 637 64 20 •
krzychu@cafe.bci.pl or louis@cafe.bci.pl • www.cafe.bci.pl

Location and Access
Located near Market Place,
  Old City.
Bus: 124, 424, 501, 511 ask
  for Bagatela.
Tram/Trolley: 1, 2, 6, 8, 18,
  ask for place
  Dominikanski.
Nearest cross street is
  Grodzka.

Hours
Mon-Sat   11am-11pm
Sun   2pm-11pm

Prices
Zl4-6 per half hour
Zl4-6 per hour
No credit cards

Nearby Places to Visit
St. Mary's Church, Wawel
  Castle

POLAND, LODZ (LODZ)

Publiczny Dostep do Internetu Cybercafe
120 Piotrkowska • tel: +48 (0)42 630 21 94 •
fax: +48 (0)42 630 21 94 • helpdesk@pdi.net • www.pdi.net

Location and Access
Located near Hortex.
Piotrkowska is the main
  street.

Hours
Mon-Fri   10am-6pm

Prices
US$0.70 per half hour
US$1 per hour
V, MC

POLAND, TORUN (TORUN)

Publiczny Dostep do Internetu Cybercafe

43 Przy Kaszowniku • tel: +48 (0)56 654 25 02 •
fax: +48 (0)56 660 64 00 • helpdesk@pdi.net • www.pdi.net

Location and Access
Phone for directions.

Hours
Mon-Fri   10am-6pm

Prices
US$0.70 per half hour
US$1 per hour
V, MC

Nearby Places to Visit
Torun itself

POLAND, WARSAW (WARSZAWA)

Daewoo Dacom Communications—62 Wspolna Street

Room 165 • tel: +48 (0)22 627 16 42 • fax: +48 (0)22 622 25 60 •
media@ddc.daewoo.com.pl or aadamows@ddc.daewoo.com.pl •
www.daewoo.com.pl/~media/media.html

Location and Access
Located in Ground 0
   Building.
Bus: 101, 127, 128, 131,
   158, 175, 407, 501, 505,
   512, 517, 519, 521, ask
   for Dworzec Centralny.
Tram/Trolley: 7, 8, 9, 22,
   24, 25, ask for Dworzec
   Centralny.
Nearest cross street is
   Jerozolimskie Al.

Hours
Mon-Fri   10am-8pm
Sat   11am-8pm

Prices
Zl3 per half hour
Zl6 per hour
No credit cards
Student discount available

POLAND, WARSAW (WARSZAWA)

Publiczny Dostep do Internetu Cybercafe

12 Nowogrodzka • tel: +48 (0)22 6226611 •
fax: +48 (0)22 6302194 • helpdesk@pdi.net • www.pdi.net

Location and Access
Located near Forum Hotel.
Underground: 1, ask for
Centrum.
Tram: Ask for Rotunda.
Nearest cross street is
Marszalkowska.

Hours
Mon-Fri   10am-9pm

Prices
US$0.70 per half hour (text
terminal)
US$1 per hour
V, MC

Nearby Places to Visit
Warsaw itself

PORTUGAL, LISBON (LISBOA)

Cyber.bica—7 Duques de Bragança Street •
tel: +351 (0)1 3225004 • fax: +351 (0)1 3225004 •
cyberbica@mail.telepac.pt • www.cyberbica.com

Location and Access
Located near Chiado Square.
Subway: Green line, ask for
Baixa/Chiado.
Tram: 28, ask for Duques de
Bragança.
Nearest cross street is Lg
Chiado.

Hours
Mon-Sat   noon-2am

Prices
Esc300 per half hour
Esc600 per hour
V, MC, AmEx
Student discount available

Nearby Places to Visit
Museum of Chiado

PORTUGAL, LISBON (LISBOA)

Webcafé—126 Rua do Diario de Noticias •
tel: +351 (0)1 3421181, mobile: +351 (0)936 2310550 • No fax •
web1@mail.esoterica.pt • www.esoterica.pt/webcafe

Location and Access
Located near Bairro Alto.
Underground: Ask for
  Restauradores.
Nearest cross street is Largo
  da Mesericordia.

Hours
Mon-Sat   4pm-4am
Sun   5pm-4am

Prices
Esc400 per half hour
Esc700 per hour
V, MC

Nearby Places to Visit
Fado Houses

RUSSIA, KIROV

Vyatka Intercom
67, Svobody Street • tel: +7 833 262 4984 • fax: +7 833 262 4984 •
webmaster@inetcafe.vyatka.ru • www.inetcafe.vyatka.ru

Location and Access
Located near Central Hotel.
Bus: 3, 5, 7, 51, ask for
  Central Hotel.
Tram/Trolley: 4, 5, ask for
  Central Hotel.
Nearest cross street is
  Moscovskaya street.

Hours
Mon-Fri   9am-6pm

Prices
rbl10 per half hour
rbl20 per hour
No credit cards

Nearby Places to Visit
Dymka Art Warehouse

art-internet-cafe SCREEN

19A, Novocherkasskiy Blvd. • tel: +7 095 349 1920 •
fax: +7 095 349 1920 • screen@screen.ru • www.screen.ru

Location and Access
Located near the Screen
   Cinema.
Bus: 641, 650, ask for the
   Screen Cinema.
Underground: Metro, ask for
   Marino.
Nearest cross street is
   Lublinskaya street.

Hours
Mon-Fri &
   Sun   noon-8pm
Sat   noon-5pm

Prices
rbl10 per half hour
rbl20 per hour
No credit cards

---

orky Ltd

24 Donskaya Street • tel: +7 095 955 9076/955 9070 •
fax: +7 095 955 9070 • orky@windoms.sitek.net • www.club.orky.ru

Location and Access
Located near Shuhovskaya
   TV Tower.
Underground: Ask for
   Shabolovskaia.
Nearest cross street is
   Leninsky Prospekt.

Hours
Mon-Sun   midnight-
              midnight

Prices
US$0.30 per half hour
US$0.50 per hour
No credit cards

Internet-cafe Etris—33, Chernyahovskogo •
tel: +7 812 325 4877/164 4877 • fax: +7 812 164 0827 •
tetris@dux.ru • www.netcafe.spb.ru

Location and Access
Located near Ligovsky
   Prospect subway station.
Bus: 3, 74, ask for Ligovsky
   Prospect Metro station.
Underground: 4, ask for
   Ligovsky Prospect.
Tram: 10, 49, ask for
   Ligovsky Prospect Metro
   station.
Nearest cross street is
   Ligovsky Avenue.

Hours
Mon-Fri   10am-9pm
Sat-Sun   1pm-9pm

Prices
rbl20 (10am-1pm) and rbl30
   (1pm-9pm) per half hour
rbl40 (10am-1pm) and rbl60
   (1pm-9pm) per hour
V, MC

El Cafe de Internet—656 Gran Via de les Corts Catalanes •
tel: +34 (9)3 4121915 • fax: +34 (9)3 3022215 •
cafe@cafeinternet.es • www.cafeinternet.es

Location and Access
Located near Plaza
   Catalunya.
Bus: Ask for Paseo de
   Gracia-Gran Via.
Underground: 1, 2, 3, 4, ask
   for Catalunya (Lines 1 and
   3) or Paseo de Gracia
   (Lines 2 and 4).
Train: All overground trains
   that stop at Plaza
   Catalunya.

Nearest cross street is Paseo
   de Gracia.

Hours
Mon-Sat   9am-midnight

Prices
Ptas600 per half hour
Ptas1,200 per hour
No credit cards
Student discount available

Nearby Places to Visit
La Pedrera, City Center

E-Mail from Spain—Pasaje Bacardí 1, 1°, 1A
(42 La Rambla) • tel: +34 (9)3 4817575 • fax: +34 (9)3 4817574 •
info@emailfromspain.es • www.emailfromspain.es

Location and Access
Located near Plaza Real.
Bus: Ask for Arc Teatre.
Underground: Ask for Liceu.
Train: Ask for FFCC
    Catalunya.
Nearest cross street is 42 La
    Rambla.

Hours
Mon-Sat   10am-8pm

Prices
Ptas500 per half hour
Ptas900 per hour
No credit cards

Nearby Places to Visit
Barrio Gòtico, Puerto, Museo
    Picasso, Casa Gaudí

Interlight Cafe Barcelona
106 Pau Claris • tel: +34 (9)33011180 • No fax •
interlight@bcn.servicom.es • www.gdesigners.com/interlight/index.htm

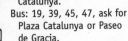

Location and Access
Located near Plaza de
    Catalunya.
Bus: 19, 39, 45, 47, ask for
    Plaza Catalunya or Paseo
    de Gracia.
Nearest cross street is Paseo
    de Gracia or Plaza
    Catalunya.

Hours
Mon-Sat   11am-10pm
Sun   5pm-10pm

Prices
Ptas500 per half hour
Ptas800 per hour
V, MC
Student discount available

Nearby Places to Visit
La Sagrada Familia, Gaudi
    Museum, La Ramblas

SPAIN, CÀCERES (EXTREMADURA)

Cybercity—Plaza de Bruselas No. 4 (Madrila alta) •
tel: +34 (9)27 626093 • fax: +34 (9)27 626046 •
cibercity@ctv.es • www.007net.com/cibercity

Location and Access
Located near Madrila
  Caceres.
Bus: 26, ask for Madrila.

Hours
Mon-Sat   1pm-2pm &
             5:30pm-10pm

Prices
Ptas400 per half hour
Ptas600 per hour
V, MC, AmEx, DC
Student discount available

Nearby Places to Visit
Gargola

SPAIN, CASTELLDEFELS BEACH (CATALUNYA)

TangaWorld Interbar Coca-Cola Club
27 Avinguda dels Banys • tel: +34 (9)3 664 5464 • No fax •
interbar@tangaworld.com • www.tangaworld.com

Location and Access
Located near the beach.
Bus: L95, L96, L97, ask for
  Platja, Avinguda dels
  Banys.
Train: Cercanias (local
  train), ask for
  Castelldefels, Apeadero
  Castelldefels.
Nearest cross streets are
  Passeig Maritim/Avinguda
  de la Marina.

Hours
Mon-Sun   5:30pm-3am

Prices
Ptas500 per half hour
Ptas800 per hour
V, MC, AmEx

Nearby Places to Visit
The beach, Castle, Avinguda
  dels Banys Comercial
  Street

SPAIN, DAIMIEL (CIUDAD REAL)

Condecosta Café—10, Màrtires •
tel: +34 (9)26 851901 • No fax • condecosta@manchanet.es •
www.manchanet.es/cr/daimiel/condecosta.htm

Location and Access
Located near Olivo
  Milenario.
Bus and Train: Madrid-
  Daimiel, Ciudad Real-
  Daimiel, ask for Daimiel.
Nearest cross street is Plaza
  de España.

Hours
Tue-Thu &
  Sun   3pm-2:30am
Fri-Sat   3pm-4am

Prices
Ptas400 per half hour
Ptas800 per hour
No credit cards

Nearby Places to Visit
Las Tablas de Daimiel, Las
  Motillas de Daimiel,
  Iglesia de Santa Maria del
  Siglo XVI

SPAIN, FUENGIROLA (MALAGA)

Servicio Internet Publico Fuengirola
Relocating, please call for new address • tel: +34 (9)52 666775 •
fax: +34 (9)52 474154 • mike@sicos.net • www.sicos.net/publico

Location and Access
Please call for directions.

Hours
Mon-Fri   11am-2pm &
          4pm-8pm
Sat   11am-2pm

Prices
Ptas500 per half hour
Ptas750 per hour
V, MC, AmEx
Student discount available
  to Spanish students

Nearby Places to Visit
Sevilla, Granada, Costa del
  Sol, Ronda, Malaga, Mijas,
  Marbella, Cordoba

SPAIN, GIJON (ASTURIAS)

El Navegante de Internet Netcom Technologies

122 Avda. de la Costa • tel: +34 (9)85 130086/344182 •
fax: +34 (9)85 130692 • wmaster@netcom.es • www.netcom.es

Location and Access
Located near Plaza de Toros
de Gijon.
Bus: 10, 15, 18, 20, ask for
Avda. de la Costa.

Hours
Mon-Fri   9am-10pm
Sat-Sun   10am-2pm &
          5pm-10pm

Prices
Ptas300 per half hour
Ptas500 per hour
V
Student discount available
for multiple hours

Nearby Places to Visit
Plaza de Toros, Parque de
Isabel la Catolica, Paseo
Maritimo, Playa de Gijon

SPAIN, MADRID (MADRID)

ASI Cybercenter

46 Castello • tel: +34 (9)1 5765097 • fax: +34 (9)1 5779563 •
asi@asiinfo.net • www.asiinfo.net

Location and Access
Autobus: 1, 9, 23, 27, 29,
51, 52.
Underground: 2, 4, ask for
Goya (2 & 4) or Velazquez
(4).
Train: Ask for Recoletos.
Nearest cross street is Goya.

Hours
Mon-Thu   9am-9pm
Fri-Sat   9am-10pm

Prices
Ptas400 per half hour
Ptas700 per hour
V
Student discount available

Nearby Places to Visit
Plaza de Colon, El Retiro

Cestein

11, C/Leganitos • tel: +34 (9)1 5482775 • fax: +34 (9)1 5412855 • cestein@cestein.es • www.cestein.es

Location and Access

Located near Hotel Coloso.
Bus: Circular, 5, 10, 23, 44, 45, 46, 75, 147.
Underground: Metro, ask for Santo Domingo/Plaza de España.
Nearest cross street is Gran Via.

Hours

Mon-Fri   8am-10pm
Sat   10am-2pm

Prices

Ptas400 per half hour
Ptas700 per hour
No credit cards
Student discount available

Nearby Places to Visit

Senate, Oriente S.O.

Cybercafe Laser Coffee Shop

21 Rosario Street • tel: +34 (9)1 3658791 • fax: +34 (9)1 3658791 • laserco@hotmail.com • www.geocities.com/MadisonAvenue/1796

Location and Access

Located near San Francisco el Grande Basilico.
Bus: Circular, 3, 41, 60, 148, ask for San Francisco Basilico.
Underground: 5, ask for Puerta de Toledo or La Latina.
Tram/Trolley: Cercanias train, ask for Piramides or Embajadores.

Nearest cross street is Bailen Street.

Hours

Mon-Fri &
Sun   10am-midnight

Prices

Ptas150 per half hour
Ptas500 per hour (with a drink)
V, MC, AmEx

Nearby Places to Visit

Royal Palace

El Argonauta Virtual

9 Gaztambide • tel: +34 (9)1 5500835 • fax: +34 (9)1 5433978 •
administrador@argonauta-virtual.com • www.argonauta-virtual.com

Location and Access

Located near El Corte Ingles
  Department Store
  (Princesa).
Bus: Circular, 1, 2, 44, 133,
  211, ask for Arguelles.
Underground: 3, 4, ask for
  Arguelles.
Nearest cross street is
  Princesa.

Hours

Mon-Sat   11am-3pm &
                   5pm-9pm

Prices

Ptas425 per half hour
Ptas700 per hour
V, MC
Student discount available

Nearby Places to Visit

The Gran Via and the Plaza
  de España

El Escribidor.es

93, Ponzano • tel: +34 (9)1 5535637 • fax: +34 (9)1 4562236 •
buzon@elescribidor.es • www.elescribidor.es

Location and Access

Located near El Corte Inglès
  (Castellana).
Bus: Circular, 5, all buses
  that go near Cuatro
  Caminos, ask for Cuatro
  Caminos.
Underground: 1, 2, 6, ask
  for Cuatro Caminos and
  Nuevos Ministerios
  Stations.
Train: Tren de Cercanias
  (local train), ask for

Nuevos Ministerios.
Nearest cross street is Paseo
  de la Castellana.

Hours

Mon-Fri   10am-9pm
Sat   11am-2pm

Prices

Ptas540 per half hour
Ptas1,000 per hour
V, MC, DC
Student discount available

SPAIN, MADRID (MADRID)

La Casa de Internet
20 1° C/Luchana • tel: +34 (9)1 4465541 • fax: +34 (9)1 4465670 •
lacasa@casainternet.com • www.casainternet.com

Location and Access
Located near Ratskeller–La
 Casa de la Cerveza, at
 Luchana #15.
Bus: 147, ask for Calle
 Luchana.
Underground: 4, ask for
 Bilbao.

Hours
Mon-Sat   10am-10pm

Prices
Ptas350 per half hour
Ptas600 per hour
V, MC, AmEx
Student discount available

SPAIN, OVIEDO (ASTURIAS)

Café Internet Bheta
s/n Uria • tel: +34 (9)85 965715 • fax: +34 (9)85 965715 •
info@bheta.com • www.bheta.com

Location and Access
Located near RENFE Station.
Bus: All city bus lines pass
 by Uria Street, ask for
 Calle Uria stop.

Hours
Mon-Fri   4pm-midnight
Sat-Sun   5pm-midnight

Prices
Ptas300 per half hour
Ptas500 per hour
No credit cards

Nearby Places to Visit
The gothic cathedral, the
 old city

Laser Internet Center

9 San Francisco Street • tel: +34 (9)85 200066 •
fax: +34 (9)85 212811 • info@las.es • www.las.es

Location and Access
Bus: 1, ask for Jovellanos.
Nearest cross street is Uria.

Nearby Places to Visit
The Cathedral, old
  University building

Hours
Mon-Sun   10am-11pm

Prices
Ptas300 per half hour
Ptas600 per hour
V

L@Red Cybercafe

5 Concepcion • tel: +34 (9)71 713574 • No fax •
info@laredcafe.com • www.laredcafe.com

Location and Access
Located near McDonald's.
Bus: 3, 5, ask for Jaime III.
Cafe is off Jaime III.

Prices
Ptas500 per half hour
Ptas1,000 per hour
No credit cards

Hours

Mon-Thu	3pm-midnight
Fri	3pm-2am
Sat	4pm-2am
Sun	4pm-11pm

Nearby Places to Visit
Cathedral, La Lonja, old
  town

SPAIN, PAMPLONA (NAVARRA)

Cibercafe InterNET IRU-A
28 Esquiroz • tel: +34 (9)48 260151 • No fax •
cafenet@cin.es • www.cin.es/cafenet

Location and Access
Located near Iturrama.
Bus: 2, ask for Iturrama or
the Hotel Ciudad de
Pamplona stop.

Hours
Mon-Sun   9am-2pm &
                3:30pm-11pm

Prices
Ptas400 per half hour
Ptas700 per hour
V, MC, AmEx
Student discount available

Nearby Places to Visit
Fueros, Castillo

SPAIN, SALT (GIRONA)

Cibercafé Nupi de Salt
163 Major • tel: +34 (9)7 2230842 • No fax •
cibercafenupi@passeig.com • www.passeig.com

Location and Access
Located near Policia
Municipal/Ayuntamiento.
Bus: Linea Salt-Girona, ask
for Plaça Llibertat.
Nearest cross street is Calle
Major.

Hours
Mon-Sat   10am-11pm
Sun   4pm-11pm

Prices
Ptas400 per half hour
Ptas500 per hour
No credit cards
Student discount available

Nearby Places to Visit
Deveses de Salt

SPAIN, SANTIAGO DE COMPOSTELA (LA CORUNA)

CiberDreams
5 Diego de Muros • tel: +34 (9)81 553550 • No fax •
ciberdreams@ctv.es • www.ctv.es/users/ciberdreams

Location and Access
Located opposite the Parque de Ramirez.
Bus: All city buses, ask for stop 1 (parada 1).
Nearest cross street is Plaza Roja.

Hours
Mon-Sun   midnight-
                   midnight

Prices
Ptas150 per half hour
Ptas300 per hour
No credit cards

Nearby Places to Visit
Cathedral of Santiago

SPAIN, TERRASSA (BARCELONA, CATALUNYA)

Cafe Via Zero
408 Paseo 22 de Juliol • tel: +34 (9)3 7838443 • No fax •
viazero@valser.es • www.valser.es/viazero

Location and Access
Located near the RENFE Station (main railway).
Bus: Many buses, ask for Estacion del Norte.
Train: RENFE, ask for Estacion Del Norte, Terrassa.

Hours
Mon-Sat   8am-11pm

Prices
Ptas500 per hour (minimum)
No credit cards
Student discount available

Nearby Places to Visit
Iglesia Romanicas San Pedro

SPAIN, TORRE DEL MAR (MALAGA)

Locutorio Internet Center Boot
8 Severo Ochoa • tel: +34 (9)5 2547016 • No fax •
info@centerboot.com • www.centerboot.com/locutorio

Location and Access
Located near Hotel Las
  Yucas.
Nearest cross street is Avda
  de Andalucia.

Hours
Mon-Sun   5pm-midnight

Prices
Ptas300 per half hour
Ptas600 per hour
V, MC, AmEx

SPAIN, VALENCIA (COMMUNIDAD VALENCIAN)

Cyber Pub Andromeda—37 Calle Salamanca •
tel: +34 (9)6 3353070 • No fax • andromeda@arrakis.es •
www.arrakis.es/~luisatan or www.galaxycorp.com/cyberandromeda

Location and Access
Located near Canovas.
Bus: 1, 2, 3, 4, 19, 41, ask
  for Plaza de Canovas.
Underground: Ask for
  Alameda.
Nearest cross street is Gran
  Via Marquez del Turia.

Hours
Tue-Sun   6:30pm-3:30am

Prices
Ptas500 per hour
  (minimum)
V, MC, AmEx, DC, D
Student discount available

Nearby Places to Visit
Historical Center, Ciudad de
  las Ciencias and las Artes,
  Palau de la Musica

SPAIN, ZARAGOZA (ZARAGOZA)

CiudadRobot—4, Plaza San Francisco •
tel: +34 (9)76 557312 • fax: +34 (9)76 562688 •
info@ciudadrobot.com • www.ciudadrobot.com/cibercafe

Location and Access
Located near the University.
Bus: 23, 40, ask for Plaza
San Francisco.
Nearest cross street is Fdo.
El Catolico.

Hours
Mon-Fri   10am-1pm &
           5pm-8pm

Prices
Ptas350 per half hour
Ptas650 per hour
V, MC
Student discount available

Nearby Places to Visit
Palacio de la Aljaferia

SWEDEN, BORGHOLM (OLAND, COUNT OF KALMAR)

Café ISSCO AB
27 A Storgatan • tel: +46 (0)485 10110 • fax: + 46 (0)485 13610 •
anne.milling-erichsen@issco.se • www.issco.se/internet.htm

Location and Access
Located near the center of
the city.
Bus: KLT buses from all over
the county, ask for
Borgholms Forngard.

Hours
Tue-Wed   10am-2pm
Thu   noon-4pm

Prices
Skr30 per half hour
Skr60 per hour
No credit cards
Student discount available

Nearby Places to Visit
Borgholms Slottsruin (old
ruined castle)

Internet Café Nybak@t

6 Malmgatan • tel: +46 (0)413 10220 • No fax •
staff@nybakat.com • www.nybakat.com

Location and Access
Located near Hotel Sten
  Stennson Sten.
Bus: Ask for the central
  stop.
Train: Ask for Eslöv.
Nearest cross streets are
  Sodergatan and
  Kanalgatan.

Hours
Mon-Thu   10am-10pm
                (or later)

Fri-Sat   10am-11pm
                (or later)
Sun   11am-10pm
                (or later)

Prices
Skr25 per half hour
Skr50 per hour
V, MC
Student discount available

Nearby Places to Visit
Trollsjøn, castles, manor
  houses, golf course, parks

Globe Internet Center

Viktoriagatan 7 • tel: +46 (0)31 139888 • fax: +46 (0)31 139888 •
ma@globe.nu • www.globe.nu

Location and Access
Tram/Trolley: 1, 2, 3, ask for
  Vasagatan.
Nearest cross street is
  Vasagatan.

Hours
Mon-Fri &
  Sun   noon-10pm
Sat   noon-6pm

Prices
Skr30 per half hour
Skr50 per hour
No credit cards
Student discount available

Nearby Places to Visit
Haga, the oldest part of
  Gothenburg

Cyberspace Café Helsingborg
9 Karlsgatan • tel: +46 (0)42 211301 • No fax •
helsingborg@cyberspace.se • www.cyberspace.se

Location and Access
Located near Roda kvarn,
  tourist information.
Bus: All buses, ask for
  Knutpunkten (central sta-
  tion) or Statsbiblioteket
  (city library).
Train: All trains to
  Helsingborg, ask for
  Knutpunkten/Helsingborg
  Central Station.
Nearest cross street is
  Jarnvagsgatan.

Hours
Mon-Fri   noon-10pm
Sat-Sun   1pm-10pm

Prices
Skr25 per half hour
Skr50 per hour
No credit cards

Nearby Places to Visit
Karnan

CyberSpace Café Landskrona
14 Idrottsvdgen • tel: +46 (0)418 21475 • fax: +46 (0)418 21479 •
landskrona@cyberspace.se • www.cyberspace.se

Location and Access
Bus: 2, ask for
  Pilangstorget.
Nearest cross street is
  Ringvagen.

Hours
Mon-Fri   10am-10pm
Sat-Sun   noon-10pm

Prices
Skr15 per half hour
Skr30 per hour
No credit cards

Nearby Places to Visit
Indoor water-adventure,
  indoor ice-skating rink,
  small animal park

SWEDEN, LINKOPING (OSTERGOTLANDS)

berZyber IT-café—25 Gustav Adolfsgatan •
tel: +46 (0)13 207421 • fax: +46 (0)13 205605 •
berzyber@edu.linkoping.se • www.linkoping.se/bit/projekt/cybercafe

Location and Access
Located near Linkoping
  Cathedral.
Bus: 201, ask for
  Banergatan.

Nearest cross street is
  Vasavaegen (Vasastreet).

Hours
Mon-Sat   8am-8pm
(Closed July 1-August 9 for
  summer holiday)

Prices
Skr5 per half hour
Skr10 per hour
No credit cards

Nearby Places to Visit
Linkoping Museum, Old
  Linkoping, Linkoping
  Airplane Museum

SWEDEN, LUND (SKANE)

CyberSpace Café Lund
6 Bantorget • tel: +46 (0)46 389550 • No fax •
lund@cyberspace.se • www.cyberspace.se

Location and Access
Located near central
  station, Domkyrkan.
Bus: All buses, ask for
  Bantorget.

Train: To Malmö, ask for
  Lund.
Nearest cross street is
  Bangatan, Klostergatan.

Hours
Mon-Fri   10am-10pm
Sat-Sun   noon-10pm

Prices
Skr25 per half hour
Skr50 per hour
V, MC, AmEx, DC

Nearby Places to Visit
Domkyrkan

CyberSpace Café Malmö
13 Engelbrektsgatan • tel: +46 (0)40 302755 •
fax: +46 (0)40 302755 • malmo@cyberspace.se • www.cyberspace.se

Location and Access
Located near Gustav Adolfs
  Torg.
Bus: Ask for Gustav Adolfs
  Torg.
Nearest cross street is Stora
  Nygatan, Gustav Adolfs
  Torg.

Prices
Skr25 per half hour
Skr50 per hour
No credit cards

Nearby Places to Visit
Malmö City

Hours
Mon-Sun   10am-10pm

Kajplats 305
5 Norra Neptunigatan • tel: +46 (0)40 342574 •
fax: +46 (0)40 342648 • info@kajen.com • www.kajen.com

Location and Access
Located near Central Station
  in Malmö.
Bus: 21C, ask for
  Nordenskioldsgatan.
Train: Paagataaget, ask for
  Malmö Central.
Nearest cross street is
  Citadellsvägen.

Prices
Skr25 per half hour
Skr25 per hour
No credit cards

Nearby Places to Visit
City of Malmö

Hours
Mon-Fri   2pm-10pm
Sun   2pm-8pm

SWEDEN, MALMÖ (SKANE)

Kajplats 305, the Computersection
Bassängkajen 8 • tel: +46 (0)40 342574 • fax: +46 (0)40 342648 •
info@kajen.com • www.kajen.com

Location and Access
Located near Central
  Station.
Bus: 20, ask for
  Nordenskjoldsgatan.
Train: Ask for Malmö.

Hours
Mon-Thu   2pm-10pm
Fri & Sun   2pm-8pm

Prices
Skr15 per half hour
Skr30 per hour

(25 SEK minimum)
No credit cards
Student discount available
  with youth membership
  card

Nearby Places to Visit
Kajplats 305 is a place of
  music and culture.

SWEDEN, STOCKHOLM (STOCKHOLM)

Nine Studios
44 Odengatan • tel: +46 (0)8 6129009 • fax: +46 (0)8 6129020 •
desk@nine.nu • www.nine.nu

Location and Access
Located near Hard Rock
  Café.
Bus: Ask for Odenplan.
Underground: 17, 18, 19,
  ask for Odengatan.
Nearest cross street is
  Sveavägen.

Hours
Mon-Fri   10am-1am
Sat-Sun   11am-1am

Prices
Skr30 per half hour
Skr60 per hour
V, MC, DC, D
Student discount available
  before 3pm

Nearby Places to Visit
City Library

SWITZERLAND, BIEL/BIENNE (JURA)

Cyberhouse—9 Waffengasse, 9 rue des Armes •
tel: +41 (0)32 322 62 30 • No fax •
bb@cyberhouse.ch • www.cyberhouse.ch

Location and Access
Located near Migros super-
   market.
Bus: Ask for Place Guisan.
Train: Ask for Bienne.
Nearest cross street is
   Bahnhofstrasse.

Hours
Tue-Thu   9am-11:30pm
Fri-Sat   9am-12:30am
Sun   2pm-8:30pm

Prices
CHF6 per half hour
CHF12 per hour
No credit cards
Student discount available

Nearby Places to Visit
Old town, Lake of Bienne,
   Sport Resort Magglingen,
   Swatch Factory

SWITZERLAND, FRIBOURG (FRIBOURG)

Scottish Bar—47, Route du Jura •
tel: +41 (0)26 466 8 02 • fax: +41 (0)26 466 82 03 •
office@scottish.mcnet.ch • scottish.mcnet.ch

Location and Access
Located near Parc Ste-
   Thérèse (near UBS Bank).
Bus: 5 Torry, ask for Jura
   SBS.
Tram: 3 Jura, ask for Jura
   SBS.
Nearest cross street is
   Direction Fribourg Centre.

Hours
Mon-Fri   8am-1:30am
Sat   9am-1:30am
Sun   9am-11:30pm

Prices
CHF0.16 per minute
CHF10 per hour
No credit cards

Nearby Places to Visit
Old City and Cathedral

ESF—Espace Saint-François

12, Place Saint-François (1st floor) • tel: +41 (0)21 320 41 60 •
fax: +41 (0)21 320 41 61 • esf@esf.ch • www.esf.ch

Location and Access
Located opposite the
    Banque Cantonale
    Vaudoise.
Bus: Most buses, ask for
    Saint-François.

Hours
Wed-Sat   10am-6:30pm

Prices
CHF5 per half hour
CHF10 per hour
No credit cards

Nearby Places to Visit
Center of the town

In Comm—Innovative Communication

32 Petit-Chêne • tel: +41 (0)21 320 10 60 • fax: +41 (0)21 351 11 92 •
cyberpoon@incomm.ch • www.incomm.ch.net

Location and Access
Located near Railway
    Station.
Bus: Most buses go nearby.
Tram: Ask for Place de la
    Gare or St. François.
Train: Metro, ask for Place
    de la Gare.

Hours
Mon-Sat   2pm-6:30pm

Prices
CHF10 per half hour
CHF15 per hour
No credit cards
Student discount available

Nearby Places to Visit
Olympic Museum

SWITZERLAND, MARTIGNY (VALAIS)

CyberCasino
17, Av. de la Gare • tel: +41 (0)27 722 13 93 •
fax: +41(0) 27 722 04 51 • info@omedia.ch • www.cybercasino.ch

Location and Access
Located near post office and
  Credit Suisse Bank.
Nearest cross street is the
  St. Bernard Pass from
  Switzerland to Italy.

Hours
Mon   9am-midnight
Tue-Sun   7am-midnight

Prices
CHF10 per half hour
CHF20 per hour
No credit cards
Student discount available

Nearby Places to Visit
Verbier, Montana, Chamonix
  (France), Aosta (Italy)

SWITZERLAND, ST. MORITZ (GRISON/GRAUBUENDEN)

Bobby's Pub
50, Via dal Bagn • tel: +41 (0)81 834 42 83 •
fax: +41 (0)81 834 42 82 • info@bobbys-pub.ch • www.bobbys-pub.ch

Location and Access
Located in the Gallaria
  Caspar Badrutt Building.
Bus: Local Bad-Dorf, ask for
  Union Bank of Switzerland
  stop.

Hours
Mon-Sat   10am-1am
Sun   noon-1am

Prices
CHF6 per half hour
CHF12 per hour
V, MC, AmEx

Nearby Places to Visit
The mountains (nice view)

SWITZERLAND, ZUCHWIL

IntroNet Cafe

24 Langfeldstrasse • tel: +41 (0)32 686 86 11 •
fax: +41 (0)32 686 86 79 • admin@intro.ch • www.intro.ch

Location and Access
Bus: Zuchwil, ask for
  McDonald's.

Nearby Places to Visit
Shopping Center

Hours
Mon-Sat   9am-6:30pm

Prices
First hour free, then CHF10
  per hour
V, MC
Student discount available

SWITZERLAND, ZURICH (ZURICH)

acXess Computerstube AG—79 Scheuchzerstrasse •
tel: +41 (0)1 350 22 33 • fax: +41 (0)1 362 22 44 •
peretti@axcomp.ch • www.axcomp.ch/axcomp

Location and Access
Located near
  Schaffhauserplatz.
Bus: 33, ask for
  Scheuzerstrasse.
Tram/Trolley: 7, 9, 10, 15,
  ask for Ottikerstrasse (7 &
  15) or Seilbahn Rigiblick
  (9 & 10).
Nearest cross street is
  Winterthurerstrasse.

Hours
Mon-Tue &
  Fri   10am-6:30pm
Wed-Thu &
  Sat   call to reserve

Prices
CHF5 per half hour
CHF10 per hour
V

SWITZERLAND, ZURICH (ZURICH)

Internet Café Urania Zürich
3, Uraniastrasse • tel: +41 (0)1 210 33 11 •
fax: +41 (0)1 210 33 13 • info@cafe.ch • www.cafe.ch

Location and Access
Located near Parking
Urania, Sternwarte, Zurich
Main Station.
Bus and Underground: Ask
for Hauptbahnhof (Main
Station) and Paradeplatz.
Train: 3, 6, 7, 11, ask for
Zurich Main Station.
Nearest cross street is
Bahnhofstrasse.

Hours
Mon-Thu &
  Sun   10am-11pm
Fri-Sat   10am-midnight

Prices
CHF7.50 per half hour
CHF15 per hour
V, MC

Nearby Places to Visit
Bahnhofstrasse, the Old
Town, Lindenhofpatz,
various churches

TURKEY, BODRUM (MUGLA)

Palmiye Internet Cafe—196 Neyzen Tevfik Caddesi •
tel: +90 (0)252 313 9184 • fax: +90 (0)252 313 9181 •
palmiye1@efes.net.tr • www.sailturkey.com/internetcafe

Location and Access
Located near Bodrum Karada
Yacht Marina.
Bus: Gumbet Dolmus, ask
for Karada Marina.

Hours
Mon-Sun 9am-midnight

Prices
TL750,000 per half hour
TL1,250,000 per hour
  (about US$3.50)
V, MC

Nearby Places to Visit
The Mausoleum of
Halicarnassus, the Castle
of St. John

TURKEY, ISTANBUL (ISTANBUL)

The Orient Hostel—13 Yeni Akbiyik Cadessi, Sultanahmet •
tel: +90 (0)212 518 0789 • fax: +90 (0)212 518 3894 •
orienthostel@superonline.com • www.hostels.com/orienthostel

Location and Access
Near the Four Seasons Hotel
  and the Blue Mosque.
Tram: Any tram, ask for
  Sultanahmet.
Train: Any suburban train on
  the Europe-side of town,
  ask for Cankurtaran.

Hours
Mon-Sun   10am-midnight

Prices
US$2.40 per half hour
US$4 per hour
V, MC

Nearby Places to Visit
Topkapi Palace, the Aya
  Sofya, the Grand Bazaar,
  numerous museums

TURKEY, ISTANBUL (ISTANBUL)

Yagmur Cybercafe—18/2 Seyhbender Sok. Asmalimescit,
Beyoglu • tel: +90 (0)212 292 3020 • fax: +90 (0)212 293 3466 •
cafe@citlembik.com.tr • www.citlembik.com.tr

Location and Access
Located near Pera Palas
  Hotel, the American
  Consulate, and Tünel
  Square.
Bus: From Eminonu or
  Yenikapi, ask for Taksim.
  From Sisli, 69A, 69E, 74A,
  ask for Tepebasi.
Underground: Ask for Tünel.
Tram: Going between Taxim
  Square and Tünel Square,
  ask for Tünel.

Nearest cross street is
  Istiklal Caddesi.

Hours
Mon-Sun   11am-11pm

Prices
TL450,000 per half hour
TL900,000 per hour
No credit cards
Student discount available

Nearby Places to Visit
Galata Tour, Pera Palas Hotel

216

Karsiyake Internet Cafe—Girne Bulvari 8 / A Karsiyaka •
tel: +90 (0)232 369 45 00 • fax: +90 (0)232 484 01 45 •
internetcafe@superonline.com • www.webglobal.net/ruken/isyerim.htm

Location and Access
Located opposite a Tuna
  Pastari Shop.
Bus: Ask for Girne.
Nearest cross street is Girne
  Street.

Hours
Mon-Sat   10am-midnight
Sun   11am-midnight

Prices
TL500,000 per half hour
TL500,000 per hour
V, MC

UK, CHANNEL ISLANDS, ST. PETER PORT (GUERNSEY)

Gaia's Web
17 Le Pollet • tel: +44 (0)1481 701 144 • fax: +44 (0)1481 721 153 •
post@gaias-web.com • www.gaias-web.com

Location and Access
Located near Town Church.
Bus: Ask for any bus going
  into town.
Nearest cross street is the
  High Street.

Hours
Mon-Sat   9am-6pm

Prices
£3.50 per half hour
£6 per hour
V, MC

Nearby Places to Visit
The island, many things to
  see

Netplay Cafe—8 Fletchers Walk, Paradise Circus •
tel: +44 (0)121 248 228 • fax: +44 (0)121 248 2229 •
info@netplaycafe.co.uk • www.netplaycafe.co.uk

Location and Access
Located underneath Adrian Bolt Hall.
Bus: Ask for New Street Station.
Tram/Trolley: Ask for New Street or the center of town.
Train: Main line trains to New Street Station,
Located between New Street and Broad Street.

Hours
Mon-Sat   10am-7pm
Sun   noon-4pm

Prices
£2.50 per half hour
£5 per hour
No credit cards

Nearby Places to Visit
Convention Centre

Couchnet Internet Cafe
117 Charminster Road • tel: +44 (0)1202 297 222 •
fax: +44 (0)1202 297 555 • info@couchnet.com • www.couchnet.com

Location and Access
Located near Richmond Arms Pub.
Bus: 6, ask for Richmond Arms.
Nearest cross street is Alma Road.

Hours
Mon-Sun   10am-11:30pm

Prices
£3 per half hour
£6 per hour
V, MC, AmEx, DC

Nearby Places to Visit
Bournemouth, Poole, and New Forest

3W Cafe

4 Market Place • tel: +44 (0)1344 862 445 •
fax: +44 (0)0870 056 7350 • dave@3w.co.uk • www.3w.co.uk

Location and Access

Located near the 3M build-
ing.
Bus: Ask for Bracknell Bus
Station.
Train: From London, ask for
Bracknell Train Station.
Nearest cross street is
Market Street.

Hours

Mon-Sat   10:30am-7:30pm
Sun   1:30pm-7:30pm

Prices

£2.50 per half hour
£5 per hour
No credit cards
Student discount available

Nearby Places to Visit

Ascot racing, South Hill
Park Theatre, John Nike
Ice Rink Ski Centre, the
Look Out & Discovery
Centre, Coral Reef Leisure
Pool

NetGates Cafe—51 Broad Street •

tel: +44 (0)117 907 4040 • fax: +44 (0)117 927 7556 •
cafe@netgates.co.uk • www.netgates.co.uk/cafe

Location and Access

Located near St. Nicholas
Market.
Train: Ask for Bristol Train
Station.
Nearest cross street is Corn
Street.

Hours

Mon-Sat   9:30am-6:30pm

Prices

£2.50 per half hour
£5 per hour
V, MC
Student discount available

Nearby Places to Visit

SS Great Britain, Dockside

CB1

32 Mill Road • tel: +44 (0)1223 576 302 • No fax •
sturdy@cb1.com • www.cb1.com

Location and Access
Phone for directions.

Hours
Mon-Sun   10am-9pm

Prices
£3 per half hour
£6 per hour
No credit cards

Nearby Places to Visit
Cambridge University

The Greyhound Public House and Restaurant

93 Coldhams Lane • tel: +44 (0)1223 247 075 •
fax: +44 (0)1223 565 638 • greyhound@dial.pipex.com •
http://dspace.dial.pipex.com/town/plaza/gw53

Location and Access
Bus: 6 from town center,
  ask for Coldhams stop.

Nearby Places to Visit
Cambridge Colleges and city

Hours
Mon-Sat   11am-11pm

Prices
£7.50 per half hour
£15 per hour
V, AmEx

UK, ENGLAND, CROYDON (SURREY)

Cyberzone—1 Dingwall Road •
tel: +44 (0)181 681 6500 • fax: +44 (0)181 686 0356 •
gordon@cyberzone.co.uk • www.cyberzone.co.uk

Location and Access
Located near East Croydon Station.
Bus: N109, X30, 54, 64, 130, 119, 194, 198, 353, 354, 367, 600, 657, 726, ask for East Croydon Station.
Tram/Trolley: Under construction, stop will be East Croydon Station.
Train: East Croydon Mainline, ask for East Croydon Station. Nearest cross street is George Street.

Hours
Mon-Sat   9:30am-9:30pm
Sun   11am-8pm

Prices
£3.25 per half hour
£6 per hour
No credit cards
Student discount available

UK, ENGLAND, EASTBOURNE (SUSSEX)

Global Information Centre Ltd.
22 Pevensey Road • tel: +44 (0)1323 431 770 •
fax: +44 (0)1323 739 256 • mail@gic.co.uk • www.gic.co.uk

Location and Access
Located near tourist information centre.
Bus: Ask for nearby bus station.
Train: Ask for Eastbourne. Nearest cross street is Terminus Road.

Hours
Mon-Sat   10am-6pm
Sun   noon-6pm

Prices
£3.50 per half hour
£7 per hour
No credit cards
Student discount available

Nearby Places to Visit
Pevensey Marshes, Friston Forest, South Downs, seaside

Hyperactive Cafe—1B Central Station Crescent, Queen Street • tel: +44 (0)1392 201 544 • fax: +44 (0)1392 201 545 • cafe@inxpress.co.uk • www.inxpress.co.uk

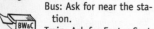

Location and Access
Located near Exeter Central Station.
Bus: Ask for near the station.
Train: Ask for Exeter Central Station.

Hours
Mon-Fri	10am-7:30pm
Sat	10am-6pm
Sun	noon-6pm

Prices
£2.50 per half hour
£5 per hour
No credit cards
Student discount available

Nearby Places to Visit
Exeter Cathedral

Cafe Internet Gatwick—Spectators Gallery, Skyview Level 4, South Terminal • tel: +44 (0)1293 568 400 • fax: +44 (0)1293 568 400 • gatwick@cafeinternet.co.uk • www.cafeinternet.co.uk

Location and Access
Located at Gatwick Airport.
Bus: C8, C80, X38, 291, ask for Gatwick South Terminal.
Train: Connex South Central and Gatwick Express, ask for Gatwick Airport.
Nearest cross street is Perimeter Road South.

Hours
Mon &
Wed-Sun 9am-4pm
(winter)
Mon &
Wed-Sun 9am-7pm
(summer)

Prices
£3 per half hour
£5 per hour
V, MC, AmEx
Student discount available

Quarks

7 Jeffries Passage • tel: +44 (0)1483 451 166 •
fax: +44 (0)1483 451 166 • asknigel@quarks.co.uk • www.quarks.co.uk

Location and Access
Located near Guildford
  Library.
Bus: Ask for Guildford
  Library.
Tram/Trolley: 6, 7, 8, 10,
  11, 408, 415, 426, 428,
  477, 478, and the Park
  and Ride, ask for North
  Street.
Train: Main line & Branch
trains, ask for Guildford
  Station.
Nearest cross street is North
  Street.

Hours
Mon-Sat   10am-9pm
Sun   noon-6pm

Prices
£2.50 per half hour
£5 per hour
V, MC

Get Surfed!

4-6 Peterborough Road • tel: +44 (0)181 426 4446 •
fax: +44 (0)181 426 4446 • info@getsurfed.co.uk • www.getsurfed.co.uk

Location and Access
Located near Harrow-on-
  the-Hill.
Bus: 182, 183, ask for
  Peterborough Road.
Underground: Metropolitan
  line, ask for Harrow-on-
  the-Hill.
Train: British Rail, ask for
  Harrow-on-the-Hill.
Nearest cross street is
  Station Road.

Hours
Mon-Sat   10:30am-7pm

Prices
£2.20 per half hour
£4.40 per hour
V, MC

Nearby Places to Visit
Historic Harrow Village and
  the School

UK, ENGLAND, HORLEY (SURREY)

The Network Club
163 Victoria Road • tel: +44 (0)1293 432 111 • No fax •
bfewtrell@networkclub.co.uk • www.networkclub.co.uk

Location and Access
Located behind the Air
   Balloon Pub.
Bus: 524, ask for Victoria
   Road, Air Balloon.
Nearest cross street is
   Brighton Road.

Hours
Mon-Sat   10am-8pm

Prices
£3 per half hour
£5 per hour
No credit cards

Nearby Places to Visit
We are at the foot of
   London Gatwick Airport.

UK, ENGLAND, HUDDERSFIELD (YORKSHIRE)

Window on the World—7 Northumberland Street •
tel: +44 (0)1484 431 289 • fax: +44 (0)1484 513 739 •
mediacentre@architechs.com • www.architechs.com/mediacentre

Location and Access
Located near railway sta-
   tion.
Bus: Metro buses, ask for
   Huddersfield.
Train: From Leeds or
   Manchester, ask for
   Huddersfield Station.

Hours
Mon-Sat   10am-6pm

Prices
£2.50 per half hour
£5 per hour
No credit cards
Student discount available

Nearby Places to Visit
Peak district, Bradford,
   Leeds

@thecafe
55 Kirkstall Lane • tel: +44 (0)113 294 4270 • No fax •
info@thecafe.co.uk • www.thecafe.co.uk

Location and Access
Located near Kirkstall
  Abbey.
Bus: 15, 15C, 41, 50, 50A,
  670, 671, 732, 733, 736,
  760, ask for Kirkstall
  Lights.
Train: Ask for Headingley.
Nearest cross street is
  Kirkstall Road.

Hours
Mon-Fri   9:30am-10pm
Sat   12:30pm-6pm

Prices
£2.50 per half hour
£5 per hour
No credit cards

@thecafe—17 Chapel Street, Headingley •
tel: +44 (0)113 294 4270 • No fax •
info@thecafe.co.uk • www.thecafe.co.uk

Location and Access
Located near the Arndale
  Shopping Center.
Bus: 1, 28, 93, 95, 96, 97,
  731, 755, 780, ask for the
  Arndale Shopping Center.
Train: Ask for Headingley.
Nearest cross street is North
  Lane.

Hours
Mon-Tue &
  Thu-Fri   12:30pm-8pm
Sat   12:30pm-6pm

Prices
£2.50 per half hour
£5 per hour
No credit cards

BiblioTech CyberCentre—631-633 Fulham Road •
tel: +44 (0)171 460 4343 • fax: +44 (0)171 736 6066 •
enquiries@bibliotech.co.uk • www.bibliotech.co.uk

Location and Access
Located near Fulham
  Broadway tube stop.
Bus: 11, 14, 211, ask for
  Fulham Broadway.
Underground: District line,
  ask for Fulham Broadway.
Nearest cross street is North
  End Road.

Hours
Mon-Fri   9am-6pm
Sat   10am-6pm

Prices
£3 per half hour
£6 per hour
No credit cards

Nearby Places to Visit
Most of London sites,
  Chelsea, Earls Court

Bytes Internet
123 Shepherds Bush Road • tel: +44 (0)171 371 6999 •
fax: +44 (0)171 371 6699 • bytes123@hotmail.com • No website

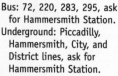

Location and Access
Located near Hammersmith
  roundabout.
Bus: 72, 220, 283, 295, ask
  for Hammersmith Station.
Underground: Piccadilly,
  Hammersmith, City, and
  District lines, ask for
  Hammersmith Station.
Nearest cross street is Brook
  Green.

Hours
Mon-Thu   9am-8pm
Fri-Sat   9am-6pm
Sun   11am-6pm

Prices
£3 per half hour
£6 per hour
No credit cards

Nearby Places to Visit
Hammersmith Odeon

Cafe Internet—22-24 Buckingham Palace Road •
tel: +44 (0)171 233 5786 • fax: +44 (0)171 233 5785 •
cafe@cafeinternet.co.uk • www.cafeinternet.co.uk

Location and Access
Located near Victoria Tube
and the Royal Mews.
Bus: Ask for Victoria.
Underground: Victoria line,
ask for Victoria Station.
Train: From Gatwick and
elsewhere, ask for Victoria
Station.
Nearest cross street is
Victoria Street.

Hours
Mon-Fri   8am-9pm
Sat-Sun   9am-8pm

Prices
£3 per half hour
£6 per hour
V, MC, AmEx
Student discount available

Nearby Places to Visit
Buckingham Palace,
Westminster

C@fe.Net
40 Sheen Lane • tel: +44 (0)181 255 4022 • fax: +44 (0)181 255 4022 •
cafemail@cafenet.uk.com • www.cafenet.uk.com

Location and Access
Located near Siam Court
Thai restaurant.
Bus: R69, 33, 337, ask for
Sheen Lane.
Underground: District line,
ask for Richmond Tube
Station.
Nearest cross street is Upper
Richmond Road.

Hours
Mon-Thu   11am-10pm

Fri-Sat   11am-7pm
Sun   noon-10pm

Prices
£2.50 per half hour
£5 per hour
V, MC, AmEx, DC
Student discount available

Nearby Places to Visit
Richmond Park, Royal
Gardens

UK, ENGLAND, LONDON (FULHAM)

The Cyber Centre—631-633 Fulham Road •
tel: +44 (0)171 460 4343 • fax: +44 (0)171 736 6066 •
tom@postmaster.co.uk • www.thecybercentre.co.uk

Location and Access
Located near Fulham
   Broadway Underground.
Bus: 11, 14, 28, 259, ask
   for Fulham Broadway.
Underground: District line,
   ask for Fulham Broardway.
Nearest cross street is
   Fulham Broadway.

Hours
Mon-Thu   9am-9pm
Fri   9am-6pm
Sat   10am-6pm

Prices
£3 per half hour
£6 per hour
V, MC, AmEx

Nearby Places to Visit
London is full of them.

UK, ENGLAND, LONDON (WEST END)

Cyberia—39 Whitfield Street •
tel: +44 (0)171 681 4200 • fax: +44 (0)171 209 0984 •
cyberia@easynet.co.uk • www.cyberiacafe.net

Location and Access
Located near Habitat.
Bus: 24, 29, 253, and all
   buses that go along
   Tottenham Court Road,
   ask for Goodge Street
   Station.
Underground: Northern line,
   Central line, ask for
   Tottenham Court Road or
   Goodge Street.

Hours
Mon-Fri   10am-8pm

Sat   11am-7pm
Sun   11am-6pm

Prices
£3 per half hour
£6 per hour
No credit cards
Student discount available

Nearby Places to Visit
Post Office Tower, Regent's
   Park, Oxford Street, Toy
   Museum, Tottenham Court
   Road

Cyberia Ealing—73 New Broadway •
tel: +44 (0)181 840 3131 • fax: +44 (0)181 840 4123 •
ealing@cyberiacafe.net • www.ealing.cyberiacafe.net

Location and Access
Located near Virgin Cinema.
Bus: E3, 83, 207, 607, ask
  for Ealing Broadway.
Underground: Central and
  District lines, ask for
  Ealing Broadway.
Train: Paddington, ask for
  Ealing Broadway.
Nearest cross street is
  Uxbridge Road.

Hours
Mon-Sat   7:30am-11pm
Sun   9am-11pm

Prices
£2.50 per half hour
£5 per hour
V, MC
Student discount available

Nearby Places to Visit
London, Ealing Film Studios,
  Chiswick House

---

declare Computer Studios—206 Camden Lock Market,
Top Floor • tel: +44 (0)171 482 0102 • fax: +44 (0)171 482 0104 •
camden@declare.com • www.declare.com

Location and Access
Located opposite Fusilier &
  Firkin Pub.
Bus: 24, 27, 31 pass by the
  shop; 29, 134, 135, ask
  for Camden Town Tube.
Underground: Northern line,
  ask for Camden Town.
Train: Network Southeast,
  ask for Camden Town.
Nearest cross street is
  Camden High Street.

Hours
Mon-Thu   10am-9pm
Fri   10am-5pm
Sat-Sun   noon-5pm

Prices
£2.50 per half hour
£5 per hour
V, MC
Student discount available

Nearby Places to Visit
Camden Lock Market,
  London Zoo

UK, ENGLAND, LONDON (CONVENT GARDEN)

declare Computer Studios—14 Neals Yard •
tel: +44 (0)171 379 5113 • fax: +44 (0)171 379 0135 •
coventgarden@declare.com • www.declare.com

Location and Access
Located near Neal Street, Covent Garden.
Underground: Piccadilly line, ask for Leicester Square or Covent Garden.
Located between Shorts Gardens and Monmouth Street.

Hours
Mon-Thu 10am-9pm
Fri   10am-5pm
Sat-Sun   noon-5pm

Prices
£2.50 per half hour
£5 per hour
V, MC
Student discount available with ID card

Nearby Places to Visit
Opera, Leicester Square

UK, ENGLAND, LONDON (EARLS COURT)

declare Computer Studios
58 Kenway Road • tel: +44 (0)171 835 0203 •
fax: +44 (0)171 835 0204 • earlscourt@declare.com • www.declare.com

Location and Access
Located near King's Head Pub.
Bus: 31, ask for Earls Court.
Underground: Piccadilly and District lines, ask for Earls Court.
Located between Shorts Gardens and Monmouth Street.

Hours
Mon-Thu 9am-9pm
Fri-Sat   10am-6pm

Prices
£1.25 per fifteen minutes
£5 per hour
V, MC
Student discount available

Nearby Places to Visit
Earls Court (Exhibition Hall)

IDM CyberCentre

8-14 Stanley Road • tel: +44 (0)181 542 0011 •
fax: +44 (0)181 540 2092 • training@idm.co.uk • www.idm.co.uk

Location and Access
Located near Wimbledon YMCA.
Bus: 55, 57, 93, ask for Odeon Cinema.
Underground: District and Northern lines, ask for Wimbledon and South Wimbledon.
Train: Southwest trains, ask for Wimbledon.

Nearest cross street is the Broadway (Wimbledon).

Hours
Mon-Thu   9am-8pm
Fri-Sat   9am-6pm

Prices
£2.50 per half hour
£4 per hour
V, MC, DC

London Internet Ltd.—33A Old Brompton Road •

tel: +44 (0)171 838 1199 • fax: +44 (0)171 838 0888 •
info@london-internet.net • www.london-internet.net

Location and Access
Located opposite the South Kensington Tube Station.
Bus: 14, 74, 345 ,ask for Old Brompton Road, South Kensington.
Underground: District, Circle, and Piccadilly lines, ask for South Kensington.

Hours
Mon-Fri   9am-7pm
Sat   10am-5pm
Sun   11am-4pm

Prices
£2.50 per half hour
£5 per hour
V, MC

Nearby Places to Visit
Natural History Museum, Victoria & Albert Museum, Science Museum, Harrods, Royal Albert Hall

Portobello Gold Bar, Restaurant, Internet Lounge & Online Hotel—95/97 Portobello Road •
tel: +44 (0)171 460 4906/4910 • fax: +44 (0)171 460 4911 •
mikebell@portobel.demon.co.uk • www.portobellogold.com

Location and Access
Located near Portobello Market.

Bus: Ask for Notting Hill Gate, Westbourne Grove, Ladbroke Grove.

Underground: Central, District, and Circle lines, ask for Notting Hill Gate Station.

Nearest cross street is Notting Hill Gate.

Hours
Mon-Sat   10am-9pm
Sun   noon-7pm

Prices
£3 per half hour
£5 per hour
V, MC, DC
Student discount available

Nearby Places to Visit
Portobello Market, antique shops

PubNet at the Latchmere—503 Battersea Park Road •
tel: +44 (0)171 223 3549 • fax: +44 (0)171 585 2392 •
alan@pubnet.co.uk • www.latchmere.co.uk

Location and Access
Located in the Latchmere.

Bus: 44, 49, 319, 344, 345, ask for the Latchmere.

Nearest cross street is Latchmere Road.

Hours
Mon-Sun   10:30am-10:30pm

Prices
£3.50 per half hour
£6 per hour
V, MC, DC
Student discount available

Nearby Places to Visit
Battersea Park, Battersea Dogs Home, Albert Bridge

Shoot 'n Surf Computer Games & Internet Cafe

13 New Oxford Street • tel: +44 (0)171 419 1183 •
fax: +44 (0)171 419 1184 • info@shootnsurf.co.uk •
www.shootnsurf.co.uk

Location and Access
Located near British
  Museum.
Bus: 171, ask for Holborn
  Tube.
Underground: Central and
  Piccadilly lines, ask for
  Holborn Station.
Nearest cross street is High
  Holborn.

Hours
Mon-Sun   11am-9pm

Prices
£3 per half hour
£6 per hour
V, MC
Student discount available

Surf.net Cafe—13 Deptford Church Street •
tel: +44 (0)181 488 1200 • fax: +44 (0)181 488 1200 •
richard@surfnet.co.uk • www.surfnet.co.uk/surfnet/index.html

Location and Access
Located near Deptford
  Anchor.
Bus: 47,5 3, 177, ask for
  Deptford Broadway.
Underground: East London
  line, ask for New Cross.
Train: Connex SE, ask for
  Deptford.
Nearest cross street is
  Deptford Broadway.

Hours
Mon-Fri   11am-9pm
Sat   11am-7pm
Sun   noon-4pm

Prices
£2.50 per half hour
£5 per hour
No credit cards

Nearby Places to Visit
Greenwich, the Cutty Sark,
  Royal Observatory, Queen's
  House, Rangers House, Fan
  Museum, Naval Museum,
  Royal Naval College

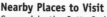

233

UK, ENGLAND, LONDON (SOHO)

Webshack—15 Dean Street •
tel: +44 (0)171 439 8000 • fax: +44 (0)171 287 0333 •
info@webshack-cafe.com • www.webshack-cafe.com

Location and Access
Located near National
Westminster Bank.
Bus: 7, 73, ask for near
Tottenham Court Road.
Underground: Northern,
Central, Victoria, and
Bakerloo lines, ask for
Tottenham Court Road
(Northern & Central) or
Oxford Circus (Victoria &
Bakerloo).

Nearest cross street is
Oxford Street.

Hours
Mon-Sat   11am-11pm
Sun   11am-8pm
          (please call
          first)

Prices
£3 per half hour
£5 per hour
V, MC, AmEx, DC
Student discount available

UK, ENGLAND, LONDON (ANGEL ISLINGTON)

The World C@fe—394 St. John Street •
tel: +44 (0)171 713 8883 • fax: +44 (0)171 713 8883 •
theworldcafe@earthling.net • www.worldcafe.smallplanet.co.uk

Location and Access
Located near Angel
Underground Station.
Bus: 18, 19, 38, 43, ask for
Angel.
Underground: Northern line,
ask for Angel.
Train: Intercity Main Line
north, ask for Kings Cross
Station.
Nearest cross street is City
Road.

Hours
Mon-Fri   noon-9pm
Sat   12:30pm-6pm

Prices
£3 per half hour
£5 per hour
V, MC, AmEx
Student discount available

Nearby Places to Visit
Sadlers Wells Theatre, Upper
Street shopping, Chapel
Street Market

UK, ENGLAND, LUTON (BEDFORDSHIRE)

Hard Drive Cafe
16 King Street • tel: +44 (0)1582 485 621 • No fax •
hdc@hardcafe.co.uk • www.hardcafe.co.uk

Location and Access
Located near Town Hall.
Bus: Ask for George
  Street/Town Hall stop.
Nearest cross street is
  George Street.

Prices
£2.50 per half hour
£5 per hour
No credit cards

Hours
Mon-Fri   11am-8pm
Sat   10am-6pm

UK, ENGLAND, MANCHESTER (MANCHESTER)

Cafe Internet—The Brand Centre, 1 Stanley Road, Whitefield •
tel: +44 (0)161 796 2494 • fax: +44 (0)161 796 2496 •
cafe@cafeinternet.co.uk • www.cafeinternet.co.uk

Location and Access
Located near the Whitefield
  train station.
Bus: Routes going between
  Manchester and Bury on
  the A56, ask for
  Whitefield Brand Centre.

Prices
£3 per half hour
£6 per hour
V, MC, AmEx
Student discount available

Nearby Places to Visit
The Brand Centre is a
  leading fashion outlet.

Hours
Mon-Thu   8am-10pm
Sat-Sun   10am-9pm

UK, ENGLAND, MANCHESTER (MANCHESTER)

Cyberia—12 Oxford Street •
tel: +44 (0)161 950 2233 • fax: +44 (0)161 950 2233 •
manchester@easynet.co.uk • www.manchester.cyberiacafe.net

Location and Access
Located near Central Library.
Bus: 9, 11, 41, 40, 42, 43,
46, 47, 48, 85, 86, 111,
ask for Central Library.
Tram: Ask for Central
Library/St. Peters Square.
Train: Ask for Oxford Road
Station.
Nearest cross street is
Portland Street.

Hours
Mon-Thu   11am-9pm
Fri-Sat   11am-2am
Sun   2pm-9pm

Prices
£3 per half hour
£6 per hour
V, MC
Student discount available

Nearby Places to Visit
Museum of Science and
Industry

UK, ENGLAND, MARLOW (BUCKINGHAMSHIRE)

Crusoes Internet Cafe—Cherry Tree House & Dean Street,
Unit 2 • tel: +44 (0)1628 488 376 • fax: +44 (0)1628 488 387 •
sales@crusoes.com • www.crusoes.com

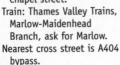

Location and Access
Located opposite Cross Keys
Pub.
Bus: 328 (Reading to High
Wycombe), ask for Marlow,
Chapel street.
Train: Thames Valley Trains,
Marlow-Maidenhead
Branch, ask for Marlow.
Nearest cross street is A404
bypass.

Hours
Tue-Fri   10am-6pm

Prices
£4 per half hour
£6 per hour
V, MC

Nearby Places to Visit
Windsor Castle, Henley
Regatta on River Thames
(seasonal)

UK, ENGLAND, NEW MILLS, HIGH PEAK (DERBYSHIRE)

Peak Art Cyber Cafe—30, Market Street •
tel: +44 (0)1663 747 770 • fax: +44 (0)1663 747 159 •
info@peakcafe.demon.co.uk • www.peakcafe.demon.co.uk

Location and Access
Located near Peak District
  National Park, Lyme Park.
Bus: 199, 358, 361, ask for
  New Mills Bus Station.
Train: Hope Valley Line
  (Manchester-Sheffield) or
  Buxton Line
  (Manchester/Blackpool-
  Buxton), ask for New Mills
  Central or New Mills
  Newtown.

Hours
Mon-Tue &
  Thu-Sat 9:30am-5pm
Wed   9:30am-2pm
Sun   10:30am-5pm

Prices
£3 per half hour
£6 per hour
No credit cards
Student discount available

UK, ENGLAND, NORWICH (NORFOLK)

Play It Buy 'Ere Records & Interconnect—The
Workshop, Jolly Butchers Yard, Ber Street • tel: +44 (0)1603 630 223 •
fax: +44 (0)1603 667 775 • anne@nbd-recordings.demon.co.uk •
www.nbd-recordings.demon.co.uk

Location and Access
Located two minutes from
  McDonald's and opposite
  the 24-hour BP station.

Nearby Places to Visit
Norwich Castle

Hours
Mon-Sat   10am-7pm

Prices
£3 per half hour
£6 per hour
No credit cards
Student discount available

Electr@net & Kino New Media Ltd.

316 High Street • tel: +44 (0)1689 877 878 •
fax: +44 (0)1689 877 239 • info@electranet.com • www.electranet.com

Location and Access
Located near Brands Hatch
   Racing Track.
Bus: 51, ask for Orpington
   High Street.
Train: From London, ask for
   Orpington Station.

Prices
£2.50 per half hour
£4.50 per hour
V, MC, AmEx, DC

Hours
Mon-Sat   9am-7pm

Project Cosmic—The Station, Exeter Road •
tel: +44 (0)1404 813 226 • fax: +44 (0)1404 813 226 •
info@cosmic.org.uk • www.cosmic.org.uk

Location and Access
Located near St. Saviour's
   Bridge.
Bus: Ottery-Exeter,
   Axminster-Exeter, ask for
   St Saviour's Bridge.
Nearest cross street is A30.

Prices
£1.75 per half hour
£3.50 per hour
No credit cards
Student discount available

Nearby Places to Visit
Ottery St Mary's Church,
   Sidmouth, Honiton, Exeter

Hours
Mon-Wed &
   Fri   10am-5pm
Thu   10am-2pm
Sat   10am-1pm

UK, ENGLAND, RADSTOCK (SOMERSET)

Cafenet—Norton Radstock College, South Hill Park •
tel: +44 (0)1761 438 532 ext. 306 • fax: +44 (0)1761 436 173 •
phollocombe@nortcoll.ac.uk • www.nortcoll.ac.uk/cafenet.htm

Location and Access
Bus: 84 Bath to Frome, 173
Bath to Wells, 176 Bath
to Shepton Mallet, 177
Bath to Paulton, 178 Bath
to Bristol, ask for Wells
Road.
Nearest cross street is Wells
Road.

Hours
Mon   9:30am-5pm

Tue-Thu   9:30am-7pm
Fri   9:30am-4pm

Prices
£2.50 per half hour
£4 per hour
No credit cards
Student discount available

Nearby Places to Visit
Bath and Wells (within ten
miles)

UK, ENGLAND, ST. ALBANS (HERTFORDSHIRE)

Netcel Internet—45 Grosvenor Road •
tel: +44 (0)1727 813 623 • fax: +44 (0)1727 813 644 •
info@netcel.co.uk • www.netcel.co.uk or www.hertfordshire.co.uk

Location and Access
Located in the Business
Link Hertfordshire
Building.
Bus: 602 Operator
University Bus, ask for B.
Train: Kings Cross to
Bedford, ask for St. Albans.
Nearest cross street is
London Road.

Hours
Wed   5:30pm-9pm

(more hours
planned)

Prices
£3 per half hour
£5 per hour
No credit cards

Nearby Places to Visit
St. Albans Cathedral, St.
Albans Museum (Roman
relics), Verulamium,
Roman Hypercaust

UK, ENGLAND, ST. AUSTELL (CORNWALL)

Planet 13—19-21 High Cross Street •
tel: +44 (0)1726 75013 • fax: +44 (0)1726 627 026 •
gary@planet13.co.uk • www.planet13.co.uk

Location and Access
Located opposite Main Post
Office.
Bus: Ask for bus station.
Train: London/Paddington-
Penzance, ask for St.
Austell.
Nearest cross street is
Church Street.

Hours
Mon-Sat   11am-7pm
Sun   10:30am-5pm
           (some Sundays
           only)

Prices
£2.50 per half hour
£5 per hour
No credit cards

Nearby Places to Visit
The beach, harbours,
Cornish scenery

UK, ENGLAND, SALISBURY (WILTSHIRE)

Salisbury Cyber Café—62 Winchester Street •
tel: +44 (0)1722 505 519 • fax: +44 (0)1722 505 199 •
salisbury_cyber@hotmail.com • www.welcome.to/salisbury

Location and Access
Located near McDonald's.
Everything is within
walking distance in town.
Train: Ask for Salisbury
Station.
Nearest cross street is
Market Square.

Hours
Mon & Fri 10am-11pm
Tue & Thu 9am-11pm
Wed   11am-11pm
Sat   9am-10pm

Sun   If the lights are
           on

Prices
£3 per half hour
£5 per hour
MC, AmEx, DC, D
Student discount available
to local language school
students

Nearby Places to Visit
Salisbury Cathedral,
Stonehenge

Net-Zone Internet Cafe

6 Newton Road • tel: +44 (0)1803 291 215 • No fax •
cafe@net-zone.co.uk • www.net-zone.co.uk

Location and Access
Located near South Devon College & Kwik-Fit Garage.
Bus: X80, 6, 12, ask for College.

Hours
Mon-Thu   8:30am-9:30pm
Fri   8am-5:30pm
Sat   11am-8pm

Prices
£2.50 weekdays & £2 evenings & weekends per half hour
£5 weekdays & £4 evenings & weekends per hour
No credit cards

Nearby Places to Visit
English Riviera Centre, Torre Abbey Sands, beach, marina, harbour

---

Global Lounge—Unit 13, Lemon Street Market •
tel: +44 (0)1872 274 037 • fax: +44 (0)1872 274 037 •
info@globallounge.co.uk • www.globallounge.co.uk

Location and Access
Located near Cinema.
Bus: Many.
Train: South West, ask for Truro.

Hours
Mon-Sat   9am-5pm

Prices
£2.50 per half hour
£5 per hour
No credit cards
Student discount available

Nearby Places to Visit
Truro Cathedral, Cornwall County Museum

UK, ENGLAND, TWICKENHAM (MIDDLESEX)

Deckers Coffee Shop—Internet Cafe—49 London
Road • tel: +44 (0)181 891 5600 • fax: +44 (0)181 891 5600 •
cafe@rivernet.co.uk • www.rivernet.co.uk/cafe

Location and Access
Located near Twickenham
    Train Station.
Bus: H22, R68, R70, 33,
    267, 281, 290, 490, ask
    for King Street
    Twickenham.
Tram/Trolley: 267, 281, ask
    for Moon under Water Pub.
Train: From Waterloo, ask
    for Twickenham.

Hours
Mon-Fri   9am-7pm
Sat   10am-4pm

Prices
£3 per half hour
£6 per hour
No credit cards
Student discount available

Nearby Places to Visit
Twickenham Rugby Ground,
    Marble Hill House, Ham
    House, Kew Gardens

UK, ENGLAND, YORK (YORKSHIRE)

Gallery of Photography
29 Castlegate • tel: +44 (0)1904 654 724 • fax: +44 (0)1904 651 509 •
info@impressions-gallery.com • www.impressions-gallery.com

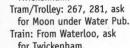

Location and Access
Located near Cliffords Tower.
Nearest cross street is
    Coppergate Centre.

Hours
Mon-Tue &
    Thu-Sat 9:30am-5:30pm
Wed   10am-5:30pm
Sun   11am-5:30pm

Prices
£2.50 per half hour
£5 per hour
V, MC

Nearby Places to Visit
Viking Centre, Castle
    Museum, York Minster

The Gateway Internet Cafe Bar

26 Swinegate • tel: +44 (0)1904 646 446 •
fax: +44 (0)1904 670 386 • gateway@ymn.net • www.ymn.net/gateway

Location and Access

Bus: Ask for Swinegate.
Train: GNER (Main North
East Line), ask for York
Station.
Nearest cross street is
Goodramgate.

Hours

Tue-Sat   10am-6pm

Prices

£3 per half hour
£5 per hour
No credit cards
Student discount available

Nearby Places to Visit

York Minster, Roman ruins,
Mediaeval York (walled
city)

Cyberia Internet Cafe

31 North Quay • tel: +44 (0)1624 617 510 • fax: +44 (0)1624 617 512 •
info@cyberia.mcb.net • www.mcb.net/cic/cyberia

Location and Access

Located near the British
Hotel.
Bus: From Douglas, ask for
near the British Hotel.
Horse Tram: To the sea ter-
minal, then walk to the
Quay.
Train: Ask for Douglas Train
Station.

Hours

Mon &
  Wed-Sat 10am-10pm
Sun   10am-6pm

Prices

£4 before 6pm, £2.50 after
6pm per half hour
£8 before 6pm, £5 after
6pm per hour
No credit cards
Student discount available

UK, NORTHERN IRELAND, BELFAST (COUNTY ANTRIM)

Revelations, The Internet Cafe—27 Shaftesbury Square • tel: +44 (0)1232 320337 • fax: +44 (0)1232 320432 • mark@revelations.co.uk • www.revelations.co.uk

Location and Access
Located near Big Video
  Screen in Shaftesbury
  Square.

Bus: Local buses.
Nearest cross street is Great
  Victoria Street.

Hours

Mon-Fri	10am-10pm
Sat	10am-8pm
Sun	noon-8pm

Prices
£2.50 per half hour
£5 per hour
No credit cards
Student discount available

Nearby Places to Visit
Queens University, wall
  murals

UK, SCOTLAND, EDINBURGH (LOTHIAN)

Cafe Internet
35-37 Shadwick Place • tel: see phone book • No fax •
cafe@cafeinternet.co.uk • www.cafeinternet.co.uk

Location and Access
Located just off the main
  Princes Street shopping
  area.

Bus: Many buses, ask for
  Shadwick Place off Princes
  Street.

Hours

Mon-Fri	8am-10pm
Sat-Sun	10am-9pm

Prices
£3 per half hour
£6 per hour
V, MC, AmEx
Student discount available

Nearby Places to Visit
Capital of Scotland, the
  Castle

Cyberia, Internet Cafe—88 Hanover Street •
tel: +44 (0)131 220 4403 • fax: +44 (0)131 220 4405 •
edinburgh@cybersurf.co.uk • www.cybersurf.co.uk

Location and Access
Located near Princes Street.
Bus: To the town center, ask
  for Hanover Street.
Train: Branch line, ask for
  Waverley Station.
Nearest cross street is
  George Street.

Hours
Mon-Sat   10am-10pm
Sun   noon-7pm

Prices
£2.50 per half hour
£5 per hour
No credit cards
Student discount available

Nearby Places to Visit
Princes Street Gardens,
  Scott Monument, the
  Botanic Gardens

---

web13—13 Bread Street •
tel: +44 (0)131 229 8883 • fax: +44 (0)131 229 9899 •
queries@web13.co.uk • www.web13.co.uk

Location and Access
Located adjacent to the ABC
  Cinema in Lothian Road.
Bus: 6, 11, 16, 27, ask for
  ABC Cinema.

Hours
Mon-Sat   9am-10pm
Sun   11am-8pm

Prices
£2.50 per half hour
£5 per hour (£3.50 per hour
  during happy hour)
V, MC, AmEx
Student discount available

Nearby Places to Visit
Edinburgh Castle, Princess
  Street Gardens

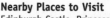

Cafe Internet—153-157 Sauchiehall Street •
tel: +44 (0)141 353 2484 • fax: +44 (0)141 353 2484 •
cafe@cafeinternet.co.uk • www.cafeinternet.co.uk

Location and Access
Located in Waterstones
  Bookshop.
Bus: All buses to the town
  center, ask for Sauchiehall
  Street.
Underground: Ask for
  Cowcaddens.
Train: Any Glasgow line, ask
  for Glasgow Central,
  Glasgow Queen Street.

Hours
Mon-Fri   8am-10pm
Sat-Sun   10am-9pm

Prices
£3 per half hour
£6 per hour
V, MC, AmEx
Student discount available

Nearby Places to Visit
Gallery of Modern Art,
  George Square, Maclellan
  Galleries, Necropolis

Internet C@fe
569 Sauchiehall Street • tel: +44 (0)141 564 1052 •
fax: +44 (0)141 564 1054 • tim@linkcafe.co.uk • www.linkcafe.co.uk

Location and Access
Located near the Mitchell
  Library.
Bus: One-way street buses
  returning to city centre
  only, ask for Charing
  Cross.
Underground: Ask for
  Charing Cross.
Nearest cross street is
  Charing Cross.

Hours
Mon-Fri   9am-11pm
Sat   10am-7pm
Sun   noon-11pm

Prices
£2.50 per half hour
£5 per hour
V, MC, AmEx, DC
Student discount available

Nearby Places to Visit
Loads, see http://www.
  glasgow.gov.uk

Dimensiwn 4
4 Bangor Street • tel: +44 (0)1286 678 777 • No fax •
info@dimensiwn4.co.uk • www.dimensiwn4.co.uk

Location and Access
Located near Lloyds and Barclays Banks.
Bus: Ask for Turf Square (opposite the cafe).
Nearest cross streets are Bridge Street, Bangot Street, Turf Square.

Hours
Mon-Fri	10am-6pm
Sat	10am-5:30pm

Prices
£2 per half hour
£4 per hour
No credit cards
Student discount available

Nearby Places to Visit
Caernarfon Castle and Old Walled Town, Segontium Roman Fort, Seiont II Maritime Museum

---

The Cardiff CyberCafe Ltd.
9 Duke Street • tel: +44 (0)1222 235 757 • fax: +44 (0)1222 235 758 •
info@cardiffcybercafe.co.uk • www.cardiffcybercafe.co.uk

Location and Access
Located near Cardiff Castle.
Bus: Many, ask for St. Mary Street, Kingsway, Cardiff Castle.
Train: Valley Lines, Great Western (South Wales), ask for Cardiff Central, Queen Street.
Nearest cross streets are Queen Street, St. Mary Street.

Hours
Mon-Fri	11am-7pm
Sat	10am-6pm

Prices
£2.50 per half hour
£4.50 per hour
V, MC, DC

Nearby Places to Visit
Cardiff Castle, Bute Park, Queen Street Shopping Centre, Ice Skating Rink, National Museum

North
America

CANADA, BOISSEVAIN (MANITOBA)

Boissevain & Morton Regional Library
436 South Railway Street • tel: +1 204-534-6478 • No fax •
mbom@mail.techplus.com • www.town.boissevain.mb.ca

Location and Access
Located near Civic Centre
  Main Street.
Nearest cross street is
  Broadway.

Hours
Wed-Fri	9am-5pm
Tue	9am-8pm
Sat	9am-noon &
	1pm-5pm

Prices
Can$1 per half hour
Can$2 per hour
No credit cards

Nearby Places to Visit
Moncur Gallery of
  Prehistory, Outdoor Art
  Gallery, Turtle Mountain
  Provincial Park,
  International Peace
  Garden

CANADA, CALGARY (ALBERTA)

Wired—The Cyber Cafe Inc.
1032 17 Avenue SW • tel: +1 403-244-7070 • No fax •
webmeister@wired-cafe.com • www.wired-cafe.com

Location and Access
Located near Mount Royal
  Village Shopping Centre.
Bus: 2, 6, ask for 17 Avenue
  and 10 Street.
Nearest cross street is 8th
  Street SW.

Hours
Mon-Thu	9am-10pm
Fri	9am-midnight
Sat	10am-midnight
Sun	noon-8pm

Prices
Can$5 per half hour
Can$10 per hour
MC
Student discount available

Nearby Places to Visit
Calgary Tower, Canada
  Olympic Park, Banff

CANADA, COURTENAY (BRITISH COLUMBIA)

Joe Read's Bookstore & Internet Cafe
#5-2760 Cliffe Avenue • tel: +1 250-334-9723 •
fax: +1 250-338-1395 • nikki@joereads.com • www.joereads.com

Location and Access
Located near Driftwood
  Mall.
Bus: Cross Town 10, ask for
  Driftwood Mall.
Nearest cross street is 26th
  Street.

Prices
Can$3 per half hour
Can$6 per hour
V, MC

Nearby Places to Visit
Estuary Park

Hours
Mon-Fri	7am-midnight
Sat	8am-midnight
Sun	10am- 10pm

CANADA, COWANSVILLE (QUEBEC)

Internet au Virtuel
434 rue Sud • tel: +1 450-263-2264 • fax: +1 450-263-0346 •
webmaster@virtuel.qc.ca • www.virtuel.qc.ca

Location and Access
Located near Royal Bank.
Bus: From Montreal,
  Voyageur route, ask for
  Cowansville, rue Sud at
  Church Street.
Nearest cross street is
  Church Street.

Hours
Mon-Thu	9:30am-10pm
Fri-Sat	9:30am-11pm
Sun	11am-10pm

Prices
Can$2.50 per half hour
Can$5 per hour
V, MC

CANADA, EDMONTON (ALBERTA)

Bistro.Web
8711-82 White Avenue • tel: +1 780-468-6983 •
fax: +1 780-468-1599 • bistro@bistro.net • www.bistro.net

Location and Access
Phone for directions.

Hours
Mon-Fri	9am-8pm
Sat	noon-8pm

Prices
Can$2.50 per half hour
Can$5 per hour
V, MC

Nearby Places to Visit
White Avenue has many shops, cafes, pubs, clubs, restaurants, and theaters. The Du Maurier Jazz festival and Fringe Festival are in summer.

CANADA, FREDERICTON JUNCTION (NEW BRUNSWICK)

Sunbury West Community Access Centre—100
Pride's Landing Road • tel: +1 506-368-1119 • fax: +1 506-368-1119 •
indiana@brunnet.bet • http://cap.unb.ca/nb/sunburywest

Location and Access
Located inside Sunbury West School.
Nearest cross street is Sunbury Drive.

Hours
Mon-Thu	6pm-10pm
Fri & Sun	1pm-5pm
Sat	9am-5pm

Prices
Can$2 flat fee

Nearby Places to Visit
Fredericton, Saint John

CANADA, GRAND MANAN (NEW BRUNSWICK)

MananNet Community Access Centre—Room 5 Grand
Manan High School, Grand Harbour • tel: +1 506-662-7057 •
fax: +1 506-662-7007 • grmancac@nbnet.nb.ca •
www.angelfire.com/hi/MananNet/index.html

Location and Access
Located at Grand Manan
  High School.
Nearest cross street is Main
  Road on Grand Manan
  Island.

Hours
Mon-Thu   2:30pm-10pm
  (during school year)
Sat   10am-5pm
  (during school year)

Sun   1pm-4pm
  (during school year)

Prices
Can$3 per half hour
Can$3 per hour
No credit cards

Nearby Places to Visit
Grand Manan Museum

CANADA, KELOWNA (BRITISH COLUMBIA)

Mind Grind Internet Cafe and Bookstore
1340 Water Street • tel: +1 250-763-2221 • No fax •
cafe@mindgrind.ca • www.mindgrind.ca

Location and Access
Located near Grand
  Okanagan Hotel.
Bus: Main routes, ask for
  Grand Okanagan Hotel.

Prices
Can$3.21 per half hour
Can$5.89 per hour
No credit cards

Hours
Mon-Thu   7:30am-9pm
Fri-Sat   7:30am-10pm
Sun   9am-5pm

CANADA, KELOWNA (BRITISH COLUMBIA)

Mind Grind II

1340 Water Street • tel: +1 250-763-2221 • No fax •
cafe@mindgrind.ca • www.mindgrind.ca

Location and Access
Located on the Grand
  Okanagan Resort.
Bus: Main routes, ask for
  the resort.

Hours
Mon-Thu	7:30am-9pm
Fri-Sat	7:30am-10pm
Sun	9am-5pm

Prices
Can$3.21 per half hour
Can$5.89 per hour
No credit cards

CANADA, LONDON (ONTARIO)

Abacus Café

417 Richmond Street • tel: +1 519-679-9812 • No fax •
abacus@abacus-cafe.com • www.abacus-cafe.com

Location and Access
Located right in the heart
  of downtown.
Bus: Any bus that goes
  downtown.
Nearest cross street is
  Dundas Street.

Hours
Mon-Fri	11am-10pm
Sat	noon-10pm
Sun	noon-5pm

Prices
Can$3.21 per half hour
Can$6 per hour
No credit cards

Nearby Places to Visit
The Brunswick Hotel

CANADA, MONCTON (NEW BRUNSWICK)

Parkton Community Access Center

66 Lancaster Road • tel: +1 506-869-6447 • fax: +1 506-853-7215 • parkhcac@nbnet.nb.ca • No website yet

Location and Access
Located near Trinity Malland MLA Claudette Bradshaw's office.
Nearest cross street is Mountain Road and Katherine Street.

Hours
Mon-Fri 1pm-9pm
Sat   1pm-5pm

Prices
Can$2 per half hour
Can$2 per hour
No credit cards
Student discount available

Nearby Places to Visit
Centennial Park, Magnetic Hill Park, Trinity Drive Mall, Moncton City Museum, Bowa Park, Capital Theater, Tim Horton's Coffee shops

---

CANADA, MONTREAL (QUEBEC)

CyberGround NetCafe

3672 Boulevard St. Laurent • tel: +1 514-842-1726 • fax: +1 514-842-9123 • info@cyberground.com • www.cyberground.com

Location and Access
Bus: 55, ask for Pine and St. Laurent.
Underground: St. Laurent Subway, ask for St Laurent Station (10 min. walk to cafe).
Located between Prince Arthur and Pine Avenue.

Hours
Mon-Fri 9am-midnight
Sat-Sun 11am-midnight

Prices
Can$4 per half hour
Can$8 per hour
V, AmEx

Nearby Places to Visit
Boulevard St. Laurent is busy in the summer— bars, cafes, discos, and restaurants.

CANADA, NEW WESTMINSTER (BRITISH COLUMBIA)

The Black Dog Billiard Cafe

983 Carnarvon Street • tel: +1 604-524-2499 • fax: +1 604-524-9464 • klaus@blackdogcafe.com • www.blackdogcafe.com

Location and Access
Located near New Westminster Quay-Skytrain.
Bus: Ask for New Westminster Skytrain Station.
Underground: Skytrain, ask for New Westminster Skytrain Station.
Train: Skytrain, ask for New Westminster Skytrain Station.
Nearest cross street is 10th Street.

Hours
Mon-Fri   7:30am-midnight
Sat-Sun   10am-midnight

Prices
Can$3 per half hour
Can$6 per hour
V

CANADA, RAYMOND (ALBERTA)

Raymond Public Library

15 South Broadway • tel: +1 403-752-4785 • fax: +1 403-752-4785 • library@chinookarch.ab.ca • No website

Location and Access
Nearest big town is Lethbridge.
The library is a landmark in Raymond.
Nearest cross street is Highway 52.

Hours
Mon &
Wed   10:30am-7:30pm
Tue &
Thu-Fri   10:30am-6pm
Sat   10:30am-3:30pm

Prices
Free

Nearby Places to Visit
Waterton Park National Park, Writing on Stone Provincial Park, Head Smashed in Buffalo Jump

Café Ultimate—1852 Scarth Street • tel: +1 306-584-2112 •
fax: +1 306-584-2112 • cyclone@sk.sympatico.ca •
www3.sk.sympatico.ca/mccpau or www.cafeultimate.com

Location and Access
Located near Twin Towers.
Bus: Ask for downtown.
Nearest cross street is
  Scarth Street Mall.

Prices
Can$3.25 +tax per half hour
Can$6.50 +tax per hour
V, DC, D
Student discount available

Hours
Mon-Fri	8am-midnight
Sat	9am-midnight
Sun	1pm-11pm

Nearby Places to Visit
Victoria Park, Public Library,
  Neutral Grounds Art
  Gallery

Centre d'Accès Communautaire—Internet de St-Alphonse—134, rue Principale Ouest • tel: +1 418-388-1303 •
No fax • stalphon@globetrotter.net • No website

Location and Access
Located in the village's ele-
mentary school, on the
main street.

Hours
| Mon-Fri | 6:30pm-9pm |
| Sat | 1pm-4pm |

Prices
Can$1.25 per half hour
Can$2.50 per hour
No credit cards

Nearby Places to Visit
The Domaine des Chutes-du-
  Ruisseau-Creux, the
  Bonaventure River, salmon
  fishing, canoeing

CANADA, ST-EUSTACHE (QUEBEC)

C@fé-Informatique
32 rue Dubois • tel: +1 450-491-1754 • fax: +1 450-491-1754 •
cafe@cafe-informatique.qc.ca • www.cafe-informatique.qc.ca

Location and Access
Located near St-Eustache
  Hospital.
Bus: Ask for St-Eustache
  Hospital.
Nearest cross street is
  Arthur-Sauve Boulevard.

Hours
Mon-Thu	9am-9pm
Fri	9am-11pm
Sat	1pm-11pm

Prices
Can$3 per half hour
Can$6 per hour
No credit cards

CANADA, SIDNEY (BRITISH COLOMBIA)

Starting Point
#2 2490 Bevan Avenue • tel: +1 250-655-9383 •
fax: +1 250-655-9386 • start@klatu.com • www.klatu.com

Location and Access
Located near the pier on
  Bevan.
Bus: Many, ask for Sidney.
Nearest cross streets are
  Beacon Avenue and the
  Pat Bay Highway (17).

Hours
Mon-Wed &
  Fri-Sat   noon-7pm

Prices
Can$5.10 per half hour
Can$9 per hour
No credit cards

Nearby Places to Visit
Butchart Gardens, the City
  of Victoria, Butterfly
  World, the Royal BC
  Museum, Craighdoragh
  Castle, the Empress Hotel

Topley Elementary School
W Highway 16 • tel: +1 250-845-2522 • fax: +1 250-845-2528 •
nadclf@mail.bulkley.net • www.fortunecity.com/skyscraper/black/634

Location and Access
Nearest city is Houston.

Hours
Mon, Wed,
 Fri   9am-10:30 am
Tue & Thu 9am-10:30am &
               4:30pm-9:30pm

Prices
Free

Nearby Places to Visit
Norma Mays Collectibles,
 Sunset Lake, Babine Lake

Cyberland Cafe—257 Yonge Street, 2nd Floor •
tel: +1 416-955-9628 • fax: +1 416-955-9374 •
contact@cyberlandcafe.com • www.cyberlandcafe.com

Location and Access
Located opposite the
 Toronto Eaton Centre.
Bus: Tour buses, ask for
 Dundas Square.
Underground: Subway, ask
 for Dundas Square.
Trolley: TTC Trolley on King
 Street, ask for Yonge
 Street.
Nearest cross street is
 Dundas Street.

Hours
Mon-Wed &
 Sun   10:30am-11:30pm
Thu   10:30am-
               midnight
Fri   10:30am-1am
Sat   10:30am-1:30am

Prices
Can$5 per half hour
Can$9.99 per hour
V, MC, AmEx
Student discount available
 for multiple hours online

The CyberOffice Cafe Inc.

5855 Yonge Street • tel: +1 416-223-3100 • fax: +1 416-223-7574 • spire@cyberofficecafe.com • www.cyberofficecafe.com

Location and Access
Located in the Newtonbrook Plaza.
Bus: Yonge and Cummer routes, ask for Yonge and Cummer.
Underground: Yonge Subway, ask for Finch Avenue.
Nearest cross street is Finch Avenue.

Hours
Mon-Sat   8:30am-11pm
Sun   11am-7pm

Prices
Can$5 per half hour
Can$10 per hour
V, MC, AmEx
Student discount available for members

Insomnia Internet Bar/Cafe

563 Bloor Street West • tel: +1 416-588-3907 • fax: +1 416-588-0220 • daniel@insomniacafe.com • www.insomniacafe.com

Location and Access
Located downtown.
Bus: 5 lines, ask for Bathurst.
Underground: Ask for Bathurst.
Nearest cross street is Bathurst.

Hours
Mon-Wed &
  Sun   11am-2am
Thu-Sat   11am-4am

Prices
Can$4.50 per half hour
Can$9 per hour
V, MC, AmEx, DC

Nearby Places to Visit
Museum, planetarium, Insomnia, Shoe Musuem

CANADA, TRENTON, QUINTE WEST (ONTARIO)

CyberDome Internet Cafe
72 Dundas Street W • tel: +1 613-394-2888 • fax: +1 613-394-2888 •
info@cyberdome.net • www.cyberdome.net

Location and Access
Nearest big town is
  Belleville.
Located above the Salvation
  Army Thrift Store.
Nearest cross streets are
  Dundas & Division.

Hours
Mon-Sat   noon-9pm
Sun   noon-5pm

Prices
Can$2 per half hour
Can$4 per hour
No credit cards
Student discount available

Nearby Places to Visit
Loyalist Parkway,
  Harbourfront

CANADA, VANCOUVER (BRITISH COLUMBIA)

Digital U Cyber Cafe & Computing Centre
1595 West Broadway • tel: +1 604-731-1011 •
fax: +1 604-731-5003 • info@digital-u.com • www.digital-u.com

Location and Access
Located near Fir Street exit
  off the south end
  Granville Street Bridge.
Bus: Ask for Granville Street
  & West Broadway.
Nearest cross street is Fir
  Street.

Hours
Mon-Fri   9am-midnight
Sat   10am-1am
Sun   10am-midnight

Prices
Can$6-$9.50 per hour
V, MC

Nearby Places to Visit
Granville Island

CANADA, VANCOUVER (BRITISH COLUMBIA)

Kitsilano's Cyber-C@fe
3514 W 4th Street • tel: +1 604-737-0595 • fax: +1 604-733-7612 •
kitscafe@portal.ca • www.kitsilanoscybercafe.bc.ca

Location and Access
Located near Jericho Hostile
& University of British
Columbia.
Bus: 4th Avenue route, ask
for Collingwood.
Nearest cross street is Alma
Street.

Hours
Mon-Tue &
  Sat-Sun 8am-5pm
Wed-Fri 7am-6pm

Prices
Can$3.25 per half hour
Can$6 per hour
V

CANADA, VICTORIA (BRITISH COLUMBIA)

Cyber Station of Victoria Ltd.
1113 Blanchard Street • tel: +1 250-386-4687 •
fax: +1 250-383-8787 • cyberstation@cyber.bc.ca • www.cyber.bc.ca

Location and Access
Located near the Inner
Harbor.
Bus: Ask for any downtown
stop.
Train: E&N Dayliner, ask for
Esquimalt.
Nearest cross street is Fort
Street.

Hours
Mon-Fri 8:30am-10pm
Sat 10am-10pm
Sun 10am-5pm

Prices
Can$5.50 per half hour
Can$10 per hour
V, MC
Student discount available

Nearby Places to Visit
Royal BC Museum, Empress
Hotel, Miniature World, BC
Parliament Buildings,
Crystal Gardens, Beacon
Hill Park, Eaton's Centre

CANADA, VICTORIA (BRITISH COLUMBIA)

Victoria Cyber Cafe

1414 B Douglas Street • tel: +1 250-995-0175 •
fax: +1 250-995-2174 • questions@cybervic.com • www.cybervic.com

Location and Access
Located near City Hall.
Bus: To downtown, ask for
  Douglas Hotel.

Hours
Mon-Fri	10am-8pm
Sat	11am-7pm
Sun	noon-6pm
Mon-Sun	10am-10pm
	(summer hours)

Prices
Can$4.20 per half hour
Can$8 per hour
V, MC, AmEx
Student discount available

Nearby Places to Visit
Crystal Garden

CANADA, WAINWRIGHT (ALBERTA)

The Cyber Spot

#207 10 Street • tel: +1 780-842-6655 • fax: +1 780-842-6655 •
cyspot01@telusplanet.net • No website

Location and Access
Located near the Clock
  Tower.
Nearest cross street is 2nd
  Avenue.

Hours
Mon-Thu &	
Sun	11am-10pm
Fri-Sat	11am-midnight

Prices
Can$4 per half hour
Can$6 per hour
No credit cards
Student discount available
  with Project Excel cards

Nearby Places to Visit
Camp Wainwright (military
  base)

CANADA, WINNIPEG (MANITOBA)

Networkx, Internet Resource Center Inc.
510 Portage Avenue • tel: +1 204-779-9000 • fax: +1 204-779-9001 • info@networkx.net • www.networkx.net

Location and Access
Located near University of Winnipeg.
Nearest cross street is Colony.

Hours
Mon-Thu	10am-midnight
Fri-Sat	10am-2am
Sun	2pm-10pm

Prices
Can$5 per half hour
Can$7 per hour
V, AmEx
Student discount available

Nearby Places to Visit
The Forks Market

MEXICO, APIZACO (TLAXCALA)

ATX Automatizaciones CyberCafe
911, 5 de Mayo • tel: +52 241 76600 • fax: +52 241 70746 • cafe@apizaco.podernet.com.mx • http://atx.com.mx

Location and Access
Located near Hotel La Posada.
Nearest cross street is Emilio Carranza.

Hours
| Mon-Fri | 9am-7pm |
| Sat | 10am-2pm |

Prices
Mex$20 per half hour
Mex$35 per hour
No credit cards

264

Netzone Dr.Z's Internet, Café & Bar

Boulevard Lazaro Cardenas s/n • tel: +52 114 35390 • No fax •
netzone1@cabonet.net.mx • www.cabonet.net.mx

Location and Access
Located in front of a gas
  station.
Bus: Aguila, ask for gas
  station.

Hours
Mon-Sat   9am-6pm

Prices
Mex$75 per half hour
Mex$100 per hour
No credit cards
Student discount available

El Valle de la Luna Maya—Ecological Reef Vacation

Resort—km 35 Carrettera Mahahual-Punta Herrero, Othon P. Blanco •
tel: +52 (01) 983 23948 • fax: +52 (01) 983 23948 •
lunamaya@astro.net.mx or lunamaya@netscape.net • No website

Location and Access
Located near Caribbean
  Coral Reef and the
  Chinchorro's Atoll.
Bus: Combi Chetumal-
  Mahahual-Punta Herrero,
  ask for El Valle de la Luna
  Maya (km 35).
Nearest cross street is where
  the cruise ships dock at El
  Uvero.

Hours
Mon-Sun   10am-midnight

Prices
Mex$20 per half hour
Mex$40 per hour
V, MC, AmEx, DC

Nearby Places to Visit
Sian'Ka'an Biosphere
  Reserve, Bacalar Lagoon,
  archeological Mayan sites
  of Muyil, Cobá, Tulum,
  Kounlinch, and Dzibanché

MEXICO, CHIHUAHUA (CHIHUAHUA)

Cybercafe Canaco

1800 Av. Cuauhtemoc • tel: +52 14 16 00 00 •
fax: +52 14 15 19 28 • cfn@infosel.net.mx • No website

Location and Access
Located near the Municipal
Park.

Nearby Places to Visit
Historical Center

Hours

Mon-Fri	9am-2pm & 4pm-7pm
Sat	9am-1pm

Prices
Mex$10 per half hour
Mex$20 per hour
No credit cards

MEXICO, CUERNAVACA (MORELOS)

Axon Cyber Cafe

129-B Av. Cuauhtemoc • tel: +52 73 12 85 25 •
fax: +52 73 12 85 25 • axon@axon.com.mx • www.axon.com.mx

Location and Access
Located near the Hotel
Jacarandas & Hosteria Las
Quintas.

Bus: 8, 11, 14, ask for the
Hotel and Hostel.
Nearest cross street is Av.
Diaz Ordaz.

Hours

Mon-Fri	9am-9pm
Sat	10am-8pm

Prices
Mex$20 per half hour
Mex$40 per hour
V, MC, AmEx
Student discount available
on Saturday

Nearby Places to Visit
Plaza Cuernavaca,
Teopanzolco Pyramid,
downtown

MEXICO, FRACC, LOS PIRULES, TLALNEPANTLA (ESTADO DE MEXICO)

CyberSchool—102-B, Cerro de Cempoaltepetl •
tel: +52 (0)1 5 370 8801 • fax: +52 (0)1 5 370 8801 •
cyber_school@fcmail.com • www.skyscraper.fortunecity.com/gigo/489

Location and Access
Located near Supermarket
  Aurrera Pirules and the
  Indoamericano College.
Bus: Available.
Nearest cross street is
  Periferico Norte.

Prices
Mex$20 per half hour
Mex$20 per hour
No credit cards
Student discount available

Hours
Mon-Fri   9am-9pm
Sat   11am-8pm

MEXICO, GUADALAJARA (JALISCO)

Cybercafe Video Beer—773-203 Lòpez Cotilla, 1st floor •
tel: +52 3 826 3771 • fax: +52 3 826 5610 •
cybercafe@internet-cafe.com.mx • www.internet-cafe.com.mx

Location and Access
Phone for directions.

Nearby Places to Visit
Guadalajara historic area,
University and Cultural
Museum

Hours
Mon-Sat   10am-10pm

Prices
Mex$10 per half hour
Mex$20 per hour
No credit cards

MEXICO, HERMOSILLO (SONORA)

Arroba Cafe-Internet—Boulevard Rodriguez No. 96 Col.
Centro • tel: +52 62 14 50 70 • fax: +52 62 14 53 50 •
cafe@hermosillo.net • www.cafe-arroba.com.mx

Location and Access
Nearest big town is Cd
  Obregon.
Located opposite Kentucky
  Fried Chicken.
Bus: Boulevard, ask for
  Garmendia.
Nearest cross street is
  Garmendia.

Hours
Mon-Sat   9am-11pm
Sun   4pm-11pm

Prices
Mex$15 per half hour
Mex$30 per hour
V, MC, AmEx

MEXICO, JEREZ DE GARCIA SALINAS (ZACATECAS)

Cibercafe of Jerez—Paseo Del Poeta #20, Fracc. R.L.V. •
tel: + 52 (91) 494 54013 • fax: +52 (91) 494 54573 •
viajesam@logicnet.com.mx • www.logicnet.com.mx/~viajesam

Location and Access
Located opposite the
  General Hospital of Jerez.
Bus: Municipal, Greyhound,
  Mexicana, and Taesa lines,
  ask for General Hospital.
Nearest cross street is the
  exit off the highway to
  Guadalajara, to the south
  of Jerez.

Hours
Mon-Sun   8am-10pm

Prices
US$2 per half hour
US$2 per hour
No credit cards
Student discount available

Nearby Places to Visit
The Thermal Waters of
  Caxan, the city and airport
  of Zacatecas, Balneario
  Las Margaritas, La Sierra
  de los Cardos

Baja Net
430 Madero • tel: +52 112 59380 • fax: +52 112 59380 •
info@baja.net.mx • www.baja.net.mx

Location and Access
Located near Zócalo.
Bus: Madero Street routes,
ask for El Aramburu.
Nearest cross street is
Malecón.

Hours
Mon-Sat   8am-8pm

Prices
Mex$30 per half hour
Mex$60 per hour

V, MC
Student discount available
with identification from a
Mexican school

Nearby Places to Visit
All the beaches from La Paz
to Pichilinge, Las
Ventanas, Cabo San Lucas,
San José del Cabo,
Mulege, Pescadero, La
Lobera, El Bajo sea
mount

Cofynet Internet Cafe—Av. 1 No. 360 x 60 and Prol. Montejo.
Col. Gonzalo Guerrero • tel: +52 99 44 74 41 • fax: +52 99 44 74 41 •
cyber@cofynet.com • www.cofynet.com

Location and Access
Located near Sam's Club.
Bus: Tapetes, Carefour, ask
for Sam's Club.
Nearest cross street is 60 or
Prol. Montejo.

Hours
Mon-Sat   10am-midnight
Sun   4pm-midnight

Prices
Mex$10 per half hour 10am-
5pm; Mex$15 per half
hour 5pm-midnight
Mex$20 per hour 10am-5pm;
Mex$30 per hour 5pm-
midnight
No credit cards
Student discount available

Nearby Places to Visit
La Gran Plaza mall

MEXICO, MEXICO CITY (DISTRITO FEDERAL)

Ciberpuerto—238 Alfonso Reyes •
tel: +52 5 286 4744/286 0868 • fax: +52 5 286 0861 •
ciberpuerto@ciberpuerto.com • www.ciberpuerto.com

Location and Access
Located near Colonia
  Condesa.
Bus: Insurgentes Lane, ask
  for Baja California.
Underground: Brown (7),
  ask for Chilpancingo.
Nearest cross street is
  Insurgentes Ave.

Hours
Mon-Fri   10am-8pm
Sat   11am-3pm

Prices
Mex$20 per half hour
Mex$40 per hour
V, MC, AmEx, DC

Nearby Places to Visit
Coffee shops, restaurants,
  parks

MEXICO, MEXICO CITY (DISTRITO FEDERAL)

Internet Station—130 Arquimedes St. local #20 Colonia
Polanco • tel: +52 5 280 60 91 • fax: +52 5 280 60 91 •
isoff@altavista.net • www.amcc.org/internet-station.html

Location and Access
Located near Metro Polanco.
Underground: Metro, ask for
  Polanco.
Nearest cross street is
  Horacio.

Hours
Mon-Sat   11:30am-8pm

Prices
Mex$20 per half hour
Mex$30 per hour
No credit cards

Nearby Places to Visit
Chapultepec

ShareWeb CyberCafe—573-C Av. Madero Ote.,
Centro Histórico • tel: +52 43 29 46 14 • fax: +52 43 18 02 44 •
shareweb@morelia.teesa.com •
http://morelia.teesa.com/~shareweb/index.html

Location and Access
Located near the Library of
  University Michoacana,
  the pharmacy La Perla,
  and the hotels.
Bus: All red buses, ask for
  the Santander Bank.

Prices
Mex\$10 per half hour
Mex\$20 per hour
No credit cards
Student discount available

Nearby Places to Visit
The Tarascas, Centro
  Historico

Hours
Mon-Sat   10am-10pm
Sun   2pm-10pm

CyberNet Cafe-Bar—101 Juarez Avenida Downtown •
tel: +52 951 4 80 40 • fax: + 52 951 4 80 40 •
cnet@oax1.telmex.net.mx • www.cybernetcafebar.com.mx

Location and Access
Located near Florencia
  Travel Agency.
Bus: Any route traveling
  through Avenida Juarez,
  ask for Esquina de Avenida
  Juarez e Independencia.
Nearest cross streets are
  Independencia Avenida &
  Morelos Avenida.

Hours
Mon-Sat   10am-10pm

Prices
Mex\$15 per half hour
Mex\$30 per hour
No credit cards

Nearby Places to Visit
Santo Domingo Church &
  Museum

MEXICO, PUEBLA (PUEBLA)

Cafe Internet El Naveg@nte—2939 Avenida 15 de Mayo •
tel: +52 22 49 5045/49 5194/30 1599 • fax: +52 22 49 5258 •
afloresf@mail.mnag.com.mx • www.mnag.com.mx

Location and Access
Nearest big city is Mexico
    City.
Located near Grupo ACIR
    and Plaza San Pedro.
Nearest cross street is
    Boulevard Norte.

Hours
Mon-Sat   8am-10pm

Prices
Mex$20 per hour (minimum)
V, MC, AmEx, DC
Student discount available

MEXICO, PUEBLA (PUEBLA)

La Noria Cafe Internet—45 Poniente 1937 Local 3 •
tel: +52 22 430926 • No fax • cafeinternet@compuserve.com.mx •
www.geocities.com/SiliconValley/Pines/5213

Location and Access
Located near Sam's, Vips,
    Entretenicentro La Noria.
Nearest cross street is
    Circuito Interior at Sam's.

Hours
Mon-Sat   11am-2pm &
                5pm-9pm

Prices
Mex$15 per half hour
Mex$30 per hour
No credit cards

Centro Comunicaciones

No 1 Calle Timon, Local A • tel: +52 322 12177 •
fax: +52 322 12178 • ccpv@pvmet.com.mx • No website

Location and Access

Located near El Faro light-
house.
Bus: Marina, Vidafel, ask for
Paseo De Marina and
Timon.
Nearest cross street is Paseo
De Marina.

Hours

Mon-Fri   9am-7pm
Sat   9am-2pm

Prices

Mex$23 per half hour
Mex$45 per hour
AmEx
Student discount available

Nearby Places to Visit

Marina Golf Course,
Aquarium, Vidafel Water
Park

The Net House

232 Ignacio L. Vallarta • tel: +52 322 2 69 53 • fax: +52 322 2 69 53 •
jcoates@the-net-house.com • www.the-net-house.com

Location and Access

Located two blocks from the
beach.
Bus: All buses stop at the
corner, ask for Cardenas
and Vallarta Streets.
Nearest cross street is
Cardenas Street.

Hours

Mon-Sun   7am-2am

Prices

Mex$23 per half hour
Mex$45 per hour
No credit cards
Student discount available
for locals

Nearby Places to Visit

Too numerous to mention

MEXICO, SAN MIGUEL DE ALLENDE (GUANAJUATO)

Estacion Internet

11 Recreo Street • tel: +52 415 2 73 12 • fax: +52 415 2 61 53 •
merlin@mpsnet.com.mx • http://sma.mpsnet.com.mx

Location and Access
Located near Plaza
  Principal.
Nearest cross street is
  Correo Street.

Hours
Mon-Sat   9am-8pm
Sun   9am-2pm

Prices
Mex$30 per half hour
Mex$60 per hour
No credit cards
Student discount available

Nearby Places to Visit
The whole downtown area

MEXICO, TUXTEPEC (OAXACA)

cafe-tuxcom—Av. 3 Calle 2 Costa Verde •

tel: +52 287 52339/53706 • fax: +52 287 5339 •
biland@tuxcom.net.mx or tux@rocketmail.com • www.tuxcom.net.mx

Location and Access
Located near Fettiche Disco.
Bus: All of them, ask for
  Chedraui.

Hours
Mon-Wed   9am-8pm
Thu-Sat   9am-midnight
Sun   9am-3pm

Prices
Mex$15 per hour (minimum)
V, MC, AmEx, DC, D ($10
  minimum)
Student discount available
  sometimes

Nearby Places to Visit
Places of natural or historical interest, churches,
  pyramids, rivers

Soapy's Station—102 Gilberto Concepcion de Gracia •
tel: +1 787-289-0344 • fax: +1 787-289-0345 •
skytalk@isla.net • www.skytalkwest.com

Location and Access
Located near Wyndham
  Hotel and Pier 3.
Bus: Ask for Bus Station.
Nearest cross street is Calle
  Tanca.

No credit cards
Student discount available

Nearby Places to Visit
All of Old San Juan

Hours
Mon-Sun   9am-midnight

Prices
US$5 per half hour
US$10 per hour

Hard Drive Cafe
2492 Wedgewood Drive, Suite B • tel: +1 330-733-5282 •
fax: +1 330-733-5282 • mack@thehdcafe.com • www.thehdcafe.com

Location and Access
Nearest cross street is Route
  91, Canton Road.

Student discount available

Nearby Places to Visit
National Rock-n-Roll Hall of
  Fame, Inventors Hall-of-
  Fame, Football Hall-of-
  Fame, Sea World, Geauga
  Lake Amusement Park

Hours
Mon-Fri   7:30am-9pm
Sat   8:30am-9pm
Sun   11am-7pm

Prices
US$3 per half hour
US$6 per hour
V, MC, D

USA, ALBANY (NEW YORK)

C@fe Web
1040 Madison Avenue • tel: +1 518-438-4826 •
fax: +1 518-438-4826 • kate@cafe-web.com • www.cafe-web.com

Location and Access
Located next door to the
  Madison Theater.
Nearest cross streets are
  Allen Street and Lancaster.

Hours
Mon-Thu   noon-10pm
Fri   noon-midnight
Sat   11am-midnight
Sun   11am-10pm

Prices
US$4 per half hour
US$8 per hour
No credit cards
Student discount available
  6pm-9pm

Nearby Places to Visit
New York State Museum

USA, ALPINE (TEXAS)

caffe.net
201 E. Holland Ave. • tel: +1 915-837-7255 • fax: +1 915-837-2924 •
wired@caffe.net • www.caffe.net

Location and Access
Nearest cross street is N.
  5th (Fort Davis Highway).

Hours
Mon &
  Wed-Fri   2pm-8pm
Tue   3pm-8pm

Prices
US$5 per half hour
US$8 per hour
V, MC, D

Nearby Places to Visit
Big Bend National Park, Fort
  Davis National Historic
  Site, McDonald
  Observatory, Marfa Mystery
  Lights

ORTRACKM.net, Inc.

517-A High Street • tel: +1 417-778-7523 • fax: +1 417-778-7523 •
ortrackm@ortrackm.missouri.org • http://ortrackm.missouri.org

Location and Access
Located across the street
from Wallace & Owens.
Nearest cross street is
Highway 160 West.

Hours

Mon-Fri	8am-5pm
Sat	8am-noon

Prices
US$20 per month prepaid
US$100 per 6 months pre-
paid

Nearby Places to Visit
Eleven Point River, Greer
Spring, Falling Springs,
Cane Bluff, Riverton,
Grand Gulf, Mammoth
Spring

Tea-House of the Net

1472 S. Euclid • tel: +1 714-781-2300 • No fax •
charlie@tea-house.com • www.tea-house.com

Location and Access
Located near Disneyland.
Bus: 39, ask for Euclid and
Cerritos.
Nearest cross street is
Cerritos.

Hours

Mon-Fri	noon-9pm
Sat	10am-6pm

Prices
US$3 per half hour
US$6 per hour
No credit cards

Nearby Places to Visit
Knott's Berry Farm

Surf City, an Internet Cafe

415 L Street • tel: +1 907-279-7877 • fax: +1 888-453-0681 • surfcity@surfcafe.com • www.surfcafe.com

Location and Access
Located across from Simon & Seaforts Restaurant.
Bus: Anchorage Tour Bus, ask for 4th Avenue Theater.
Nearest cross street is 4th Avenue.

Hours
Mon-Fri   7am-midnight
Sat-Sun   10am-midnight

Prices
US$3.60 per half hour
US$7.20 per hour
No credit cards
Student discount available

Nearby Places to Visit
4th Avenue Theater, 4th Avenue street vendors, Great Alaskan Experience Theater, Anchorage Museum of Art, 5th Avenue Mall

---

Wallywerks Computer Education & Entertainment Emporium—854 9th Street, #204 • tel: +1 707-825-8803 • fax: +1 707-825-8957 • wally@wallywerks.com • www.wallywerks.com

Location and Access
Located near the Plaza.
Bus: Numbers vary, ask for the Plaza in Arcata.
Nearest cross street is H Street.

Hours
Mon-Sat   1pm-9pm
Sun   1pm-7pm

Prices
US$2 per half hour
US$4 per hour (US$1 Happy Hour 5-6pm Mon-Fri)
No credit cards

Nearby Places to Visit
The beach, redwood trees, wildlife preserves, shops, restaurants, Humboldt State University

RedLight Cafe

553 Amsterdam Avenue • tel: +1 404-874-7828 • No fax •
redlight@mindspring.com • www.redlightcafe.com

Location and Access
Located near Piedmont Park.
Bus: 27, ask for Piedmont
Park.
Subway: Ask for mid-
town/10th Street.
Nearest cross street is
Monroe Drive.

Hours
Tue-Sun   6pm-2am

Prices
US$2.50 per half hour
US$5 per hour
V, MC, D
Student discount available

Nearby Places to Visit
Carter Center

The Strand—A Cybercafe—105 East Lombard Street •

tel: +1 410-625-8944 • fax: +1 410-625-4676 •
info@thestrandcafe.com • www.thestrandcafe.com

Location and Access
Located near Baltimore's
Inner Harbor.
Bus: Many, ask for Inner
Harbor.
Metro Subway: Ask for
Charles Center.
Light Rail: Ask for
Convention Center.
Nearest cross street is
Calvert Street.

Hours
Mon-Thu   7am-9pm
Fri   7am-11pm
Sat   8am-11pm
Sun   8am-9pm

Prices
US$4 per half hour
US$8 per hour
V, MC, AmEx

Nearby Places to Visit
National Aquarium,
Columbus Center

USA, BATAVIA (ILLINOIS)

CyberHawk's Internet Cafe and Gaming Center
158 West Wilson Street • tel: +1 630-761-4440 •
fax: +1 630-761-3377 • info@CyberHawksCafe.com •
www.CyberHawksCafe.com

Location and Access
Located near Walgreens drug store.

Train: Chicago Metro Rail, ask for Geneva.
Nearest cross streets are Randall Road and Wilson Street.

Hours
Mon-Wed	8am-9pm
Thu	8am-10pm
Fri	8am-midnight
Sat	9am-midnight
Sun	9am-8pm

Prices
US$5 per half hour
US$10 per hour
V, MC, AmEx

Nearby Places to Visit
All Chicago area attractions

USA, BEDFORD (OHIO)

Cyber Pete's Internet C@fe
665 Broadway • tel: +1 440-439-5328 • fax: +1 440-439-5427 •
cyberpetes@hotmail.com • www.cyber-pete.com

Location and Access
Bus: Available.
Nearest cross street is Tarbell.

Hours
Mon-Tue & Thu	6am-11pm
Wed-Thu	6am-midnight
weekend	6am Fri-9pm Sun

Prices
US$4 per half hour
US$8 per hour
V, MC

Nearby Places to Visit
Rock and Roll Hall of Fame

Café Internet—133 SW Century Drive, Suite 204 • tel: +1 541-318-8802 • fax: +1 541-318-8841 • cafeinternet@bendcable.com • www.cafeinternet-bend.com

Location and Access
Located near Mt. Bachelor
  Ski Resort.
Nearest cross street is
  Colorado.

Hours

Mon-Thu	10am-7pm
Fri	10am-9pm
Sat	10am-6pm
Sun	11am-4pm

Prices
US$4 per half hour
US$7 per hour
No credit cards

Nearby Places to Visit
Cascade Mountains, High
  Lakes, the High Desert
  Museum, Smith Rocks
  climbing area

Cafe Internet (UC Telecommunications Company)—2569 Telegraph Avenue • tel: +1 510-649-6087 • fax: +1 510-540-5579 • pmservice@transbay.net • www.transbay.net

Location and Access
Located near University of
  California at Berkeley.
Bus: AC Transit 40, 43, ask
  for Parker Street or Blake
  Street.
Underground: BART (Bay
  Area Rapid Transit), ask
  for Berkeley Station.
Train: Amtrak, ask for
  Berkeley Station, then use
  AC Transit bus 40 or taxi,
  or take a 20-minute walk.

Nearest cross street is Blake
  Street.

Hours
Mon-Sat   10am-6pm

Prices
US$5 per half hour
US$7 per hour
V, MC, AmEx, D

Nearby Places to Visit
Tilden Regional Park,
  Oakland, San Francisco

Tie Dye Shop & CyberCafe

176 Main Street • tel: +1 607-723-2456 • fax: +1 607-771-1084 • mimi@stny.lrun.com • www.tiedyecafe.com

Location and Access
Nearest cross street is
  Laurel Avenue.

Hours
Tue   11am-11pm
Wed-Thu   11am-midnight
Fri-Sat   11am-1am
Sun   noon-6pm

Prices
US$3 per half hour
US$6 per hour
V, MC, D

Nearby Places to Visit
Carousels

CyberPlayce

7079 Overland Road • tel: +1 208-377-8701 • fax: +1 208-377-8745 • admin@cyberplayce.com • www.cyberplayce.com

Location and Access
Located near McDonald's &
  Taco Bell.
Bus: Boise Urban Stages,
  ask for Overland & Cole.

Nearest cross streets are
  Cole Road and Interstate
  84 exit 50B.

Hours
Mon-Fri   6am-midnight
weekend   9am Sat-
           midnight Sun

Prices
US$3 per half hour
US$6 per hour
V, MC, AmEx, D
Student discount available
  during holidays

Nearby Places to Visit
The mountains, Idaho State
  Capitol, Boise River,
  white-water rafting

USA, BOSTON (MASSACHUSETTS)

Designs for Living—Netcafe
52 Queensberry Street • tel: +1 617-536-6150 •
fax: +1 617-536-6150 • designs@mynet.com • www.mynet.com

Location and Access
Located near Fenway Park
and Museum of Fine Arts.
Bus: 55, ask for Queensberry
and Jersey Streets.
Underground: Green line,
ask for Kenmore Square.
Nearest cross street is
Jersey Street.

Hours
Mon-Tue &
Thu-Fri 7am-9pm

Wed	7am-noon
Sat	8am-9pm
Sun	9am-9pm

Prices
US$4 per half hour
US$8 per hour
V, MC, D
Student discount available
after 6pm

Nearby Places to Visit
Isabella Stewart Gardner
Museum

USA, BUFFALO (NEW YORK)

Common Grounds Internet Cafe
5759 Main Street • tel: +1 716-632-5282 • No fax •
spherman@cgicafe.com • http://espresso.cgicafe.com/homepage.html

Location and Access
Located near Mobil Station.
Bus: 48, 66, ask for stop
right in front of the Plaza
by Precision Bicycles.
Nearest cross street is
Garrison Road.

Hours
Mon-Sat 1pm-9pm

Prices
US$4.80 per half hour
US$7.50 per hour
V, MC, AmEx, DC, D
Student discount available

Nearby Places to Visit
Niagara Falls

USA, CAMBRIDGE (MASSACHUSETTS)

Cybersmith
42 Church Street • tel: +1 617-492-5857 • fax: +1 617-661-4214 •
hvd_gm@cybersmith.com • www.cybersmith.com

Location and Access
Located near Harvard
  University.
Bus: Ask for Harvard Square.
Underground: Red Line, ask
  for Harvard Station.
Nearest cross streets are
  Brattle & Mass Avenue.

Hours
Mon-Thu	10am-10pm
Fri-Sat	10am-midnight
Sun	9am-8pm

Prices
US$2.50 per half hour
US$4.95 per hour
V, MC, AmEx, DC, D
Student discount available

Nearby Places to Visit
Charles River—the site for
  the Head of the Charles
  boat race each fall

USA, CAPE CORAL (FLORIDA)

Coffee Haus—2323 Del Prado Boulevard #6A •
tel: +1 941-573-1882 • fax: +1 941-772-4217 •
ellie55@hotmail.com • www.freeyellow.com/members4/coffeehaus

Location and Access
Located near Midpoint
  Bridge.
Nearest cross street is
  Veterans Memorial
  Parkway.

Hours
Mon-Thu	8am-10pm
Fri	8am-11pm
Sat	9am-11pm
Sun	9am-6pm

Prices
US$3.50 per half hour
US$7 per hour
V, MC, DC, D

Coffee & @ BYTE Cyber Cafe—235 West Cocoa Beach •
Causeway • tel: +1 407-459-2233 • No fax •
webmistress@coffeeandabyte.com • www.coffeeandabyte.com

Location and Access
Located near Ron Jon Surf
  Shop and Cocoa Beach.
Nearest cross street is A1A.

V, MC, AmEx, DC, D
Student discount available

Hours
Mon-Thu   10am-11pm
Fri-Sat   10am-midnight
Sun   noon-5pm

Prices
US$4 per half hour
US$7 per hour

JaVa's Cyber Espresso Bar
1173 N. Hamilton Road • tel: +1 614-418-9228 •
fax: +1 614-855-4712 • erich@javas.com • www.javas.com

Location and Access
Located in Vista Plaza
  Center.
No public transportation but
  near Port Columbus
  Airport.
Nearest cross street is Morse
  Road.

Hours
Mon-Thu   6:30am-10:30pm
Fri   6:30am-midnight
Sat   8am-midnight
Sun   8am-9pm

Prices
US$3 per half hour
US$6 per hour
V, MC, AmEx, D

Downtown Cyber Cafe

1016 Oak Street • tel: +1 501-329-9669 • No fax •
downtown.deli@conwaycorp.net • www.bcity.com/downtown_deli

Location and Access
Located across from Bobby's
  Antiques near Toad Suck
  Plaza.

Nearest cross street is
  Chesnut Street.

Hours
Phone for hours

Prices
US$2.50 per half hour
US$5 per hour
V, MC

CyberCafé at the MAC

3120 McKinney Avenue • tel: +1 214-953-1212 •
fax: +1 214-953-1873 • info@the-mac.org • www.the-mac.org

Location and Access
Located near Hard Rock
  Cafe.
Train: 21 Dart Rail & 39

  Trolley, exit at the cafe.
Nearest cross streets are
  Lemmon Avenue or Hall
  Street.

Hours
Wed-Sat   11am-10pm
Sun   1pm-5pm

Prices
Free

Nearby Places to Visit
Quadrangle, Trolley Barn,
  McKinney Avenue, the
  Dallas Museum of Art,
  downtown Dallas

USA, DAVIE (FLORIDA)

Cybernation Internet Cafe and Computer Stores
2235 South University Drive • tel: +1 954-236-8787 •
fax: +1 954-236-6099 • glenn@cybernation.net • www.cybernation.net

Location and Access
Located in Nova University.
Bus: Ask for Oakland and
  Federal Highway.
Nearest cross street is
  Federal Highway/US-1.

Prices
US$2.50 per half hour
US$5 per hour
V, MC, AmEx, DC, D
Student discount available

Hours
Mon-Fri   9:30am-6:30pm
Sat   10am-7pm
Sun   11am-6pm

USA, DELRAY BEACH (FLORIDA)

Z Business Center's Internet Cafe—125 South Congress
Avenue • tel: +1 561-266-8520 (toll free in USA +1 800-668-3968) •
fax: +1 561-266-8505 • info@zcenter.com • www.zcenter.com

Location and Access
Train: TRI-rail, ask for
  Atlantic Avenue.

Prices
US$6.50 per half hour
US$12 per hour
V, MC, AmEx
Student discount available

Hours
Mon-Fri   7:30am-7:30pm
Sat   8am-7pm
Sun   noon-5pm

Cafe@Netherworld

1278 Pennsylvania • tel: +1 303-861-8638 • fax: +1 303-861-0416 •
info@Netherworld.com • www.netherworld.com

Location and Access
Located near the Capitol.
Bus: RTD, ask for the
    Capitol.
Nearest cross street is 13th.

Hours
Mon-Thu   11am-2am
Fri-Sun   11am-5am

Prices
US$2 per half hour
US$4 per hour
V, MC, D
Student discount available

Nearby Places to Visit
Colorado Capitol, Denver Art
    Museum, Denver Mint,
    Denver Library

Majordomo's Net Cafe

1401 Ogden Street • tel: +1 303-830-0442 • fax: +1 303-830-7034 •
info@majordomos.com • www.majordomos.com

Location and Access
Located in historic Capitol
    Hill.
Bus: Downing Street (10),
    12th Avenue (12), Colfax
    Avenue (15), ask for
    Colfax and Ogden.
Nearest cross street is
    Colfax Avenue.

Hours
Mon-Fri   7:30am-9pm
Sat   7:30am-7pm
Sun   11am-7pm

Prices
US$6 per half hour
US$12 per hour
V, MC, D
Student discount available

Nearby Places to Visit
State Capitol Building, the
    Denver Arm Museum, the
    new Denver Public Library,
    the Denver Zoo, the
    Denver Museum of Natural
    History

CyberJon's, the Durham Internet C@fe
3401 University Drive • tel: +1 919-493-3685 •
fax: +1 919-403-1597 • pepper@vnet.net • No website

Location and Access
Located near Durham
　Academy.
Bus: Ask for Academy Road
　at University Drive.
Nearest cross street is
　Academy Road.

Hours
Mon-Sat　7am-10pm
Sun　　　1pm-8pm

Prices
US$6 per half hour
US$12 per hour
V, MC AmEx, D

Nearby Places to Visit
Duke University, Sara P.
　Duke Gardens, North
　Carolina Museum of Life
　and Science, Bennett
　Place, Duke Homestead,
　Staggville Plantation

CyberLink Cafe
250 West Water Street • tel: +1 607-734-0161 • fax: +1 607-737-1028 •
info@cyberlinkcafe.com • www.cyberlinkcafe.com

Location and Access
Located near Elmira College.
Bus: Available.
Nearest cross street is
　College Avenue.

Hours
Mon-Thu　7am-8pm
Fri　　　　7am-10pm
Sat　　　　9am-10pm
Sun　　　10am-6pm

Prices
US$3 per half hour
US$5 per hour
No credit cards
Student discount available

Nearby Places to Visit
Corning Glass Center,
　Soaring Museum, Harris
　Hill (gliders)

USA, EUGENE (OREGON)

Sip 'n Surf Cybercafe

99 W. 10th, Suite 115 • No tel • No fax • cafe@sipnsurf.com •
www.sipnsurf.com

Location and Access
Located near downtown
Eugene Mall in the new
Atrium building.

Bus: Ask for Downtown
Eugene Main Station.

Hours
Mon-Fri   7am-6pm
Sat   10am-3pm

Prices
US$3 per half hour
US$6 per hour
No credit cards

Nearby Places to Visit
University of Oregon,
Oregon Coast

USA, FAIRBANKS (ALASKA)

Fairnet, Inc.

1512 Cowles Street • tel: +1 907-488-5001 • No fax •
fyfnet@uaf.edu • www.fairnet.org

Location and Access
Located near Lathrop High
School.

Bus: From Fairbanks
International Airport, take
the Blue Line to Airport
and Barnett.
Nearest cross street is
Airport.

Hours
Mon-Sat   10am-8pm

Prices
Free

USA, FAIRBANKS (ALASKA)

Fairnet, Inc.
1620 Washington Drive • tel: +1 907-488-5001 • No fax •
fyfnet@uaf.edu • www.fairnet.org

Location and Access
Located near Executive
  Estates Housing.
Bus: From the Fairbanks
  International Airport take
  the Yellow Line to Fred
  Meyers on Airport and
  University Avenue, then
  walk two blocks.
Nearest cross street is
  Airport and College.

Hours
Mon-Fri   1pm-5pm

Prices
Free

USA, FLAGSTAFF (ARIZONA)

Bookman's Cyber Cafe—1520 S. Riordan Ranch Road •
tel: +1 520-774-0005 • fax: +1 520-774-0396 •
bookmans@flagstaff.az.us • www.bookmans.com

Location and Access
Located near Northern
  Arizona University.
Nearest cross street is
  Milton/University.

Hours
Mon-Sat   9am-10pm
Sun   10am-9pm

Prices
US$3 per half hour
US$6 per hour
V, MC, AmEx, DC, D

Nearby Places to Visit
Grand Canyon, Meteor Crater

Cybernation Internet Cafe and Computer Stores

2635 East Oakland Park Boulevard • tel: +1 954-630-0223 •
fax: +1 954-630-0211 • glenn@cybernation.net • www.cybernation.net

Location and Access
Located near the Merrill
  Lynch office building and
  Sun Bank.
Bus: Ask for Oakland and
  Federal Highway.
Nearest cross street is
  Federal Highway/US-1.

Hours
Mon-Fri   9:30am-6:30pm
Sat   10am-7pm
Sun   11am-6pm

Prices
US$2.50 per half hour
US$5 per hour
V, MC, AmEx, DC, D
Student discount available

Nearby Places to Visit
The beach

The Cyb@r.club at Piere's Entertainment Center

5629 St. Joe Road • tel: +1 219-486-1979 • fax: +1 219-486-6066 •
postmaster@cybarclub.com • www.cybarclub.com

Location and Access
Located in the Marketplace
  of Canterbury.
Bus: Ft. Wayne Public Bus
  System, ask for
  Marketplace of Canterbury.
Nearest cross street is St.
  Joe Center Road.

Hours
Mon-Sat   7pm-3am
Sun   7pm-12:30am

Prices
Free

Nearby Places to Visit
The Coliseum, Wizards
  Stadium, Indiana-Purdue
  University

USA, FORT WORTH (TEXAS)

Rodeo Steakhouse
1309 Calhoun Street • tel: +1 817-332-1288 • fax: +1 817 332-4723 •
info@CyberRodeo.com • www.CyberRodeo.com

Location and Access
Located near Fort Worth/Tarrant County Convention Center.
Nearest cross streets are I-35 West and I-30.

Hours
Tue-Sat   4pm-10pm

Prices
US$5 per half hour (minimum)

US$5 per hour
V, MC, Amex, D

Nearby Places to Visit
Sundance Square, Fort Worth Zoo, Culture District, Water Gardens, Billy Bob's Texas, Stockyards, Fort Worth Rodeo, Tarantula Train

---

USA, GEORGETOWN (TEXAS)

Java Net, a Christian Coffeehouse
3010 Williams Drive #12 • tel: +1 512-819-9399 •
fax: +1 512-819-9893 • javanet@java-net.com • www.java-net.com

Location and Access
Located on the way to Sun City, 1 mile west of I-35 in Williamsburg Village Shopping Center.

Hours
Mon-Thu   7:30am-10pm
Fri-Sat   8am-11pm

Prices
US$3.50 per half hour
US$6.95 per hour
V, MC, AmEx

Nearby Places to Visit
The Square, Inner Space Caverns, Southwestern University, Sun City

USA, GRAND RAPIDS (MICHIGAN)

Four Friends Coffeehouse and Cyberlounge
136 Monroe Center • tel: +1 616-456-5356 • No fax •
4friends@iserv.net • www.iserv.net/~4friends

Location and Access
Located at the intersection
of Pearl Street and Monroe
Avenue.

Hours
Mon-Thu   7am-10pm
Fri   7am-midnight
Sat   9:30am-midnight

Prices
US$2 per half hour
US$4 per hour

No credit cards

Nearby Places to Visit
Amway Grand Plaza Hotel,
Gerald R. Ford Museum,
Van Andel Public Museum,
Grand Rapids Art Museum

USA, GRASS VALLEY (CALIFORNIA)

j@ck's internet cafe
115 S. Church St. • tel: +1 530-477-7873 • fax: +1 530-477-2968 •
jack@jackscafe.com • www.jackscafe.com

Location and Access
Look for big blue mural on
the side of the building.
Bus: Ask for Church Street.
Nearest cross street is Main
Street.

Hours
Mon-Sun   6am-11pm

Prices
US$3 per half hour
US$6 per hour

No credit cards
Student discount available

Nearby Places to Visit
Northstar Mining Museum,
Empire Mine Historic Park,
Nevada County
Fairgrounds, Malekoff
Diggind State Park, Tahoe
National Forest, Scott Flat
Lake, Rollins Lake

The Looking Glass . . . A Cyber Cafe
133 Main Street • tel: +1 908-813-8390 • fax: +1 908-813-9749 •
tlg@goes.com • www.the-looking-glass.net

Location and Access
Bus: Ask for Hackettstown.
Train: Amtrack, ask for
  Hackettstown.
Nearest cross street is Rt.
  517.

Hours
Mon-Sat   8am-11pm
Sun   11am-8pm

Prices
US$4 per half hour
US$8 per hour
V,MC, AmEx, DC, D
Student discount available

Nearby Places to Visit
Waterloo Village, Delaware
  Water Gap

PC Coffee Shop
Rt. 590 • tel: +1 717-689-0481 • fax: +1 717-689-0899 •
pccoffeeshop@pccoffeeshop.com • www.pccoffeeshop.com

Location and Access
Located near Poconos.
Nearest cross street is
  Hamlin Corners intersec-
  tion of Rt. 590 and Rt.
  191.

Hours
Mon-Sun   noon-8pm

Prices
US$3.49 per half hour
US$6.99 per hour
V, MC

USA, HANAPEPE (KAUAI, HAWAII)

Atomic Clock Cafe
3897 Hanapepe Road • tel: +1 808-335-5121 • fax: +1 808-335-5355 •
atomicclock@hawaiian.net • www.atomic-clock.com

Location and Access
Located in the Hanapepe Clinic.
Bus: The Kauai Bus, ask for Hanapepe Town.
Nearest cross street is Ko Road.

Hours
Mon-Fri   8am-5pm

Prices
US$5 per half hour

US$10 per hour
No credit cards
Student discount available for locals

Nearby Places to Visit
Old Hanapepe Town

USA, HILO (HAWAII, HAWAII)

Bytes & Bites
223A Kilauea Avenue • tel: +1 808-935-3520 •
fax: +1 808-935-4435 • bytes1@hotmail.com • www.hilo.org/bytes

Location and Access
Bus: Hele On, ask for Kilauea/Ponahawai.
Nearest cross street is Ponahawai Street.

Hours
Mon-Sun   10am-10pm

Prices
US$5 per half hour
US$8 per hour
No credit cards

Nearby Places to Visit
Historic Hilo Waterfront, Rainbow Falls, Akaka Falls, Hawaii Volcanoes National Park where Kilauea Volcano has been erupting since 1984

Cafe Cybre, Inc.
481 Harwood Road • tel: +1 817-268-0660 • fax: +1 817-268-0667 • info@cafecybre.com • www.cafecybre.com

Location and Access
Nearest cross street is Hurstvew Drive.

Hours
Mon-Thu & Sun 2pm-midnight
Fri-Sat 2pm-1am

Prices
US$3 per half hour
US$6 per hour
V, MC, AmEx, DC, D

Nearby Places to Visit
Ft. Worth Stockyards, Billy Bob's Texas, NRH2O Water Park, Historic Grapevine, the Tarantula train

---

The Hard Drive
372 South Freeman • tel: +1 208-535-2920 • fax: +1 208-522-5473 • worp@harddrive.net • www.harddrive.net

Location and Access
Located in One Stop Ship-n-Copy, near Fourth Street Post Office, Idaho Falls High School.
Bus: CART.
Nearest cross street is Fourth Street.

Hours
Mon-Thu 9am-9pm
Fri-Sat 9am-10pm

Prices
US$2 per half hour
US$3.95 per hour
No credit cards
Student discount available while doing school work

Nearby Places to Visit
Grand Tetons, Yellowstone National Park, Craters of the Moon

USA, INDIANAPOLIS (INDIANA)

Cybersmith
6020 E. 82nd Street • tel: +1 317-913-0350 • fax: +1 317-913-0351 •
csq_gm@cybersmith.com • www.cybersmith.com

Location and Access
Nearest cross street is
  Allisonville.

Hours
Mon-Sat   10am-9pm
Sun   noon-6pm

Prices
US$0.50 per half hour
US$1 per hour
V, MC, AmEx, DC, D

Nearby Places to Visit
Indianapolis Motor
  Speedway

USA, IOWA CITY (IOWA)

Cyberbeans Internet Cafe and Lounge
126 East Washington • tel: +1 319-337-7243 • No fax •
info@cyberbeans.com • www.cyberbeans.com

Location and Access
Located near the Ped Mall,
  inside Great Midwestern
  Ice Cream Company.

Bus: All Iowa City/Coralville
  routes, ask for Old Capitol
  Mall.
Nearest cross street is
  Dubuque Street.

Hours
Mon-Sat   7am-10pm
Sun   8am-10pm

Prices
US$4.20 per half hour
US$8.40 per hour
No credit cards

Nearby Places to Visit
The Amana Colonies

USA, JOSHUA TREE (CALIFORNIA)

Jeremy's Cybercafe & Beer Haus
61597 29 Palms Highway • tel: +1 760-366-9799 • No fax •
jeremy@joshua-tree.com • www.joshua-tree.com

Location and Access
Located near Joshua Tree
   National Park next door to
   the only bank in the town
   of Joshua Tree.
Bus: Local bus from Palm
   Springs, ask for Joshua
   Tree National Park.

Hours
Mon-Thu   7:30am-midnight
Fri-Sun   6:30am-minight

Oct-Jun;
      shorter hours
   Jul-Sept

Prices
US$0.13 per minute (US$2
   minimum)
US$7.80 per hour
V, MC

Nearby Places to Visit
The Integretron, Giant Rock

USA, JUNEAU (ALASKA)

Soapy's Station
175 South Franklin • tel: +1 907-247-9191 • fax: +1 907-247-5193 •
skytalk@ptialaska.net • www.skytalkwest.com

Location and Access
Located in the Senate
   Building.
Nearest cross street is Front
   Street.

Hours
Mon-Sat   9am-9pm
Sun   8am-6pm

Prices
US$5 per half hour
US$10 per hour
No credit cards
Student discount available

Nearby Places to Visit
Red Dog Saloon

USA, KAANAPALI (MAUI, HAWAII)

Mauione at the Kaanapali Beach Hotel
Kaanapali Beach Hotel Kekaa Drive • tel: +1 808-661-0571 • No fax •
jbonline@maui.net • http://mauigateway.com/~mauione

Location and Access
Located near Kaanapali
  Beach, Tiki Bar.
Bus: All the buses stop at
  the Kaanapali Beach
  Hotel.
Train: Lahaina Kaanapali &
  Pacific Railroad, ask for
  Kaanapali.

Hours
Mon-Sun   midnight-
          midnight

Prices
US$6 per half hour
US$10 per hour
No credit cards

USA, KETCHIKAN (ALASKA)

Soapy's Station
425 Water Street • tel: +1 907-247-9191 • fax: +1 907-247-5193 •
skytalk@ptialaska.net • www.skytalkwest.com

Location and Access
Located near Sockeye Sam's
  at the Tunnel.
Bus: Only one bus in
  Ketchikan going up and
  down the road next to the
  beach, ask for Sockeye
  Sam's.

Hours
Mon-Sat   7am-9pm
Sun   8am-6pm

Prices
US$5 per half hour
US$10 per hour
V, MC, AmEx, DC, D
Student discount available

Nearby Places to Visit
Harley Shop, walking tour,
  Charter Fishing Pier

USA, KINGMAN (ARIZONA)

Netspresso Coffee House—1949 Beverly #C-104 •
tel: +1 520-692-5277 • fax: +1 520-692-5377 (call first) •
tiger1@kingman.com • www.kingman.com/~ntsprso1/index.htm

Location and Access
Located near Wal-Mart
  Shopping Plaza.
Nearest cross street is
  Interstate 40.

Hours
Mon-Sun   6am-10pm

Prices
US$3 per half hour
US$6 per hour
No credit cards

Nearby Places to Visit
Historic Route 66, Las
  Vegas, Oatman historic
  ghost town

USA, LA JOLLA (CALIFORNIA)

C@fe Cybernet
8657 Villa La Jolla • tel: +1 619-452-1600 • fax: +1 619-535-2050 •
markl@san.rr.com • www.cafecybernet.com

Location and Access
Located near Mormon
  Temple on Interstate 5.
Bus: 34, ask for Nobel and
  Villa La Jolla.
Nearest cross street is La
  Jolla Village Drive.

Hours
Mon-Sat   9am-11pm
Sun   9am-10pm

Prices
US$6 per half hour

US$12 per hour
V, MC, AmEx, DC, D
Student discount available

Nearby Places to Visit
La Jolla Cove, Steven Birch
  Aquarium, San Diego Wild
  Animal Park, San Diego
  Zoo, Sea World, La Jolla,
  Jewel of the Sea, San
  Diego Bay, Balboa Park, La
  Jolla Museum of Art, Del
  Mar Turf Club

USA, LAPORTE (INDIANA)

Temple News Agency—816 Jefferson Avenue •
tel: +1 219-362-2676 • No fax • tmplnewz@csinet.net •
http://members.tripod.com/~templenews/index.html

Location and Access
Located near County
Courthouse.
Nearest cross street is
Lincolnway & Indiana
Avenue.

Hours
Mon &
Wed-Thu 6:30am-6pm
Tue & Sun 6:30am-9pm
Fri-Sat 6:30am-7pm

Prices
US$4 per half hour
US$6 per hour
No credit cards

Nearby Places to Visit
Chicago, Notre Dame
University

USA, LAS VEGAS (NEVADA)

Cyber City Cafe
Las Vegas Strip • tel: +1 702-555-1212 • No fax •
info@cybercitycafe.com • www.cybercitycafe.com

Location and Access
Located on the Las Vegas
Strip between Bally's and
MGM Grand.
Bus: Ask for Las Vegas Strip.
Tram: MGM–Bally's, ask for
Las Vegas Strip.
Nearest cross street is the
Strip/Flamingo.

Hours
Mon-Sun midnight-
midnight

Prices
US$8 per half hour with
unlimited drinks during
surfing time
US$12 per hour with unlim-
ited drinks during surfing
time
V, MC, DC, D
Student discount available

Nearby Places to Visit
All the casinos on Las Vegas
Boulevard

USA, LENEXA (KANSAS)

The Netc@fe
13344 College Boulevard • tel: +1 913-339-9310 • No fax •
steve@thenetcafe-KC.com • www.thenetcafe-KC.com

Location and Access
Located near Johnson
   County Community
   College.
Nearest cross street is
   Pflumm.

Hours
Mon-Thu   10am-10pm
Fri-Sat   10am-11pm

Prices
US$4 per half hour
US$7 per hour
No credit cards
Student discount available

Nearby Places to Visit
Worlds of Fun, Kansas City
   Royals, Kansas City Chiefs,
   Kansas City Zoo, The Plaza
   (shopping district)

USA, LEWISTON (NEW YORK)

WNY Internet Partners
790 Center Street • tel: +1 716-754-0048 • fax: +1 716-754-0049 •
info@wnyip.net • www.wnyip.net

Location and Access
Bus: 50, ask for 8th Street.
Nearest cross street is 8th
   Street.

Hours
Mon-Thu   10am-8pm
Fri   10am-5pm
Sat   noon-4pm
closed on weekends June-
   August

Prices
US$5 per half hour
US$5 per hour
V, MC

Nearby Places to Visit
Niagara Falls, Historic
   Lewiston, Historic
   Youngstown, the entire
   Niagara Frontier

USA, LONG BEACH (CALIFORNIA)

Megabyte Coffeehouse
4135 E Anaheim Street • tel: +1 562-986-6892 • No fax •
mark@megabytecoffee.com • www.megabytecoffee.com

Location and Access
Located near the Queen
  Mary.
Bus: 142, 143, ask for
  Anaheim/Ximeno.
Nearest cross street is
  Ximeno.

Prices
US$3 per half hour
US$6 per hour
No credit cards

Hours
Mon-Thu   10am-midnight
Fri   10am-1am
Sat   9am-1am
Sun   9am-midnight

USA, LOS ANGELES (CALIFORNIA)

Cyber Java @ Hollywood
7080 Hollywood Boulevard • tel: +1 323-466-5600 •
fax: + 1 310-388-1313 • info@cyberjava.com • www.cyberjava.com

Location and Access
Located near Mann's Chinese
  Theatre, Walk of Fame.
Bus: Ask for Hollywood and
  La Brea.
Underground: MTA, ask for
  Hollywood.
Nearest cross street is North
  La Brea Boulevard.

Hours
Mon-Tue &
  Sun   7am-midnight
Wed-Sat   7am-3am

Prices
US$5 per half hour
US$9 per hour
V, MC
Student discount available

USA, MANAHAWKIN (NEW JERSEY)

Telecottage
193 East Bay Avenue • tel: +1 609-597-0410 •
fax: +1 609-597-2410 • info@telecottage.com • www.telecottage.com

Location and Access
Located near Manahawkin
Autosales (purple
awning).
Nearest cross street is Route
9 and Bay Avenue.

Hours
Mon-Thu 10am-6pm
Fri-Sun by appointment

Prices
US$6 per half hour

US$10 per hour
V, MC, AmEx

Nearby Places to Visit
Long Beach Island (5
miles), Chatsworth (25
miles), Smithville (30
miles), Basto (30 miles),
Atlantic City (40 miles)

USA, MIAMI (FLORIDA)

Cafe & Internet of America
12536 North Kendall Drive • tel: +1 305-412-0100 •
fax: +1 305-412-0102 • cafe@cafeina.net • www.cafeina.net

Location and Access
Nearest cross street is 127th
Avenue.

Hours
Mon-Sat noon-8pm

Prices
US$5 per half hour
US$9 per hour
V, MC, AmEx, DC, D

USA, MINNEAPOLIS (MINNESOTA)

CyberX

3001 Lyndale Avenue, South • tel: +1 612-824-3558 • No fax •
webmaster@cyberx.com • www.cyberx.com

Location and Access
Located near Uptown.
Bus: 4, 21, ask for corner of
  Lake and Lyndale.
Nearest cross street is Lake.

Hours

Mon-Sat	8am-midnight
Sun	9am-midnight

Prices
US$3-$3.50 per half hour
US$6-$7 per hour
No credit cards

Nearby Places to Visit
Lynlake area, theaters, art
  galleries, shopping,
  restaurants, entertainment

USA, MONON (INDIANA)

Palaver

332 North Market Street • tel: +1 219-253-8131 •
fax: +1 219-253-6800 • webmaster@palaver.net • www.palaver.net

Location and Access
Located near Indiana Beach.

Hours
Tue & Thu noon-8pm

Prices
US$4 per half hour
US$8 per hour
No credit cards

Interlink

545 Morgan Mill Road • tel: +1 704-283-1903 • fax: +1 704-283-9453 • hostmaster@interlink-cafe.com • www.interlink-cafe.com

Location and Access
Located just down the street from Quincey's Restaurant.
Nearest cross street is Highway 74.

Hours
Mon-Sat   9am-6pm

Prices
US$3.50 per half hour
US$7 per hour
V, MC, AmEx, D
Student discount available

Nearby Places to Visit
Charlotte

Java Java—860 Fifth Avenue South •
tel: +1 941-435-1180 • fax: +1 941-435-0878 • scott@javajavanaples.com • www.javajavanaples.com

Location and Access
Located near Naples Fifth Avenue visitor center.
Trolley: Ask for Trolley depot/main station.
Nearest cross street is US 41.

Hours
Mon-Fri   7am-11pm
Sat   8am-midnight

Prices
US$4 per half hour
US$8 per hour
V, MC, AmEx, D
Student discount available

Nearby Places to Visit
Naples Pier, Tin City, Historic District, Jungle Larry's Caribbean Gardens, Everglades National Park, Corkscrew Swamp Sanctuary

Bean Central

2817 West End Avenue • tel: +1 615-321-8530 • No fax •
bean@isdn.net • www.beancentral.com

Location and Access
Located near Vanderbilt
  University & the
  Parthenon.
Cafe owners don't recom-
  mend mass transit in
  Nashville.
Nearest cross street is
  I-440.

Hours
Mon-Sat   7am-11pm

Prices
US$2 per half hour
US$4 per hour
V, MC, AmEx

Nearby Places to Visit
Music Row

Bean Central

3770 Hillsboro Road • tel: +1 615-321-8530 • No fax •
bean@isdn.net • www.beancentral.com

Location and Access
Located across from Green
  Hills Mall.
Cafe owners don't recom-
  mend mass transit in
  Nashville.
Nearest cross street is
  I-440.

Hours
Mon-Fri   7am-6pm
Sat   8am-5pm
Sun   10am-5pm

Prices
US$2 per half hour
US$4 per hour
V, MC, AmEx

Nearby Places to Visit
Music Row

USA, NEWBURYPORT (MASSACHUSETTS)

The Cybercafe
257 Low Street • tel: +1 978-462-6798 • fax: +1 978-465-8698 • rosemar@tiac.net • www.tiac.net/users/rosemar

Location and Access
Located near Friendly's Restaurant.
Nearest cross street is Route 95.

Prices
US$4 per half hour
US$8 per hour
V, MC, D

Hours
Mon-Fri   8:30am-7pm
Sat   10am-3pm

USA, NEW ORLEANS (LOUISIANA)

Realm of Delirium—New Orleans First Cyber Cafe
941 Decatur Street (upstairs) • tel: +1 504-523-2923 • fax: +1 504-523-3541 • RODInfo@RealmOfDelirium.com • www.RealmOfDelirium.com

Location and Access
Located near French Market.
Nearest cross street is St. Phillip.

Prices
US$4.50 per half hour
US$7.50 per hour
No credit cards

Hours
Mon-Thu &
  Sun   10am-midnight
Fri-Sat   10am-2am

Nearby Places to Visit
The French Quarter

Cyber Cafe
273A Lafayette Street • tel: +1 212-334-5140 • fax: +1 212-334-6436 • partners@cyber-cafe.com • www.cyber-cafe.com

Location and Access
Located near SoHo Guggenheim, SoHo, Little Italy, China Town.
Underground: 6, N, R (BMT), B, D, F, Q, ask for Spring Street (6), Prince Street (N, R) or Broadway/Lafayette (B, D, F, Q).
Nearest cross street is Prince Street.

Hours
Mon-Sat   8:30am-10pm
Sun   10am-10pm

Prices
US$6.40 per half hour
US$12.80 per hour
V, MC, AmEx, DC, D

---

cyberfelds internet cafe
20 East 13 Street, 2nd Floor • tel: +1 212-647-8830 • No fax • cyberfelds@cyberfelds.com • www.cyberfelds.com

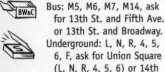

Location and Access
Located near 14th Street, Union Square Park, above the Village Copier.
Bus: M5, M6, M7, M14, ask for 13th St. and Fifth Ave. or 13th St. and Broadway.
Underground: L, N, R, 4, 5, 6, F, ask for Union Square (L, N, R, 4, 5, 6) or 14th Street (F).
Nearest cross streets are University and Fifth Ave.

Hours
Mon-Fri   8am-midnight
Sat-Sun   noon-10pm

Prices
US$5 per half hour
US$10 an hour
Student discount available with purchase of 8-hour time block

Nearby Places to Visit
Greenwich Village

The Internet Cafe

82 East 3rd Street • tel: +1 212-614-0747 • fax: +1 212-614-9342 •
lizzie@bigmagic.com • www.bigmagic.com

Location and Access
Located in the East Village.
Bus: M15, M21, ask for 2nd
   or 3rd Street (M15) or 1st
   or 2nd Avenue (M21).
Underground: 6, F, ask for
   Bleecker Street (6) or 2nd
   Avenue (F).
Nearest cross streets are
   First and Second Avenues.

Hours
Mon-Sat   11am-2am

Prices
US$5 per half hour
US$10 per hour
V, MC
Student discount available

Nearby Places to Visit
East Village

The Cyber Tower Connection

164 Broadway • tel: +1 401-846-5296 • fax: +1 401-846-7161 •
cybertower@efortress.com • No website

Location and Access
Located across from the
   Broadway Post Office on
   one of the main streets
   entering town.
Bus: Almost all of the city
   buses run by the cafe, ask
   for the post office.

Hours
Mon-Sat   9am-9pm

Prices
US$5.70 per half hour
US$12 per hour
V, MC, AmEx, D

Nearby Places to Visit
Newport is an international
   city by the sea, popular
   tourist area

USA, NORMAL (ILLINOIS)

Cyberi@

213 W. North Street • tel: +1 309-452-0028 • fax: +1 309-454-2273 •
cyberia@cyberianet.com • www.cyberianet.com

Location and Access
Located near Normal Theater
and Waterson Towers.
Bus: All buses in Normal
stop across the street, ask
for Waterson Towers.
Nearest cross street is Fell.

Hours
Mon-Sun   11am-10pm

Prices
US$2.70 per half hour

US$5 per hour
V, MC, AmEx, D

Nearby Places to Visit
Illinois State University

USA, PALO ALTO (CALIFORNIA)

Cybersmith

353 University Avenue • tel: +1 650-325-2005 • fax: +1 650-325-2125 •
pal_gm@cybersmith.com • www.cybersmith.com

Location and Access
Located near Stanford
University.
Train: Caltrain, from San
Francisco to San Jose, ask
for Stanford University
station.
Nearest cross street is
Florence Avenue.

Hours
Mon-Thu   10am-11pm
Fri-Sat   10am-midnight
Sun   11am-9pm

Prices
US$2.50 per half hour
US$4.95 per hour
V, MC, AmEx, DC, D

Nearby Places to Visit
Stanford University, Rodin
sculptures

USA, PITTSFIELD (MASSACHUSETTS)

The Hard Drive Cafe
19 Cheshire Road • tel: +1 413-496-9488 • No fax •
info@hard-drive-cafe.com • www.hard-drive-cafe.com

Location and Access
Located in the Allendale
  Shopping Center.
Bus: Berkshire Mall, ask for
  Allendale Shopping Center.
Nearest cross street is the
  junction of Routes 8 & 9.

Hours
Mon-Fri   10:30am-9pm
Sat   10:30am-6pm

Prices
US$4 per half hour
US$6 per hour
V, MC, AmEx

Nearby Places to Visit
Tanglewood, Arrowhead,
  Williamstown Theater, Mt.
  Greylock, Berkshire
  Museum

USA, PORT TOWNSEND (WASHINGTON)

Cafe Internet™
2021 Sims Way • tel: +1 360-385-9773 • fax: +1 360-385-2736 •
cafeinet@cafe-inet.com • www.cafe-inet.com

Location and Access
Located next to Mail Boxes
  Etc.
Tram/Trolley: Jefferson
  Transit Park & Ride, ask
  for Sims Way near Mail
  Boxes Etc.

Hours
Mon, Wed, &
  Fri   9am-5pm
Tue & Thu 9am-7pm
Sat   noon-5pm

Prices
US$6 per half hour
US$9.50 per hour
No credit cards

Nearby Places to Visit
Fort Worden State Park, Port
  Townsend's Historic
  Victorian Seaport

BrewChats Cyber Cafe, Inc.
6660 SW Capitol Highway • tel: +1 503-977-2336 • No fax •
info@brewchats.com • www.brewchats.com

Location and Access
Located between Multnomah
  and Hillsdale.
Bus: 1, 5, 45, ask for the
  Jewish Community Center.
Nearest cross street is
  Vermont.

Hours
Mon-Fri   6:30am-8pm
Sat-Sun   8:30am-4pm

Prices
US$1.50 per half hour (food
  or drink purchase applies)
US$2.50 per hour (food or
  drink purchase applies)
V, MC, AmEx
Student discount available

Nearby Places to Visit
Multnomah and Hillsdale
  both have neat shops and
  restaurants

Millennium Cafe
2633 SE 21st Avenue • tel: +1 503-235-9945 • No fax •
info@millennium-cafe.com • www.millennium-cafe.com

Location and Access
Bus: In order of proximity:
  10-Harold, 4-Division, 9-
  Powell, ask for 21st &
  Clinton (10), 21st &
  Division (4), or 21st &
  Powell (9).
Nearest cross street is SE
  Clinton Street.

Hours
Mon-Fri   7am-8pm
Sat-Sun   9:30am-4pm

Prices
US$2.25 per half hour
US$4.50 per hour
No credit cards

Internet Snack Shack
303 East Main • tel: +1 307-856-9500 • No fax •
patricio@walkingcrow.com • www.internetsnackshack.com

Location and Access
Nearest big town is Casper.
Nearest cross street is
  Federal.

Hours
Mon-Sun   10am-10pm

Prices
US$3 per half hour
US$5 per hour
No credit cards
Student discount available

Info C@fe
3922 14th Avenue • tel: +1 309-786-1618 • fax: +1 309-786-6530 •
info@1infocafe.com • www.1infocafe.com

Location and Access
Nearest cross street is 38th
  Street.

Hours
Mon-Thu   7:30am-11pm
Fri   7:30am-midnight
Sat   9am-midnight

Prices
US$3 per half hour
US$5 per hour
No credit cards
Student discount available
  for Augustana students

Nearby Places to Visit
Casino boats on the river

USA, ROYAL OAK (MICHIGAN)

Cafe Domain

308 South Washington • tel: +1 248-545-7165 •
fax: +1 248-545-2585 • info@cafedomain.com • www.cafedomain.com

Location and Access
Located near Detroit Zoo at
the corner of 4th and
Washington.
Bus: Smart Bus, ask for
South Washington at the
I-696.
Nearest cross street is I-696
or 11 Mile Road.

Hours
Mon-Thu   8am-11pm

Fri-Sat   8am-2am
Sun   10am-11pm

Prices
US$1.20 per 10 minutes
US$7.50 per hour (families
surf free on Sundays)
No credit cards
Student discount available

USA, SAINT LOUIS (MISSOURI)

The Grind

56 Maryland Plaza • tel: +1 314-454-0202 • No fax •
grind@icon-stl.net • www.icon-stl.net/~grind

Location and Access
Located in the Central West
End.
Nearest cross street is
Kingshighway.

Hours
Mon-Sun   3pm-3am

Prices
Free

USA, SAN BRUNO (CALIFORNIA)

On Line Cafe.Net
428 San Bruno Avenue West • tel: +1 650-615-9985 • No fax •
robin@onlinecafe.net • www.onlinecafe.net

Location and Access
Located near San Francisco
  International Airport.
Bus: 3B, 5L, 5M, 19F, 30B,
  ask for West San Bruno
  Avenue in San Bruno.
Nearest cross street is El
  Camino Real.

Prices
US$5 per half hour
US$10 per hour
No credit cards

Hours
Mon-Fri   6:30am-6pm
Sat   7:30am-5pm
Sun   8am-3pm

USA, SAN DIEGO (CALIFORNIA)

*espresso*NET
7770 Regents Road, #109 • tel: +1 619-453-5896 •
fax: +1 619-453-5307 • info@espressonet.com • www.espressonet.com

Location and Access
Located in the Golden
  Triangle/UTC area.
Bus: Available.
Nearest cross street is La
  Jolla Village Drive.

Prices
US$3 per half hour
US$6 per hour
V, MC, AmEx, DC, D

Nearby Places to Visit
La Jolla Cove

Hours
Mon-Fri   7am-10pm
Sat-Sun 8am-10pm

USA, SAN DIEGO (CALIFORNIA)

Internet Coffee
800 Broadway • tel: +1 619-702-2233 • fax: +1 619-702-2233 •
info@internet-coffee.com • www.internet-coffee.com

Location and Access
Nearest cross street is 8th
Street.

Hours
Mon-Sun   10am-midnight

Prices
US$3.50 per half hour
US$7 per hour
No credit cards

Nearby Places to Visit
The Gas Lamp Quarter

USA, SAN FRANCISCO (CALIFORNIA)

Club-i
850 Folsom Street • tel: +1 415-777-2582 • fax: +1 415-777-1447 •
info@club-i.com • www.club-i.com

Location and Access
Located near Moscone
Center and Lulu's
Restaurant.

Bus: Muni 9X, 12, 14, 15,
27, 30, 45, ask for Folsom
and 4th Street.

Streetcar: F, J, K, L, M, N,
ask for Powell Station.
Cable car: Powell/Hyde,
Powell/Mason, ask for
Powell Station.

Located between 4th and
5th Streets.

Hours
Mon-Thu   7am-midnight
Fri   7am-2am
Sat   8:30am-2am
Sun   10am-10pm

Prices
US$4.75 per half hour
US$8.95 per hour
V, MC
Student discount available

The CoffeeNet
744 Harrison Street • tel: +1 415-495-7447 • No fax • roastmaster@coffeenet.net • www.coffeenet.net

Location and Access
Located near Moscone Convention Center.
Bus: 15 Third, 30 Stockton, ask for Harrison Street.
Underground: J Church, K Ingleside, L Taraval, M Oceanside, N Judah, F Market, ask for Powell Street.
Cable car: Ask for Powell Street station.

Nearest cross street is 4th Street.

Hours
Mon-Wed   7am-9pm
Thu-Fri   7am-11pm
Sat   10am-11pm
Sun   11am-9pm

Prices
Free with food or drink purchase over $5
V, MC

Internet Alfredo
790-A Brannan •   tel: +1 415-437-3140 • fax: +1 415-437-3149 • staff@ialfredo.com • www.ialfredo.com

Location and Access
Bus: 19, 42, ask for 7th and Brannan.
Nearest cross street is 7th Street.

Hours
Mon-Sat   noon-midnight
Sun   noon-6pm

Prices
US$3.75 per half hour
US$7.50 per hour
V, MC, AmEx

Nearby Places to Visit
SOMA, bars, restaurants, nightclubs

USA, SAN FRANCISCO (CALIFORNIA)

Seattle Street Coffee
456 Geary Street • tel: +1 415-922-4566 • fax: +1 415-922-0369 •
bro3@ix.netcom.com • No website

Location and Access
Located near Union Square.
Bus: Muni 38, ask for near
   Geary Theater.
Cable Car: Powell/Hyde,
   Powell/Mason, ask for
   Union Square.
Located between Mason and
   Taylor Streets.

Hours
Mon   6am-10pm
Tue-Fri   6am-11pm
Sat   7am-11pm
Sun   7am-9pm

Prices
US$4 per half hour
US$8 per hour
No credit cards

Nearby Places to Visit
Union Square, theaters,
   downtown shops, bars,
   restaurants

USA, SAN MATEO (CALIFORNIA)

Cafe Cybercaptive—851 N San Mateo Drive •
tel: +1 650-342-6162 • fax: +1 650-348-4810 •
kireau@cybercaptive.com • www.cybercaptive.com

Location and Access
Located across the street
   from Shen Lincoln-
   Mercury.
Bus: SamTrans 7B.
Train: Caltrain, ask for
   Burlingame station.
Nearest cross street is
   Peninsula Avenue.

Hours
Mon-Fri   8am-8pm
Sat   10am-7pm
Sun   11am-7pm

Prices
US$3 per half hour
US$6 per hour
V, MC

Nearby Places to Visit
San Francisco International
   Airport

USA, SAN RAFAEL (CALIFORNIA)

LineXpress Cyber Lounge
1122 4th Street • tel: +1 415-451-1500 • No fax •
info@linexpress.com • www.linexpress.com

Location and Access
Located near San Rafael
  Mission, Rafael Theater.
Bus: Golden Gate Transit
  from San Francisco, ask
  for 4th & Court Streets.
Nearest cross street is A
  Street.

Hours
Mon-Wed &
  Sun   10am-10pm
Thu-Sat 10am-midnight

Prices
US$3 per half hour
US$6 per hour
No credit cards

Nearby Places to Visit
Sausalito, San Francisco,
  Napa Valley

USA, SANTA ROSA (CALIFORNIA)

Higher Grounds Cyber Cafe
1899 Mendocino Avenue • tel: +1 707-525-8125 • No fax •
cafe@highergrounds.com • www.highergrounds.com

Location and Access
Located near the Santa Rosa
  Junior College.
Bus: Golden Gate Transit
  from San Francisco 72, 74,
  80; Santa Rosa City Transit
  10, 14; Sonoma County
  Transit 20, 30, 44, 48, 60,
  62, 64, ask for Mendocino
  Avenue and Steele Lane.
Nearest cross street is
  Steele Lane.

Hours
Mon-Fri   6am-midnight
Sat-Sun   7am-midnight

Prices
US$3 per half hour
US$6 per hour
V, MC, AmEx, D
Student discount available

Nearby Places to Visit
The Wine Country

Capitol Hill Internet Lounge and Cafe—219 Broadway

Avenue E., #23 • tel: +1 206-860-6858 • fax: +1 206-860-6858 •
cafe@capitolhill.net • www.capitolhill.net

Location and Access
Located in the center of
Capitol Hill.
Bus: 7, 9, 43, ask for any
Broadway stop.

Located between Thomas
and John Streets.

Hours
Mon-Sun   10am-midnight

Prices
US$3 per half hour
US$6 per hour
V, MC, AmEx

Nearby Places to Visit
Volunteer Park

Speakeasy Cafe

2304 2nd Avenue • tel: +1 206-728-9770 • fax: +1 206-728-2172 •
cafe@speakeasy.org • www.speakeasy.org

Location and Access
Bus: 1, 2, 3, 6, 13, 16, 360,
ask for 3rd and Bell.
Nearest cross street is Bell.

Hours
Mon	11am-7pm
Tue-Thu	11am-midnight
Fri	11am-1am
Sat	noon-1am
Sun	noon-10pm

Prices
US$4.50 per half hour
US$9 per hour
V, MC, AmEx

Nearby Places to Visit
Space Needle, Seattle
Center, Monorail, shop-
ping, Pioneer Square

Sheffield Pub and Pizza—Internet/Sport Bar

223 Main St., Route 7 • tel: +1 413-229-8880 • fax: +1 413-229-3293 •
info@sheffield-pub.com • www.sheffield-pub.com

Location and Access
Bus: Bonanza, ask for Miller
and Main Streets.
Nearest cross streets is
Maple Avenue.

Hours
Mon-Sat   11am-midnight
Sun   noon-11pm

Prices
Free

Nearby Places to Visit
Covered bridge within 2
miles

CoffeeNet

10030 Silverdale Way • tel: +1 360-613-4093 •
fax: +1 360-698-3169 • coffinet@coffinet.com • www.coffinet.com

Location and Access
Located near Kitsap Mall
and Schuck's Auto Parts.
Bus: To and from the Kitsap
Mall, ask for Silverdale
Mall.
Ferry: From Seattle to
Bainbridge Island, drive
(or bus) to Silverdale Mall.
Nearest cross street is
Hilltop Boulevard.

Hours
Mon-Fri   9am-7:30pm
Sat   noon-6pm

Prices
US$3 per half hour
US$6 per hour
V, MC

Nearby Places to Visit
Olympic Mountains and Rain
Forest

USA, SIOUX FALLS (SOUTH DAKOTA)

Z Coffee House
1107 W. 11th Street • tel: +1 605-339-7207 • No fax •
info@zcoffee.com • www.zcoffee.com

Location and Access
Located on the Loop.
Nearest cross streets are
12th Street & Grange
Avenue.

Hours
Mon-Thu	7am-11pm
Fri	7am-1am
Sat	10am-1am
Sun	noon-9pm

Prices
US$3.50 per half hour
US$7 per hour
No credit cards

Nearby Places to Visit
Corn fields, soybean fields,
wheat fields, Mitchell Corn
Palace

USA, SKAGWAY (ALASKA)

Soapy's Station
745 Broadway • tel: +1 907-983-2085 • fax: +1 907-983-9135 •
skytalk@ptialaska.net • www.skytalkwest.com

Location and Access
Nearest cross street is 7th
Street.

Hours
Mon-Sat	9am-7pm
Sun	8am-6pm

Prices
US$5 per half hour
US$10 per hour
No credit cards
Student discount available

Nearby Places to Visit
Broadway is a fascinating
look at the 1898 Gold
Rush.

USA, SLIDELL (LOUISIANA)

Coffee Online
1925 Second Street • tel: +1 504-781-4600 • fax: +1 504-781-4655 •
coffeeonline@cmq.com • www.coffeeonlineusa.com

Location and Access
Nearest big town is New Orleans.
Located opposite the post office.
Train: Main line from New Orleans, ask for Slidell.
Nearest cross street is Front Street.

Hours
Mon-Thu   8am-10pm
Fri-Sat   8am-midnight
Sun   10am-8pm

Prices
US$3 per half hour
US$6 per hour
No credit cards
Student discount available on limited promotions

Nearby Places to Visit
Located in Olde Towne Antique District, 30 minutes from French Quarter

USA, SOUTH LAKE TAHOE (CALIFORNIA)

The Cyber Stop
2227 Lake Tahoe Boulevard, Suite E • tel: +1 530-542-4209 •
fax: +1 530-542-0391 • rhatfield@oakweb.com • www.cyberstop.nu

Location and Access
Bus: Local buses and Greyhound, ask for South Lake Tahoe near the YMCA.
Nearest cross street is Tahoe Keys Boulevard.

Hours
Mon-Sun   9am-9pm

Prices
US$4 per half hour
US$7 per hour
V, MC, AmEx, D
Student discount available

Nearby Places to Visit
Lake Tahoe, casinos

USA, STAUNTON (VIRGINIA)

Cybercafe & Training Center—105 East Beverley Street •
tel: +1 540-887-8402 • fax: +1 540-887-8403 •
mail@cybercafe.cfw.com • www.cybercafe.cfw.com

Location and Access
Located near Mary Baldwin
College and the Woodrow
Wilson Birthplace &
Museum.
Train: Amtrack, ask for
Staunton/Shenandoah
Valley.
Nearest cross street is New
Street.

Hours
Mon-Thu   9:30am-7pm
Fri   9:30am-5pm
Sat   10am-5pm

Prices
US$5 per half hour
US$10 per hour
V, MC, D

Nearby Places to Visit
Museum of American
Frontier Culture, Historic
Downtown Staunton,
Statler Brothers Museum,
Skyline Drive

USA, TAMPA (FLORIDA)

Cybercup Cafe
6914 E. Fowler Avenue • tel: +1 813-980-0860 • No fax •
No e-mail • www.cybercup.com

Location and Access
Nearest cross street is I-75.

Hours
Mon-Thu   noon-4am
Fri   noon-midnight
Sat   midnight-
            midnight
Sun   noon-2am

Prices
US$2 per half hour
US$4 per hour
No credit cards

Nearby Places to Visit
Busch Gardens

USA, TUCSON (ARIZONA)

Library of Congress, Cybercafe
311 E Congress Street • tel: +1 520-622-2708 • fax: +1 520-792-6366 •
slutes@libcong.com • www.hotcong.com/libcong

Location and Access
Located within the historic
  Hotel Congress in the
  heart of downtown
  Tucson.
Bus: Ask for Ronstadt
  Transit Center.

Hours
Mon-Sun   11am-1am

Prices
US$3 per half hour
US$6 per hour
V, MC, AmEx, D

Nearby Places to Visit
Downtown Tucson

USA, UPPER MONTCLAIR (NEW JERSEY)

@Alans computer cafe
617 Valley Road • tel: +1 973-783-2200 • No fax •
alan@alans.com • www.alans.com

Location and Access
Located near Montclair
  State University.
Bus: DeCamp 66 route from
  Port of Authority in NYC,
  ask for Bellevue Ave in
  Upper Montclair.
Nearest cross street is
  Bellevue Avenue.

Hours
Mon-Thu   11am-9pm
Fri-Sat   11am-9:30pm
Sun   1pm-6pm

Prices
US$5 per half hour
US$10 per hour
V, MC, AmEx
Student discount available

Nearby Places to Visit
New York City

Internet Cafe Ventura—4711-3 Telephone Road •
tel: +1 805-289-0129 • fax: +1 805-644-1012 •
internetcafe@vrone.net • www.vrone.net/internetcafe

Location and Access
Located near Barnes and
    Noble.

Bus: SCAT 6B, 10, ask for
    Telephone and Main.
Nearest cross street is Main.

Hours
Mon-Sat   10am-7:30pm

Prices
US$3 per half hour
US$6 per hour
V, MC, AmEx

Nearby Places to Visit
The beatiful tourist town of
    San Buena Ventura

Surfnet Cafe
1445 Donlon Street, Suite 14 • tel: +1 805-658-1287 •
fax: +1 805-642-2560 • surfnet@jetlink.net • www.surfnetcafe.com

Location and Access
Located near Target in
    Anacapa Business Center.

Bus: South Coast Area
    Transit, ask for Market &
    Donlon.
Nearest cross streets are
    Main and Market Streets.

Hours
Mon-Wed   7am-5pm
Thu-Fri   7am-9pm

Prices
US$3 per half hour
US$6 per hour
V, MC, AmEx, DC, D

Nearby Places to Visit
The beach

BitsQuick Cafe Inc.
311 West Main Street • tel: +1 716-742-1578 • fax: +1 716-742-2085 • byran@mail.bitsquick.com • www.bitsquick.com

Location and Access
Located near Eastview Mall.
Nearest cross street is I-90.

Nearby Places to Visit
Ganondagon Native
    American Historic Site

Hours
Mon-Fri   6:30am-5pm
Sat   8:30am-2pm

Prices
US$3 per half hour
US$6 per hour
V, MC, D

WebCity Cybercafe—116 South Independence Boulevard,
Suite 103 • tel: +1 757-490-8690 • fax: +1 757-490-8704 • info@webcitycybercafe.com • www.webcitycybercafe.com

Location and Access
Located near Pembroke Mall.
Bus: Ask for Pembroke Mall.
Nearest cross street is
    Virginia Beach Boulevard.

US$6.95 per hour
V, MC, D
Student discount available

Nearby Places to Visit
Beaches, Waterside,
    Amphitheater, Nauticus,
    Navy ships, Marine Science
    Museum, Pavilion, Scope,
    Hampton Coliseum,
    Colonial Williamsburg

Hours
Mon-Thu   10am-10pm
Fri-Sat   10am-11pm
Sun   noon-9pm

Prices
US$4.50 per half hour

cyberSTOP cafe

1513 17th Street NW • tel: +1 202-234-2470 • fax: +1 202-234-2478 •
feedback@cyberstopcafe.com • www.cyberstopcafe.com

Location and Access
Located near Dupont Circle Metro.
Underground: Red Line, ask for Dupont Circle.
Nearest cross street is P Street NW.

Hours
Mon-Thu & Sun	7:30am-midnight
Fri-Sat	7:30am-2am

Prices
US$4 per half hour
US$6 per hour
V, MC, AmEx, D

Nearby Places to Visit
White House, Capitol Building, Washington Monument, Lincoln Monument

---

Get Wired Cybercafe—399 Cypress Gardens Boulevard SE •
tel: +1 941-291-0246 • fax: +1 941-294-2092 •
wired@mail.getwiredcafe.com • www.getwiredcafe.com

Location and Access
Located near Cypress Gardens.
Bus: New bus route to shopping center, ask for Wal-Mart.
Nearest cross street is Highway 17.

Hours
Mon-Thu	7am-9pm
Fri-Sat	7am-11pm
Sun	noon-6pm

Prices
US$2.25 per half hour
US$4.50 per hour
V, MC

Nearby Places to Visit
Cypress Gardens, Disney World, Universal Studios, Sea World

About the Author

Cyberkath did not grow up around computers. Born in the north of England thirty-something years ago, her formative years took place before being wired was a part of everyday life. She studied languages in London and ended up teaching English as a second language for twelve years, ultimately on three continents. She discovered e-mail and cybercafes in San Francisco while on an around-the-world trip, and has been hooked ever since. She is currently of no fixed abode in Europe somewhere.

Index by Cafe Name

333

335

Index by City

Index by U.S. State and Canadian Province